Strategic Planning for Local Government

Strategic Planning for Local Government

A Handbook for Officials and Citizens

EDITED BY
ROGER L. KEMP

McFarland & Company, Inc., Publishers
Jefferson, North Carolina, and London

The present work is a reprint of the library bound edition of Strategic Planning for Local Government: A Handbook for Officials and Citizens, *first published in 1993 by McFarland.*

For Jonathan Kemp,
who will help shape the future

LIBRARY OF CONGRESS CATALOGUING-IN-PUBLICATION DATA

Strategic planning for local government : a handbook for officials and
   citizens / Roger L. Kemp.
      p.   cm.
   Includes bibliographical references and index.

   ISBN 978-0-7864-3873-0
   softcover : 50# alkaline paper ∞

   1. Political planning — United States.   2. Strategic planning —
United States.   3. Local government — United States.   4. Public
administration — United States.   I. Kemp, Roger L.
JS344.F4S77   2008
352'.000472'0973 — dc20   92-50949

British Library cataloguing data are available

Cover art ©2008 Shutterstock

Manufactured in the United States of America

*McFarland & Company, Inc., Publishers
   Box 611, Jefferson, North Carolina 28640
   www.mcfarlandpub.com*

Contents

PART THREE : THE FUTURE

Acknowledgments

Grateful acknowledgment is made to the following organizations and publishers for granting permission to reprint the articles in this volume: American Planning Association; American Society for Public Administration; Communication Channels, Inc.; The Council of State Planning Agencies; County Supervisors Association of California; Government Finance Officers Association; International City Management Association; Marcel Dekker, Inc.; Missouri Municipal League; National Civic League; Nevada League of Cities; New Jersey State League of Municipalities; The Ohio Municipal League; San Francisco Chamber of Commerce; The University of Connecticut; Urban Land Institute; World Future Society.

Preface

While strategic planning is a common practice in the corporate world, it has only recently been applied to the public sector. Local governments, like their business counterparts, operate in a turbulent and uncertain environment. Cities, regardless of the size of their population or geographic location, are having increasing difficulty coping with an unprecedented degree of change, uncertainty, and risk. Recent external factors, such as inflation, revenue shortages, soaring energy and health costs, fewer grants from higher levels of government, and the public's skepticism of government in general, have altered traditional planning practices in local governments throughout the nation.

These factors, when coupled with rising public expectations for more services and lower taxes, set the contemporary context in which local governments must operate and survive. In order to improve planning for the future direction of local public sector organizations, and to establish more viable and effective strategies for achieving community goals, local public officials must understand the dynamics of developing and applying successful strategic planning programs in their local government organizations. This principle also holds true for other persons interested in, and able to influence, the future of their municipal organizations.

Gone are the more predictable and stable days for local governments. When revenues were plentiful and public officials could merely adjust tax rates to balance their annual budgets, life was relatively simple and routine. The outside environment did not pose any significant challenges, opportunities, and threats. Public programs were merely increased in response to citizen demand for more services. In addition to basic services — police, fire, and public works — most local governments added new recreational, cultural, and social services to better serve their citizens. The public now not only expects but demands that these services be provided.

Currently, both the scale and mix of public services are being reevaluated in response to changes in the external environment. Traditional long-range planning practices, designed for more stable periods of steady growth and predictable change, are now becoming outdated. Without such predictability, the common practice of merely projecting past activities into the future lacks both accuracy and credibility, and is no longer a useful and practical planning model. Strategic planning is quickly becoming a valuable tool to assist local governments as they strive to overcome the constraints and shortcomings imposed by traditional government planning practices.

Based on techniques developed in the private sector over the past few decades in response to similar environmental challenges, strategic planning focuses on a process to assess environmental conditions, analyze organizational strengths and weaknesses, and posture public agencies to take advantage of external challenges, opportunities, and threats. The use of strategic planning helps government organizations take advantage of opportunities created by change and uncertainty. Lacking such strategic planning initiatives, local governments will continue to rely on outdated planning practices that are threatened by the very dynamics of the environment in which they must operate.

While strategic planning is a fairly common and routine management function in the private sector, caution must be taken when applying these practices to the public sector. Traditional strategic planning models in the private sector, which typically emphasize profit maximization and environmental control, cannot merely be superimposed on municipal organizations. Due to the unique qualities of individual local governments, extreme care should be exercised when adapting such planning practices to public sector organizations. It should be emphasized that strategic planning programs in the public sector must be tailored to the unique political, administrative, and organizational characteristics of the government in which they are designed, developed and implemented.

Many cities and counties throughout the nation have undertaken strategic planning projects. Others are in the process of developing and implementing similar long-range planning programs. Many of the strategic planning practices in local governments have been diverse, fragmented, and piecemeal in their development and application. For the most part, each local government is "doing its own thing" in this dynamic and rapidly evolving planning discipline.

The purpose of this book is to review proven and sound public sector strategic planning theories, to demonstrate different, yet successful, strategic planning practices used in local governments, and to assess the future direction and application of strategic planning in America's local governments. It is hoped that the codification of strategic planning knowledge in this book — the first of its kind dealing solely with local governments — will help public officials and citizens alike as they strive to manage government in the public's interest.

Roger L. Kemp   Clifton, New Jersey   Fall, 1992

Introduction

Roger L. Kemp

The Future

Dynamic changes are now under way that will have a dramatic impact on our cities — both politically and managerially. Forces of change are now in motion that will require cities to change in order to meet the public's rightful expectations for effective governing. The milestone changes examined in this book are based on predictable trends that will have a measurable impact on municipalities across the nation. They will also test the abilities of public officials as they strive to maintain their constituencies.

Gone are the more stable days for local governments. When revenues were plentiful and public officials could merely adjust tax rates to balance budgets, life was relatively simple and routine. The outside environment did not pose significant challenges, opportunities, or threats. Public programs were merely increased in response to citizen demands for more services. In the future, both the scale and mix of public services, as well as how they are financed, will be reevaluated in response to changes presently taking place in our society.

Traditional planning practices, designed during more stable periods of steady growth and routine change, are being replaced by new planning techniques. Without predictability, the common planning practice of merely projecting past trends into the future will be found to lack both reliability and credibility.

The Forces of Change

The changes occurring in society have a profound impact on our cities and how they are governed. How public officials adapt to their environment will reflect on their ability to successfully cope with the future. Public officials are typically preoccupied with the present, and are usually reactive

1

to change. Most of the time governments, at all levels, attempt to respond to change after the fact. Nowadays, events are changing so rapidly that the traditional planning and management practices of the past are quickly becoming obsolete.

The magnitude of these changes, and their momentum, will have a direct influence on the type of public services provided in the future, how they are financed, and the extent to which they fit the needs of the citizens being served. By proactively planning for the future, our elected and appointed officials can create a smooth transition into the future. If this does not occur, public meeting halls throughout the nation will become forums for "debating" citizen demands for greater government responsiveness and change.

To illustrate the extent of these changes, and to make them easier to understand, they have been separated into five broad categories. These categories are emerging political trends, major demographic shifts, evolving urban patterns, rapid technological changes, and new economic factors influencing our municipalities. The dramatic changes in each of these areas, and their influence on our organizations, are highlighted below.

Political Trends

- More state and federal laws, and court decisions of all types, will greatly usurp the home-rule powers of elected officials and serve to limit their discretion in many areas.
- While special interest groups typically pursue their own narrow goals, these groups will increasingly form coalitions around major community issues of mutual interest.
- Brought about by limited revenues, many political issues will have no clear-cut response, such as the pros and cons of service reductions, tax increases, and user fees and charges.
- Citizens will demand more services, but not want increased taxation, making it more difficult for public officials to set program priorities and balance their annual budgets.
- Public officials will stress economic development as a vehicle to raise revenues without increasing taxes. Highly urbanized cities will have to resort to redevelopment for their financial survival.
- Responsibility will continue to shift from the federal and state governments to cities, leaving them to solve their own problems. Because of the mismatch between revenues and problems, cities with low tax bases may have to resort to service reductions.
- More minority group representatives, including women and immigrants, will get involved in the political arena, placing greater demands for their representation in the workplace.

Demographic Shifts

- There will be a growing number of senior citizens who, because of their available time, will become more politically active.
- Since nearly every community provides the "hard" services (police, fire, and public works) there will be an increasing demand for the so-called "soft" services (recreation, museums, libraries, and cultural programs).
- A greater number of smaller households will require more high-density residential developments, such as condominiums, townhouses, and apartments, placing greater demands on existing public services.
- There will be a greater number of women in the workforce, and they will become more politically active in the workplace. Such issues as comparable worth and sexual harassment will increase in importance.
- A greater number of minority and immigrant groups will create new demands for specialized public services and more bilingual public employees.
- There will be more minority groups involved in the political process, creating growing demands for district elections and greater minority representation in the political arena.
- Public officials will feel the increasing influence of these new special interest groups (e.g., seniors, women, immigrants, and other minorities).
- Any new federal grants will be limited to those programs that help achieve national goals, such as affordable housing, lower unemployment, and shelters for the homeless.

Urban Patterns

- Urban sprawl will be on the increase but will be located primarily along major vehicle transportation corridors and public mass-transit routes.
- Cities will witness greater "in-fill" development in already urbanized areas. Land areas that once were marginal will be purchased and upgraded for new development.
- Older land uses, such as outdated industrial plants and commercial centers, will be upgraded and or retrofitted with new amenities to make them more marketable.
- In central city areas, continuing high land values will lead to increased gentrification, further exacerbating the need for affordable housing for low to moderate income citizens.
- Immigrant and refugee groups will relocate primarily to center city areas in large metropolitan centers in the southwest and northeast portions of the United States.
- New "ethnic centers" will evolve in metropolitan areas. Residents will

stress maintaining the cultural traditions, values, and customs of their homelands.

- Higher energy costs and greater traffic congestion will create more political pressure for public mass-transit systems. Emphasis will be placed on multi-modal systems which offer greater transportation options to the public.
- Public services will increasingly be tailored to better represent growing urban minority and ethnic population centers.

Technological Changes

- There will be an increased use of microcomputers in the workplace, brought about by more sophisticated systems, lower costs, and more user-friendly software.
- Information management will become necessary as computers make more information networks and data bases available. The emphasis will switch from receiving more information to receiving quality information.
- Computer management systems will become a common technique to monitor and limit energy consumption in public buildings and grounds.
- More public meetings will be aired on public-access cable television stations. These stations will also be used to educate citizens on available services and key issues facing their community.
- Greater energy costs will continue to shape our technology (e.g., smaller cars, less spacious offices, new energy-saving devices, and more sophisticated building techniques).
- Advanced telecommunication systems, such as those with conference calling and facsimile transmission capabilities, will reduce the number of business meetings and related personnel and travel costs.
- Increased public pressure for mass-transit, and greater construction costs, will lead to shorter routes in more densely populated high-traffic areas. Light-rail systems will replace the expensive underground subways of the past.

Economic Factors

- Ever-increasing energy costs will require the greater use of energy conservation techniques, including computerized energy management and monitoring systems.
- Citizens will increasingly demand higher standards and accountability for air and water quality, especially in densely populated urban areas.
- The public's aversion to new taxes, and higher user fees and charges, will severely limit the growth of government services.

- Taxpayers will increasingly acknowledge that it is the legitimate role of government to provide "safety-net" services to citizens (i.e., essential sustenance to the truly needy).
- Limited new government revenues will be earmarked for those public services and programs with the highest payoff—from both a political and productive standpoint.
- The availability of federally funded grant programs will be limited, and greater competition will exist among cities for these funds. They will be earmarked for those cities with large low-income populations and related social and housing problems.
- The public will continue to advocate for the "controlled growth" of government by opposing increased taxation and the growth of user fees and charges. They will demand greater accountability and productivity for existing services.

The Need for Planning

The tempo of change in American society is unprecedented. Public officials must treat the future as an opportunity. Those who refuse to are doomed to react to events as if they were mere destiny. Proper planning will help public officials and local governments exploit the future—by limiting external threats, taking advantage of opportunities, and being able to respond to issues and problems proactively in a positive manner.

Traditional planning practices are quickly becoming obsolete in our complex and changing environment. Typical government planning has been characterized as being reactive, short-range, staff-oriented, dominated by single issues, hierarchical in nature, and generally lacking in community support. The events and issues that now must be addressed require new planning techniques. New models are essential in times of fewer grant programs, complex and interrelated issues, rising citizen expectations regarding public services, and the public's aversion to increased taxation.

Long-range strategic planning has become a common practice in the private sector over the past few decades. Strategic planning must be applied to the public sector to enable government officials to successfully adapt to the future. New planning models are available to enable cities to optimize their human and financial resources. Unlike traditional planning, strategic planning is proactive, long-range, and community-oriented. Additionally, it involves multiple issues, is nonhierarchical in nature, and helps achieve a public concensus on the issues and problems facing a municipality.

It is imperative that public officials provide a strategic vision for their community and its municipal organization. A shared understanding of issues and goals not only provides a unified vision of the future, but also helps mobilize all available resources to effectively manage change. It is only through such modern planning practices that public confidence in government can be restored and our local governments can successfully adapt to the future.

Characteristics of
Traditional vs. Strategic Planning
in Local Governments

Traditional Planning	Strategic Planning
Short-range	Long-range
Single Issue	Multiple Issues
Organizational Issues	Community Issues
Hierarchical	Non-hierarchical
Low Involvement	High Involvement
Directive-based	Concensus-based
Staff Oriented	Community Oriented
Management Orientation	Political Orientation
Staff Awareness	Community Awareness
Operational Focus	Policy Focus

Source: Center for Strategic Planning, Clifton, NJ

PART ONE
The Theory

A Public Planning Perspective on Strategic Planning

Jerome L. Kaufman and Harvey M. Jacobs

Twenty-five years ago, at a planning conference session on the newly minted Community Renewal Program — in which many in the room spoke enthusiastically about the potential of this new program — a skeptic got up and stated bluntly: "The Community Renewal Program is just the latest fad to hit town. Sooner or later it, too, will fade away into oblivion." Whether or not the corporate strategic planning approach to planning in the public sector will prove to have been another passing fad remains to be seen. But there is no doubt that it is the center of a lot of attention nowadays.

In the past five years a rash of articles have called on state and local governments to use the strategic planning approach developed in the corporate world (Olsen and Eadie 1982; Eadie 1983; Boyle 1983; Sorkin, Ferris, and Hudak 1984; Toft 1984; Denhardt 1985; Bryson, Van de Ven, and Roering 1986; Eadie and Steinbacher 1985; Tomazinis 1985). During the same period, strategic plans based on the corporate model have been undertaken for an increasing number of governmental jurisdictions: cities such as San Francisco, San Luis Obispo, and Pasadena, California, Philadelphia, Pennsylvania, Albany, New York, Memphis, Tennessee, and Windsor, Connecticut; counties such as Hennepin in Minnesota, Dade in Florida, Prince Georges in Maryland, and Prince William in Virginia; and states such as California, Ohio, and Wisconsin. The number of conferences on how to do strategic planning in the public sector is also on the rise. Even the Reagan administration has become a strong supporter of the strategic planning approach for communities. A key section in the administration's 1982 National Urban Policy Report, "Strategies for Cities," reads as if it were taken from a textbook on corporate strategic planning, with its liberal use of terms such as "strategic approach," "external factors,"

Reprinted with permission from Journal of the American Planning Association, *Vol. 53, No. 1, Winter 1987. Published by the American Planning Association, Chicago, Illinois.*

"threats and opportunities," "internal strengths and weaknesses," "comparative advantages," "strategic issues," and the like. The emergence of corporate strategic planning in public planning parallels the rise of economic development in the late 1970s as a focus of local planning. But corporate strategic planning is not limited to economic development planning. It can be and has been applied to transportation, health, environmental, and other functional planning areas. Likewise, it can be and has been applied to planning at the regional and state levels as well as at the city level.

Proponents of corporate strategic planning claim numerous benefits will accrue to communities that follow it. The authors of the *Strategic Planning Guide* funded by the U.S. Department of Housing and Urban Development (Sorkin, Ferris, and Hudak 1984), for example, contend that the approach can result in getting important things accomplished, educating the public, building consensus, developing a shared vision that extends past the next election, positioning a community to seize opportunities, shedding new light on important issues, identifying the most effective uses of resources, and providing a mechanism for public-private cooperation. Some academics contend that, "when done well, strategic planning offers one approach to the revitalization and redirection of governments and the public service" (Bryson, Van de Ven, and Roering 1986).

But there is another side of corporate strategic planning that directly challenges the public planning profession. Some proponents of the approach explicitly or implicitly fault traditional public planning for not having done the job, accusing it of falling short of the mark. They see the corporate strategic planning approach as better suited than more traditional public planning to helping communities cope with changes induced by a dwindling resource base. Given the criticism of traditional public planning approaches and the growing popularity of the corporate strategic planning approach, the field of urban and regional planning may well face crises of both relevance and professional identity.

It is the purpose of this article to examine strategic planning from a public planning perspective, stressing the application of this approach to communitywide planning, the traditional focus of public planning. This is distinct from the application of strategic planning to organizations, which might focus on how the city as a public corporation or a single city agency can accomplish its missions more effectively. We first define the corporate strategic planning approach examined in this article. Then we examine the approach in terms of its similarities to and differences from other public planning approaches, based on a review of literature familiar to most public planners. We supplement the literature review with an exploratory study of 15 public-sector planners who work in communities where corporate strategic planning is under way, in order to assess practitioners' perspectives on how this approach is similar to and different from other public planning approaches. We close with speculations on how public-sector planners might view the advent of strategic planning.

A Definition

Strategic planning originated about 20 years ago in the private sector. Its roots are tied to the need of rapidly changing and growing corporations to plan effectively for and manage their futures, when the future itself appeared increasingly uncertain. By the end of the 1960s, Steiner (1969) estimated, three-quarters of the large industrial corporations in the United States had formal strategic planning in place. By the mid–1980s more than half of the publicly traded companies were using some form of strategic planning (Denhardt 1985).

As it developed, strategic planning began taking a variety of paths. Taylor (1984) identifies five main styles of corporate strategic planning that have emerged in recent years: central control, framework for innovation, strategic management, political planning, and futures research. Bryson, Freeman, and Roering (1986) also distinguish five models of strategic planning: the Harvard policy, portfolio, industrial economics, stakeholder, and decision process models.

The central features of public-sector strategic planning are captured in the acronym *SWOT*, a derivative of the Harvard policy model. In general, a community assesses its *strengths*, *weaknesses*, *opportunities*, and *threats* as a basis for devising action strategies to achieve goals and objectives in certain key issue areas. Recognizing that variations are possible in the sequencing of, time spent in, and analytic depth devoted to each phase of the strategic planning process, Sorkin, Ferris, and Hudak (1984) identify the following as the basic steps in strategic planning at the community level:

1. Scan the environment.
2. Select key issues.
3. Set mission statements or broad goals.
4. Undertake external and internal analyses.
5. Develop goals, objectives, and strategies with respect to each issue.
6. Develop an implementation plan to carry out strategic actions.
7. Monitor, update, and scan.

In this conception of corporate strategic planning, opportunities and threats are assessed in step 1 and used as the basis for action in steps 2 and 3. Strengths and weaknesses are developed most pointedly in step 4, but they also serve as the basis for refining decisions in steps 2 and 3 and formulating strategies in steps 5 and 6. Strengths, weaknesses, opportunities, and threats are used together in step 7 to evaluate a plan and determine its continued viability.

For our purpose, we use the above conception as the definition of strategic planning as it is applied in the public sector. Our concern is with the application of strategic planning to communitywide planning, the traditional domain of public planners. Eadie and Steinbacher (1985) and Bryson, Freeman, and Roering (1986) note that strategic planning can be, and has been, applied to both communitywide and line agency planning. The approach outlined above applies broadly to both. The strong history of strategic planning, however, is as a management tool for organizations. It is the proposed application of strategic planning to communitywide issues that is new and raises issues of theory and method for public planners.

The View from the Planning Literature

Consider the following scene: Two rooms adjoin each other with a door between them. In one room, people are busily at work developing and refining the strategic planning model for use by private corporations. In the other room, a similar intensity of activity goes on as people work at developing and refining planning process models for use in the public sector. No movement, however, takes place between occupants of the two adjoining rooms. The door between the rooms is shut tightly.

This metaphor is intended to describe what we believe went on from the 1960s to the early 1980s in the respective spheres of corporate strategic planning and public planning. People were hard at work in both spheres, but little or no interaction took place between them. We doubt that more than a handful of corporate strategic planners ever read the articles and books that were cornerstones of reading lists in graduate planning theory courses — for example, Altshuler (1965), Davidoff and Reiner (1962), Etzioni (1967), Meyerson (1956), and Friedmann (1973). Likewise, readings on the corporate strategic planning approach probably were never assigned to students who took planning theory courses before 1980 — for instance, the works of Drucker (1954), Chandler (1962), Ansoff (1965), Steiner (1969), and Steiner and Miner (1977).

But in the 1980s the door between the two rooms has opened, and some of the occupants are moving between them. Some planning academics are walking into the corporate strategic planning room, looking around, and coming to the conclusion that the corporate strategic planning model has applicability for public planning (Bryson, Van de Ven, and

Roering 1986; Lang 1986; Tomazinis 1985). Likewise, some proponents of the corporate strategic planning approach (Eadie 1983; Sorkin, Ferris, and Hudak 1984; Toft 1984; Denhardt 1985) are strolling into the public planning room, gazing around, and arriving at a similar conclusion — that the corporate strategic planning approach can be of benefit to communities that public planners traditionally have served.

Some proponents of strategic planning point to significant differences between this approach and the conventional public planning approach. A few are taking some healthy whacks at public planning for its shortcomings. One, for example, says city and regional planning has lost "its flexibility to change dramatically the subject matter of its concerns, the process of its explorations, and the tools of its inquiries" (Tomazinis 1985, 14). Another is even more sweeping and caustic in his criticism: "The history of public planning is replete with tales of overexpectation, underestimation of costs, and disillusionment.... [It] has proved increasingly less useful" (Eadie 1983, 447–48).

Rather than focus on the harsher criticisms of public planning, we want to look more carefully at the distinctions that proponents of strategic planning draw between that approach and public planning. We want to assess whether these distinctions are real or imagined and, if they are real, whether they are only differences of emphasis or raise truly new points. We will draw on an analysis of the public planning literature with which most graduates of planning schools are familiar.

What, then, are the main distinctions that proponents of the corporate strategic planning approach see between it and conventional public planning?

- Corporate strategic planning is oriented more toward action, results, and implementation;
- it promotes broader and more diverse participation in the planning process;
- it places more emphasis on understanding the community in its external context, determining the opportunities and threats to a community via an environmental scan;
- it embraces competitive behavior on the part of communities; and
- it emphasizes assessing a community's strengths and weaknesses in the context of opportunities and threats.

We believe proponents of corporate strategic planning are essentially correct in contending that their approach differs significantly from conventional planning in those ways, if by "public planning" they mean long-range comprehensive or master planning. And there is reason to believe that that is the conception many strategic planning proponents hold of public planning (Eadie and Steinbacher 1985; Denhardt 1985; Toft 1984; Eadie 1983; Sorkin, Ferris, and Hudak 1984).

But that conception of public planning has been the subject of long-standing critiques in the planning literature — critiques that have been widely recognized. Several strong strands in the planning literature have moved beyond the notion that public planning should be long-range comprehensive or master planning. Strategic planning proponents may be fixing on a model of public planning that planning authors no longer acknowledge as representative of contemporary planning thought or professional practice. In fact, we contend that most of the principal distinctions that strategic planning proponents draw between their approach and public planning are, as evidenced by contemporary planning literature, much less pronounced or do not exist.

Action and Results Orientation

A major claimed distinction between corporate strategic planning and public planning is that the former is more oriented toward action and results, in other words more relevant for decision making. Yet the call for more decision-relevant planning information and analysis has been the basis of the first important set of critiques of comprehensive planning that began in the 1950s and continue into the present. Walker (1950) raised questions about the organizational position of planners and the independent planning commission and called for a more direct link with decision making and decision makers. Beginning with their groundbreaking study of planning practice Meyerson and Banfield (1955), Meyerson (1956), Banfield (1959), and then others (e.g., Altshuler 1965; Bolan 1967) began to argue that, even if comprehensive planning was a good idea in theory, it was largely unattainable in the real world of politics and policy.

In his well-known critique, Lindblom (1959) argued that comprehensive planning was an impossible undertaking. It required more intelligence and information than was ever available. Banfield (1959) argued further that, in many cases, organizations neither wanted to nor could engage in rational comprehensive planning. As a result, these authors and others (e.g., Meyerson 1956; Bolan 1971; Benveniste 1972; Catanese 1974) began to articulate models of more decision-relevant planning that were also more limited in scope, shorter-range in time frame, and more sensitive to the decision environment in which planners operate. One of these authors (Meyerson 1956) specifically warned planners that their role could be usurped if they did not move in these directions.

On this one point, then, we contend that planners have long had their attention drawn to the need for being more oriented toward action and results and have been presented various ways of achieving those ends. The abundance of applied policy analysis techniques in planning curriculums, the actual philosophical shift of certain planning schools in that direction, and the support of planners for middle-range, action-oriented programs like the Community Renewal and Model Cities programs suggest that practitioners and academics have gotten the message. We believe the need for policy relevancy has been widely recognized and is, with perhaps only recent dissension (e.g., Isserman 1985; Kreditor 1985), the mainstream of opinion about the appropriate role of planning.

Participation

A second claimed distinction of corporate strategic planning is that it broadens the basis of participation in planning. Denhardt (1985) is an example of a strategic planning proponent who suggests that the constituency for planning is too narrow. Again, as in the above discussion, Denhardt (1985), Eadie (1983), and others seem unaware of the many calls for broadening participation in planning from planning academics (Burke 1968; Friedmann 1973; Rosener 1978) and planning practitioners (AICP Code of Ethics 1981).[1] Advocate and progressive planners, in particular, stress the need to bring people into the planning process who, by design or practice, have not participated (Davidoff 1965; Arnstein 1969; Goodman 1971; Clavel 1983). Like proponents of corporate strategic planning, all these authors argue that diverse participation will lead to more insightful and responsive planning.

So, as with the issue of policy relevancy, the call by strategic planning proponents for more participation in planning is not, in and of itself, a new call to the public planning profession. For more than 20 years we have had vigorous debates on and experiments in participation in planning. What is emphasized more by some strategic planning proponents is the suggestion that we might need greater participation from selected segments of the private business community, although the call for public-private partnership is not absent from the planning literature (Catanese 1974; Branch 1983).

Environmental Scanning

An important contribution that corporate strategic planning has to offer public planning is the idea of scanning the environment. According to Denhardt (1985, 175), under strategic planning "the organization is not assumed to exist in a vacuum, but rather both the organization's objectives and steps to achieve those objectives are seen in the context of the resources and constraints presented by the organization's environment." This environmental sensitivity allows the organization to do smarter, more focused planning and improves its ability to understand the relative risks associated with alternative courses of action. The environmental scan encourages an organization to look beyond itself in space and time.

This basis for planning fits well with the interest in futures studies in general and the work of Naisbitt (1982) in particular. The world is understood to comprise limited resources and certain unchangeable circumstances that need to be accepted and creatively used. Within the context of an environmental scan, an organization then assesses its strengths and weaknesses. That is, strengths and weaknesses are determined relative to opportunities and threats, which are themselves given and essentially unchangeable.

Although the emphasis on environmental scanning is both well developed and, from our perspective, well deserved, it also is not entirely new, though it is perhaps less well accepted within the planning community. As far back as the 1920s and 1930s Lewis Mumford, Benton MacKaye, and their associates in the Regional Planning Association of America wrote plans and developed planning theory that explicitly called for planning within broad social-economic-technological contexts (Stein 1926; MacKaye 1928; Mumford 1938). Under the Roosevelt administration, the work of the National Reserve Planning Board, especially in its early years, similarly reflected the importance to planning of broad trend analysis (National Resources Board 1934a; 1934b; National Resources Committee 1937; Clawson 1981).

More recently, planners from many different subfields have stressed the importance of understanding and planning for an organization within a broad context. Environmental planners base much of the justification for their practice on the relation of local activities to broader environmental systems and activities (e.g., McHarg 1969). Planning for air pollution, water pollution, groundwater contamination, farmland preservation, wildlife habitat, and forest management, for example, all require planners to examine resource use and economics regionally, nationally, and even internationally. Likewise, in the field of economic development, planners have available ample literature that stresses the importance of planning for plant location within an understanding of intra- and international changes in population, economics, and technological investment (Perry and Watkins 1977; Bluestone and Harrison 1982). Similarly, in social planning, the definition of key problem areas and target populations for service delivery is commonly based on analysis of broad demographic and economic trends. Etzioni (1967) has formulated an approach to planning in general that stresses what corporate strategic planning proponents call environmental scanning. As noted earlier, Etzioni's work is a source common to graduate planning theory courses, and thus environmental scanning is an idea to which public planners have been long exposed.

Competitive Behavior

Another feature of corporate strategic planning is how it encourages a community to embrace competitive behavior. Its proponents are quite explicit in this regard. For example, Toft argues that "what is called for in most situations . . . is competitive strategy. A successful community must view itself as a competitive product." In the 1980s, "governments and community organizations . . . must be proactive given a more erratic and uncertain environment where there will be winners and losers" (Toft 1984, 6, 7).

That cities, counties, states, and regions are in a competitive position with each other is no news to planners. It is the basis of much of the frustration in planning; to wit, communities searching for an ever-increasing tax base, the related inability to rein in municipal boundaries, the difficulty in managing regional environmental resources, and the companion proposals these frustrations have engendered: tax sharing, councils of governments, and regional and state land use planning reform (Williams 1970; Long 1977; Scott 1975). Practicing planners have long acknowledged the competition of a city with surrounding suburban communities (Catanese and Farmer 1978; Krumholz 1982). Recently, planners have become more acutely aware of interregional and even international competition for jobs and industrial plant location (Perry and Watkins 1977; Bluestone and Harrison 1982).

What is different about corporate strategic planning is not its recognition of competition but its perspective on that competition. The traditional perspective on competition in public planning is to view it as damaging to the economic and social health of a community. Planners and planning theory strove to seek out and foster cooperative, shared solutions. Under strategic planning, competition is seen as inevitable. Communities therefore are exhorted to identify their competitive niche and exploit it or suffer the consequences.

Community Strengths and Weaknesses

The final distinctive feature claimed for corporate strategic planning is the community's critical appraisal of strengths and weaknesses relative to the environmental scan of opportunities and threats and within the parameters of the other features discussed above — action orientation, public involvement process, and competitive perspective on intergovernmental relations. This, too, we conclude, is not an entirely new idea for the planning community, though the exact terms used to describe the exercise and the emphasis accorded this phase of planning may be different under corporate strategic planning.

According to proponents of strategic planning, traditional public planning (i.e., long-range comprehensive or master planning) too often perceives the world around and within as one-dimensional. That is, goals, objectives, and policies that are developed and stated in a plan too often seem to cover all topics of possible concern to the locality and assume that the planning, policy, and administrative units of the government have equal capacity and incentive to act on the plan's recommendations. In contrast, strategic planning is supposed to encourage an honest assessment of a community's capacity to act, seeking to maximize strengths and minimize weaknesses in the context of opportunities and threats. As with the points discussed above, however, this perspective is not entirely new to planning theory or practice, though it may not be as well developed, for reasons that point up one of the main differences in public and private planning.

The discussion of strengths and weaknesses borrows directly from the economic literature on competitive advantage. In fact, it can be seen as nothing more than a shifting of the competitive advantage idea from the market to the organizational and community sector. At the community level, Tiebout's (1956) formulation of local expenditures and the public choice school of economics has kept the issues of competitive advantage and strengths and weaknesses before the planning community for a long time. Practitioners such as Krumholz (1982; Krumholz, Cogger, and Linner 1975) have shown how planners with particular ethical orientations can pointedly address the strengths and weaknesses of current city planning processes and move an organization toward maximizing its strengths. Likewise, certain traditional and well-regarded plans, such as New York City's (1969), explicitly address the weaknesses of certain city agencies and activities. Other plans we are aware of, such as Chicago's (1966), had similar sections in early drafts that were later edited out to reduce organizational friction and to help generate diverse support for the plans. At one level, identifying strengths and weaknesses, especially the latter, has been a politically unwise and difficult undertaking. But it is not an idea to which planners have been accustomed.

Thus, when we examine the planning literature, we find that the components of corporate strategic planning that proponents say are fundamentally different are not really all that different. Many of the implied and explicit criticisms are directed at the comprehensive, long-range, or master planning model. Most of these criticisms are longstanding within the theory and practice of public-sector planning. Planners have been told of the need to be more policy relevant, to involve more and different types of people in the planning process, and to do their planning within a realistic assessment of the systems and networks of which they are part. Planners also are aware both of competition and of the idea of identifying and acting on strengths and weaknesses.

What, then, is different about strategic planning from the point of view of the planning literature? We note two differences. The first is the framework of corporate strategic planning, which brings all the above points together. It may be true that the literature has drawn planners' attention to most or all of the points that proponents claim are distinctive about strategic planning. The strategic approach is distinctive, however, in pulling all those elements together into a coherent planning structure. Continuing to highlight the importance of individual elements and stressing their interrelationship may help planners to do better planning.

The second difference is the ideological and programmatic usefulness of corporate strategic planning. By introducing a model of planning that is seen to come out of the private sector, the practice of planning — which nowadays is under attack in some quarters — may be seen as more legitimate. Corporate strategic planning thus may be shifting the debate in public-sector planning from *whether* to do it to *how* to do it. In these times, that would be a significant shift.

The View from the Planning Trenches

Strategic planning applied to the public sector is a relatively recent development. The preceding analysis of literature indicates that key features of the strategic planning approach, which proponents claim are distinct from the conventional public planning approach, are well ensconced in planning theory and recognized in some of the writings on planning practice. But the exhortations of academics are not necessarily guideposts that all practitioners follow. As we know, the gap between what planning theorists say and what planning practitioners do can be wide (Krueckeberg 1971; Kaufman 1974).

For that reason we decided to examine how planning practitioners view strategic planning as it has been applied at the communitywide level. We wanted to get firsthand information about how planners steeped in the public planning tradition felt about a planning approach that, although nurtured in the corporate world, is being implanted in the public-sector vineyard. Do planners see important differences between strategic planning efforts and the approaches followed in public planning? If so, what are these differences? What are planners' attitudes toward community-based strategic planning ventures — enthusiasm? acceptance? skepticism? hostility?

To answer these questions, we conducted phone interviews with 15 public planners about their views of strategic planning efforts under way at the communitywide level. Each planner interviewed worked either in a community where a strategic planning program was under way or in one where such a program had been completed recently.[2] These planners represented communities for which strategic planning was far enough along to allow for an informed interview. Therefore, they could give opinions about the contrast, if any, of the strategic planning process with other, more traditional planning approaches. It was important to the validity of the study that each planner had held his or her position long enough before the introduction of strategic planning that they could discuss its differences and similarities with other forms of public planning in the community. The interview group was small, reflecting the newness of corporate strategic planning. Given the size of the group, we want to stress the exploratory nature of these interviews and to offer these data as the basis for more extensive research in the future.

In a recent paper, Tomazinis (1985, p. 14) said, "Strategic planning has the potential to revitalize public planning . . . by invigorating the planning agencies, revitalizing the interest in planning of top elected officials, and helping cities and regions rediscover and redefine their crucial problems." We read this positive statement about strategic planning to the group of planners as the opening to our telephone interview, asking whether and why they agreed or disagreed with it.

In general, these planners were divided in their opinion about strategic planning. A few were quite positive about its value. Others were mildly supportive, seeing some benefits but also having some reservations. And some were downright skeptical.

One enthusiast, for example, stated that he unequivocally agreed with the Tomazinis statement. Another supporter saw strategic planning as an opportunity to put planning on a more vigorous footing. Still another commented that the strategic planning program in his community definitely had value in revitalizing elected officials' interest in planning.

Skeptics responded differently to the Tomazinis statement. One said planning in his community was already vigorous, top elected officials already had a strong interest in planning, and crucial problems were being addressed continually by his agency; strategic planning therefore was not really needed. Another said strategic planning "was just an advertising gimmick to sell the old stuff in a new way." Other skeptics saw it as trendy. As one put it, "Nowadays it's the way to get federal bucks for planning. You have to use the right buzz words to get a share of the dwindling dollars."

Going beneath these surface reactions, we sensed that a planner's attitude toward strategic planning was conditioned principally by two factors: the planner's educational background and the perceived status of the planning function in the community where the planner worked.

We observed that planners with degrees from planning schools were generally less sanguine about strategic planning than those with degrees in fields other than planning. As one planner with a graduate planning degree said, "I don't see the strategic planning process as significantly different from what I learned in planning school." Another planning school graduate put it this way: "Strategic planning is like pouring old wine into new bottles."

In contrast, a supporter of strategic planning who had a degree in economic geography justified his support by criticizing the planning done in his agency as producing "too many plans that are just damn inventories." He went on to say, "Just as one of Congress' problems is that it has too many lawyers, one of the problems with planning agencies is that they have too many planners." Likewise, an economist who has worked as a planner for many years suggested that "comprehensive plans that planners prepare tend to be too illusionary. The interconnectedness of goals, objectives, and policies is not always clear. Strategic planning avoids these pitfalls."

A cross-cutting factor affecting a planner's attitude toward strategic planning was the perceived status of the planning function in the community. Where public planning was perceived to be more vigorous, respected, and involved in community issues, planners viewed strategic planning as unnecessary or redundant. Where the public planning function was perceived to be weak, then strategic planning efforts took on a rosier complexion in the planner's view.

The following comments about strategic planning were made by planners who saw their planning programs as strong and healthy:

> In our community, we have an ongoing and lively discussion of issues. Interest in public affairs is high. I don't think we need a strategic planning approach.

> An aggressive planning department like ours is already doing the things that strategic planning proponents are saying strategic planning does. I don't think the strategic planning done by the Chamber of Commerce has much value. It's regarded as a business advocacy plan. It has neither been adopted nor has it had much influence on public policy.

> In our agency, which has lots of professionals who are broadly educated and policy-sensitive, strategic planning is not needed.

This last planner, however, acknowledged that in a community where the planning function is weak, "strategic planning might help to invigorate the planning agency." Likewise, one planner, who admitted he worked for an agency that was not well regarded, saw definite advantages to the strategic planning approach: "It pushes us to be more focused on issues, and it increases our chances of getting things implemented." Another who worked in a community where planning was not considered strong liked the strategic planning approach because it emphasized community strengths as well as weaknesses. He claimed it had led to the realization that "we have some good things going for us in our community, counteracting the tendency to knock ourselves too much."

Whether they were favorable or unfavorable toward strategic planning, the planners we interviewed agreed that it was *not* fundamentally different from good traditional public planning.

Some skeptics offered these contentions:

> Strategic planning doesn't strike me as much different than the kind of middle-range, policy-sensitive planning we do now in our community.

> We do essentially the same things in our planning program that proponents of corporate strategic planning claim that approach accomplishes.

> Strategic planning doesn't represent much of a change from what we already do. For the last 10 years in our agency we've been taking a strategic approach, looking at strengths and weaknesses of our city, focusing on crucial issues, developing action strategies. Strategic planning is not a new direction.

Even strong supporters of strategic planning saw no fundamental differences:

> Intuitively we were doing strategic planning before. But we didn't have a model that we could specifically cite, like strategic planning, to give a name to what we were doing.

> Although we're doing strategic planning for economic development, the approach is not new; the basis of it isn't any different from what you expect from good comprehensive planning.

Although in agreement that the two planning approaches are not fundamentally different, both the supporters and the skeptics of corporate strategic planning cited differences in emphasis between the two approaches. Both groups seemed to be shorter-range in focus and targeted on more realistic and feasible proposals. In addition, they were in agreement that strategic planning efforts at the local level emphasized marketing of communities attractively, packaging action proposals in ways designed to excite the public and policymakers, and highlighting the community's competitive advantages — all ideas consistent with the private-sector origins of the model. Differences of opinion did surface, however, between the supporters and the skeptics. Whereas supporters tended to assess strategic planning efforts as more analytically rigorous, as involving a broader cross section of the community in planning, and as achieving more implementation success, skeptics — as befitted their label — disagreed with those contentions.

Differences of opinion were sharpest over the limitations of the corporate strategic planning approach. Although supporters acknowledged that strategic planning had some weaknesses (e.g., it can be very time-consuming, it's difficult to maintain the interest level of top decision makers in the process, and it can be a costly undertaking), their criticisms were decidedly tamer than those of the skeptics. The latter were especially blunt in their contentions that strategic planning programs were too narrowly based, reflected too much of a business community agenda, had much less influence on policy decisions than its advocates credited it, and seriously underestimated the problem of implementing priority decisions than its advocates credited it, and seriously underestimated the problem of implementing priority actions in the decentralized, pluralistic decision-making system of the public sector. Given their contention that their planning agencies were already active both in identifying crucial community issues and in thinking and acting strategically long before strategic planning came on the scene, one senses that planners who hold strong reservations about strategic planning see little value in it. Quite clearly, their views are not shared by all the planners we interviewed. As we said, a few were quite enthusiastic about the strategic planning efforts under way in their communities, and more who were lukewarm were still positive about some features of the approach.

Conclusion

It is the purpose of this article to examine, from a public planning perspective, the adaptation of the corporate strategic planning model to communitywide planning. We have examined five points that proponents of corporate strategic planning put forth as distinguishing it from traditional public planning. We argue that the implied or explicit critique of so-called traditional planning is, at base, a critique of comprehensive, long-range, or master planning; that this is only one mode of planning; and that it is a mode that has long sustained criticism for the very points highlighted by proponents of corporate strategic planning. From the planning literature, we find that the critiques and suggestions embodied in strategic planning are longstanding, well developed, and well known. We note, though, that corporate strategic planning is distinctive in bringing these points together into a coherent planning process model.

In addition, we conducted telephone interviews with 15 planners around the United States whose communities have engaged in strategic planning. We found them divided in their assessment of the approach. A few were quite supportive, some had mixed feelings, and still others were decidedly skeptical. All, however, found that strategic planning was not significantly different from good comprehensive planning; it was different in emphasis, they said, but not different in kind.

We are aware of the limitations of the methods used to arrive at the above and subsequent conclusions. Our examination of planning literature, founded in the survey by Klosterman (1981), represents the material we believe is central to debate and development in planning theory. Others whose assessment of the literature is different may find our argument less compelling. In terms of the interviews with practicing planners, the size of the study population was small and necessarily non-random. As such our data are exploratory. A more verifiable assessment of what practicing public planners think about strategic planning efforts at the local level would require a larger group of interviewees and a more rigorous interview structure. Nevertheless, we believe the phone interviews provide an accurate snapshot of how selected public planners with exposure to strategic planning view it today. Further, these data provide a basis for developing hypotheses about planners' perceptions of corporate strategic planning and its application in current planning practice.[3]

In the way of general conclusions, we offer the following thoughts. First, recent introspection about corporate strategic planning (e.g., Kiechel 1982; *Business Week* 1984; Hayes 1985) reflects an emerging skepticism toward its application to the management of corporations. Bryson, Van de Ven, and Roering (1986) and Eadie (1983), proponents of corporate strategic planning, show a growing sensitivity to the complexities of transferring this approach to the public sector.

Second, we stress that, at least in the short term, strategic planning will remain an issue in the public sector. Especially in the area of economic development, strategic planning has become an important technique to develop a program of action based on a public-private partnership. As noted earlier, in certain ways we believe that is good for public planning. In a time of fiscal constraint and possible crisis, strategic planning is redefining the nature of the public planning debate. It may be that corporate strategic planning will help turn the discussion from *whether* to do planning to *how* to do planning.

This suggests our third set of thoughts. The public planning community can look at the advent and popularity of corporate-style strategic planning in any of three ways: as a threat, as an opportunity, or as another fad. As a threat, strategic planning seems poised to replace the way public planners have done planning and even the planners themselves (e.g., Denhardt 1985, p. 175). Even if planners embrace strategic planning, however, it is possible that, although they may become more integrated into decision making, the planning they do may be little different from the management-type planning undertaken by public administrators. Success with strategic planning thus might be bittersweet. Seen in that light, strategic planning is something to be either avoided or fought against so as to preserve the place and style of existing public planning. How successful this posture would be is unclear, especially given the strong support that corporate strategic planning receives from influential members of the private sector and political communities.

On the other hand, strategic planning seems to offer significant opportunities for public planners. If we are correct in our assessment of the components of strategic planning and its relation to existing planning theory, planners already should be well exposed to its concepts and techniques. Even its jargon is becoming familiar to planners. In this case, public planners should be well positioned to play significant roles in strategic planning programs at the community level. They can stress their skills in facilitation, communication, analysis of secondary data, and forecasting. If strategic planning in the future follows the examples of the recent past, substantial amounts of money will be available for such programs. If they look at strategic planning as an opportunity, public planners could be central to deciding how and for what those funds get used. Otherwise, the torch for planning will be carried by other professionals and groups.

Finally, corporate-style strategic planning may be just another passing fad. Like planning-programming-budgeting systems, it may be bursting onto the scene with a great deal of fanfare only to slip into relative obscurity later (So 1984). That is an unknown now, and we attempt no prediction. Instead, we close by noting that, since it is unknown, planners would do well to treat the advent of strategic planning seriously and to view it, in the parlance of the approach, as an opportunity rather than as a threat.

Ultimately public planners will need to wait for more data before making definitive judgments about corporate strategic planning. More strategic plans need to be prepared, and existing strategic plans need to be acted on. Only then will it be known if strategic planning can bring about more effective public planning.

Notes

1. The American Institute of Certified Planners Code of Ethics (1981) states clearly that planners "must strive to give citizens the opportunity to have meaningful impact on plans and programs." Participation is defined as "broad enough to include people who lack formal organization or influence."

2. Interviews were conducted with top-level planners in San Francisco; the Philadelphia area; the Minneapolis–St. Paul area; Dade County, Florida; Fort Collins, Colorado; Pittsburgh; Madison, Wisconsin; Memphis, Tennessee; Oxford, Ohio; and Albany, New York. For the purposes of this article, the names, titles, and positions of the interviewees are omitted.

3. A broad range of research questions could be pursued with regard to applications of corporate strategic planning in the public sector. For instance, why is strategic planning used in some communities but not in others? Is it a function of leadership, organization, business influence? Who benefits from strategic planning efforts, and how are those benefits realized? Do strategic planning efforts strengthen the planning function? Do strategic planning programs that involve widespread public participation reflect broader consensus or more watered-down compromise? Is the idea of regionalism advanced or weakened when communities follow a strategic planning approach that emphasizes competition?

References

Altshuler, Alan A. 1965. *The city planning process: A political analysis.* Ithaca, N.Y.: Cornell University Press.

American Institute of Certified Planners. 1981. Code of ethics and professional conduct. Washington: AICP.

Ansoff, Igor. 1965. *Corporate strategy: An analytic approach to business policy for growth and expansion.* New York: McGraw-Hill.

Arnstein, Sherry R. 1969. A ladder of citizen participation. *Journal of the American Institute of Planners* 35, 4: 216–24.

Arthur Anderson & Co. n.d. *Guide to public-sector strategic planning.* Chicago: Arthur Anderson & Co.

Banfield, Edward C. 1959. Ends and means in planning. *International Social Science Journal* 11, 3: 361–68.

Beneviste, Guy. 1972. *The politics of expertise.* Berkeley, Calif.: Glendessary Press.

Bluestone, Barry, and Bennett Harrison. 1982. *The deindustrialization of America.* New York: Basic Books.

Bolan, Richard. 1967. Emerging views of planning. *Journal of the American Institute of Planners* 33, 4: 234–46.

_____. 1971. The social relations of the planner. *Journal of the American Institute of Planners* 37, 6: 386–95.

Boyle, M. Ross. 1983. The strategic planning process: Assessing a community's economic assets. *Economic Development Commentary* 7, 2: 3–7.

Branch, Melville C. 1983. *Comprehensive planning: General theory and principles.* Pacific Palisades, Calif.: Palisades Publishers.

Bryson, John M., Andrew H. Van de Ven, and William D. Roering. 1986. Strategic planning and the revitalization of the public service. In *Toward a New Public Service* (Robert C. Denhardt and Edward Jennings, eds.) Columbia, Mo.: University of Missouri Press. In press.

_____, R. Edward Freeman, and William D. Roering. 1986. Strategic planning in the public sector: Approaches and future directions. In *Strategic Approaches to Planning Practice,* (Barry Checkoway, ed.) Lexington, Mass.: Lexington Books. Forthcoming.

Burke, Edmund C. 1968. Citizen participation strategies. *Journal of the American Institute of Planners* 34, 5: 287–94.

Business Week. 1984. The new breed of strategic planner. *Business Week* September 17: 62–68.

Catanese, Anthony James. 1974. *Planners and local politics: Impossible dreams.* Beverly Hills, Calif.: Sage Publications.

_____, and W. Paul Farmer, eds. 1978. *Personality, politics, and planning.* Beverly Hills, Calif.: Sage Publications.

Chandler, Alfred. 1962. *Strategy and structure.* Boston: MIT Press.

Chicago Department of Development and Planning. 1966. *The comprehensive plan of Chicago.* Chicago: CDDP.

Clavel, Pierre. 1983. *Opposition planning in Wales and Appalachia.* Philadelphia: Temple University Press.

Clawson, Marion. 1981. *New Deal planning*. Baltimore: Johns Hopkins University Press.
Davidoff, Paul. 1965. Advocacy and pluralism in planning. *Journal of the American Institute of Planners* 31, 4: 331–38.
_____, and Thomas Reiner. 1962. A choice theory of planning. *Journal of the American Institute of Planners* 28, 2: 103–15.
Denhardt, Robert B. 1985. Strategic planning in state and local government. *State and Local Government Review* 17, 1: 174–79.
Drucker, Peter. 1954. *The practice of management*. New York: Harper and Row.
Eadie, Douglas C. 1983. Putting a powerful tool to practical use: The application of strategic planning in the public sector. *Public Administration Review* 43, 5: 447–52.
_____, and Roberta Steinbacher. 1985. Strategic agenda management: A marriage of organizational development and strategic planning. *Public Administration Review* 45, 3: 424–30.
Etzioni, Amitai. 1967. Mixed scanning: A "third" approach to decision-making. *Public Administration Review* 27, 5: 385–92.
Friedmann, John. 1973. *Retracking America: A theory of transactive planning*. New York: Anchor Press/Doubleday.
Goodman, Robert. 1971. *After the planners*. New York: Simon and Schuster.
Hayes, Robert H. 1985. Strategic planning—Forward in reverse? *Harvard Business Review* 63, 6: 111–19.
Isserman, Andrew M. 1985. Dare to plan: An essay on the role of the future in planning practice and education. *Town Planning Review* 56, 4: 483–91.
Kaufman, Jerome L. 1974. Contemporary planning practice: State of the art. In *Planning in America: Learning from Turbulence* (D. Godschalk, ed.) Washington: American Institute of Planners.
Kiechel, Walter. 1982. Corporate stategists under fire. *Fortune* 106, 13: 34–39.
Klosterman, Richard E. 1981. Contemporary planning theory education: Results of a course survey. *Journal of Planning Education and Research* 1, 1: 1–11.
Kreditor, Alan. 1985. Dilemmas in planning education: Dichotomies between visionary and utilitarian. Paper presented at the annual meeting of the Association of Collegiate Schools of Planning, Atlanta, Georgia. November.
Krueckeberg, Don. 1971. Variations in behavior of planning agencies. *Administrative Science Quarterly* 16, 2: 192–202.
Krumholz, Norman. 1982. A retrospective view of equity planning: Cleveland 1969–1979. *Journal of the American Planning Association* 48, 2: 163–74.
_____, Janice M. Cogger, and John H. Linner. 1975. The Cleveland policy planning report. *Journal of the American Institute of Planners* 41, 5: 298–304.
Lang, Reg. 1986. Achieving integration in resource planning. In *Integrated Approaches to Resource Planning and Management* (Reg Lang, ed.) Calgary, Alberta: University of Calgary Press. In press.
Lindblom, Charles E. 1959. The science of muddling through. *Public Administration Review* 19, 2: 79–88.
Long, Norton E. 1977. How to help cities become independent. In *How Cities Can Grow Old Gracefully*, prepared for the Subcommittee on the City, Committee on Banking, Finance and Urban Affairs, U.S. House of Representatives. Washington: U.S. Government Printing Office.
MacKaye, Benton. 1928. *The new exploration: A philosophy of regional planning*. New York: Harcourt, Brace and Co.
McHarg, Ian. 1969. *Design with nature*. Garden City, N.Y.: Doubleday and Co.
Meyerson, Martin. 1956. Building the middle-range bridge for comprehensive planning. *Journal of the American Institute of Planners* 22, 2: 58–64.
_____, and Edward Banfield. 1955. *Politics, planning and the public interest*. New York: Free Press.
Mumford, Lewis. 1938. *The culture of cities*. New York: Harcourt Brace Jovanovich.
Naisbitt, John. 1982. *Megatrends*. New York: Warner Books.
National Resources Board. 1934a. *Report of the land planning committee*. Washington: U.S. Government Printing Office.

_____. 1934b. *Report of the National Resources Board.* Washington: U.S. Government Printing Office.

National Resources Committee. 1937. *Our cities: Their role in the national economy.* Washington: U.S. Government Printing Office.

New York City Planning Commission. 1969. *Plan for New York City: Critical issues.* New York: NYCPC.

Olsen, John B., and Douglas C. Eadie. 1982. *The game plan: Governance with foresight.* Washington: Council of State Planning Agencies.

Perry, David C., and Alfred J. Watkins, eds. 1977. *The rise of the sunbelt cities.* Urban Affairs Annual Reviews, vol. 14. Beverly Hills, Calif.: Sage.

Rosener, Judy. 1978. Matching method to purpose: The challenges of planning citizen-participation activities. In *Citizen Participation in America,* (Stuart Langdon, ed.) Lexington, Mass.: Lexington Books.

Scott, Mel. 1969. *American city planning since 1890.* Berkeley: University of California Press.

Scott, Randall W., ed. 1975. *The management and control of growth.* Vol. 1–3. Washington: Urban Land Institute.

So, Frank S. 1984. Strategic planning: Reinventing the wheel? *Planning* 50, 2: 16–21.

Sorkin, Donna L., Nancy B. Ferris, and James Hudak. 1984. *Strategies for cities and counties: A strategic planning guide.* Washington: Public Technology, Inc.

Stein, Clarence. 1926. *Report of the New York State Commission of Housing and Regional Planning.* Albany, N.Y.: New York State Legislature.

Steiner. George A. 1969. *Top management planning.* London: Macmillan.

_____, and J. B. Miner. 1977. *Management policy and strategy: Text, readings, and cases.* New York: Macmillan.

Taylor, Bernard. 1984. Strategic planning—Which style do you need? *Long Range Planning* 17, 3: 51–62.

Tiebout, Charles M. 1956. A pure theory of local expenditures. *Journal of Political Economy* 64, 5: 416–24.

Toft, Graham S. 1984. Strategic planning for economic and municipal development. *Resources in Review* 6, 6: 6–11.

Tomazinis, Anthony R. 1985. The logic and rationale of strategic planning. Paper presented at the annual meeting of the Association of Collegiate Schools of Planning, Atlanta. November.

Walker, Robert. 1950. *The planning function in urban government.* Chicago: University of Chicago Press.

Williams, Norman Jr. 1970. The three systems of land use control. *Rutgers Law Review* 25, 1: 80–101.

Applying Private-Sector Strategic Planning to the Public Sector

John M. Bryson and William D. Roering

Strategic planning approaches developed in the private sector can help governments and public agencies become more effective — at least that is the claim of many authors, including us. Its proponents claim that strategic planning provides a set of concepts, procedures, and tools that can help public-sector organizations deal with the recent dramatic changes in their environments. As two early proponents of strategic planning by governments note, "Strategic planning is a disciplined effort to produce fundamental decisions shaping the nature and direction of governmental activities within constitutional bounds" (Olsen and Eadie 1982, p. 4).

What distinguishes strategic planning from more traditional planning (particularly traditional long-range comprehensive or master planning for a community) is its emphasis on (1) action, (2) consideration of a broad and diverse set of stakeholders, (3) attention to external opportunities and threats and internal strengths and weaknesses, and (4) attention to actual or potential competitors (Bloom 1986; Kaufman and Jacobs 1987).

That does not mean, however, that all approaches to what might be called corporate-style strategic planning (that is, strategic planning approaches developed in the private sector) are equally applicable to the public sector. The purposes of this article, therefore, are (1) to compare and contrast six approaches to corporate-style strategic planning, (2) to discuss their applicability to the public sector, and (3) to identify the most important contingencies that govern the successful use of these approaches in the public sector. (Actually, we present nine approaches, grouped into six categories.)

Reprinted with permission from Journal of the American Planning Association, *Vol. 53, No. 1, Winter 1987. Published by the American Planning Association, Chicago, Illinois.*

Before beginning, we should note that corporate strategic planning typically focuses on an *organization* and what it should do to improve its performance, and not on a *community*, the traditional object of attention for comprehensive planners, or on a *function*, such as transportation or health care within a community (Tomazinis 1985). We, too, focus primarily on a government corporation or agency and on how it might plan to improve its performance. But we also note where applications to communities or functions seem appropriate.

We must observe as well that careful tests of corporate-style strategic planning in the public sector are few in number. (The same, of course, can be said about approaches to comprehensive, functional, and project planning; see Bryson 1983.) Nevertheless, there is enough experience with corporate strategic planning in the private sector — and increasingly in the public sector — to reach some tentative conclusions about what seems to work under what conditions.

The rest of this article is divided into three main sections. The first presents an outline of a public-sector strategic planning process that can incorporate the six private-sector approaches to strategic planning. The second is a discussion of the six approaches: the Harvard policy model, strategic planning systems, stakeholder management, content models (portfolio models and competitive analysis), strategic issues management, and process strategies (strategic negotiations, "logical incrementalism," and innovation). We compare and contrast those approaches along several dimensions, including their key features, assumptions, strengths, weaknesses, applicability to the public sector, and contingencies governing their use in the public sector.

The third section presents conclusions about the applicability of private-sector strategic planning to public-sector organizations and purposes. The principal conclusions are (1) that public-sector strategic planning is important and probably will become part of the standard repertoire of public planners and (2) that, nevertheless, public planners must be very careful how they engage in strategic planning, since not all approaches are equally useful and since a number of conditions govern the successful use of each approach.

A Public-Sector Strategic Planning Process

Author John Bryson has developed an outline of a public-sector strategic planning process that provides a framework for discussing the six corporate-style strategic planning approaches and their applicability to the public sector (see Figure 1). The process begins with an initial agreement (or "plan for planning") among decision makers whose support is necessary for successful plan formulation and implementation. Typically they would agree on the purpose of the effort, who should be involved, what should be taken as "given," what topics should be addressed, and the form and timing of reports. Most authors agree that the support and commitment of management and the chief executive are vital if strategic planning in an organization is to succeed (Olsen and Eadie 1982). Further, the involvement of key decision makers outside the organization usually is crucial to the success of public programs if implementation will involve multiple parties and organizations (McGowan and Stevens 1983).

The second step is identification of the mandates, or "musts," confronting the government corporation or agency. Third comes clarification of the organization's mission and values, or "wants," because they have such a strong influence on the identification and resolution of strategic issues, as discussed below (Peters and Waterman 1982; Gilbert and Freeman 1985). The process draws attention in particular to similarities and differences among those who have stakes in the outcome of the process and in what the government's or agency's mission ought to be in relation to those stakeholders. "Stakeholder" is defined as any individual, group, or other organization that can place a claim on the organization's attention, resources, or output or is affected by that output. Examples of a government's stakeholders are citizens, taxpayers, service recipients, the governing body, employees, unions, interest groups, political parties, the financial community, and other governments.

Next comes two parallel steps: identification of the *external* opportunities and threats the organization faces, and identification of its *internal* strengths and weaknesses. The distinction between what is "inside" and what is "outside" hinges on whether the organization controls the factor, which places it inside, or does not, which places it outside (Pfeffer and Salancik 1978). To identify opportunities and threats one might monitor a variety of political, economic, social, and technological forces and trends as well as various stakeholder groups, including clients, customers, payers, competitors, or collaborators. The organization might construct various scenarios to explore alternative futures in the external environment, a practice typical of private-sector strategic planning (Linneman and Klein 1983). To identify strengths and weaknesses the organization might monitor resources (inputs), present strategy (process), and performance (outputs).

Strategic planning focuses on achievement of the best "fit" between an organization and its environment. Attention to mandates and the external environment, therefore, can be thought of as planning from the "outside in." Attention to mission and values and the internal environment can be considered planning from the "inside out."

Together, the first five elements of the process lead to the sixth,

Figure 1. Strategic Planning Process

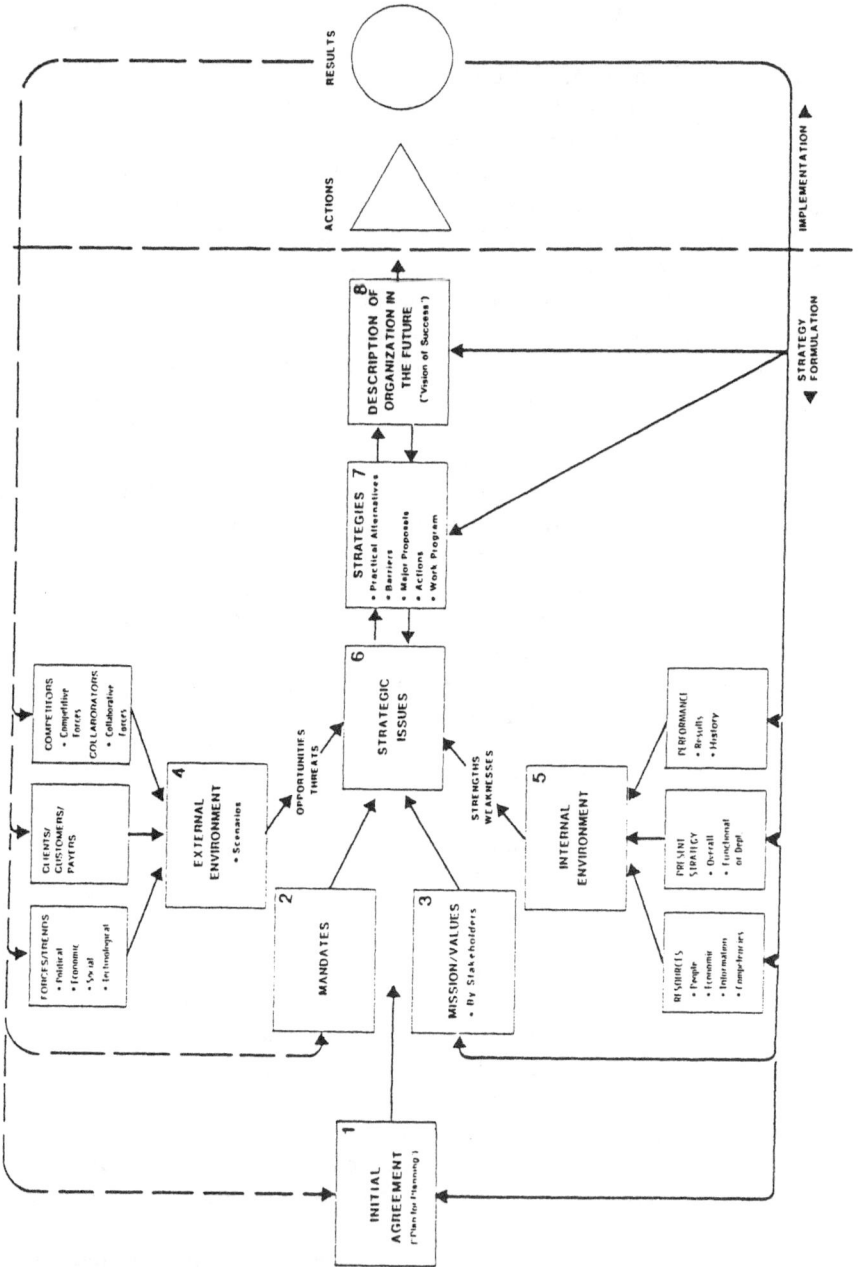

1 INITIAL AGREEMENT ("Plan for Planning")

2 MANDATES

3 MISSION/VALUES
• By Stakeholders

4 EXTERNAL ENVIRONMENT
• Scenarios

FORCES/TRENDS
• Political
• Economic
• Social
• Technological

CLIENTS/CUSTOMERS/PAYERS

COMPETITORS
• Competitive forces
COLLABORATORS
• Collaborative forces

OPPORTUNITIES
THREATS

6 STRATEGIC ISSUES

5 INTERNAL ENVIRONMENT

RESOURCES
• People
• Economic
• Information
• Competencies

PRESENT STRATEGY
• Overall
• Functional or Dept

PERFORMANCE
• Results
• History

STRENGTHS
WEAKNESSES

7 STRATEGIES
• Practical Alternatives
• Barriers
• Major Proposals
• Actions
• Work Program

8 DESCRIPTION OF ORGANIZATION IN THE FUTURE ("Vision of Success")

STRATEGY FORMULATION

IMPLEMENTATION

ACTIONS

RESULTS

identification of strategic issues (i.e., fundamental policy questions affecting the organization's mandates, mission, values, product or service level and mix, clients or users, cost, financing, or management). Usually, it is vital that strategic issues be dealt with expeditiously and effectively if the organization is to survive and prosper. Failure to address a strategic issue typically will lead to undesirable results from a threat, failure to capitalize on an important opportunity, or both.

Strategy development, the seventh step in our outline process, begins with the identification of practical alternatives for resolving the strategic issues. Then it moves to the enumeration of barriers to the achievement of those alternatives, rather than directly to development of proposals to realize the alternatives. A focus on barriers at this point is not typical but is one way of assuring that any strategies developed deal with implementation difficulties directly rather than haphazardly.

After strategy development comes an atypical eighth step: describing the organization's potential future. This description is the organization's "vision of success" (Taylor 1984), an outline of how the organization would look if it successfully implemented its strategies and achieved its full potential. The importance of such descriptions as a guide for performance has long been recognized by well-managed companies (Ouchi 1981; Peters and Waterman 1982) and organizational psychologists (Locke et al. 1981). Typically included in such descriptions are the organization's mission, its basic strategies, its performance criteria, some important decision rules, and the ethical standards expected of the organization's employees.

Those eight steps complete the strategy formulation process. Next come actions and decisions to implement the strategies and, finally, the evaluation of results.

Although our outline shows the process in a linear, sequential manner, we emphasize that the process in practice is iterative. Participants typically rethink what they have done several times before they reach final decisions. Moreover, the process doesn't always begin at the beginning. Instead, organizations typically find themselves confronted with a strategic issue that leads them to engage in strategic planning. Once engaged, the organization is then likely to go back and begin at the beginning.

The process is applicable to public organizations, functions, and communities. The only general requirement is a "dominant coalition" (Thompson 1967) willing to follow the process. For each of the approaches to corporate strategic planning we note specific contingencies that affect its application in the public sector.

Approaches to Corporate Strategic Planning

Although the roots of public-sector strategic planning are deep, most of the history and development of the concepts, procedures, and tools of strategic planning in this century have occurred in the private sector. This history has been amply documented by others (Bracker 1980). We briefly set forth six schools of thought or models of strategic planning developed in the private sector and discuss their key features, assumptions, strengths, weaknesses, applicability to the public sector, and contingencies governing their use.

As noted above, strategic planning as a concept involves general policy and direction setting, situation assessments, strategic issue identification, strategy development, decision making, action, and evaluation. We begin with the approaches that cover more of the process and highlight policy and direction setting; then we move to approaches that focus more narrowly on elements in the later stages of the process we have outlined.

The Harvard Policy Model

The Harvard policy model was developed as part of, and has been included in, the business policy course taught at the Harvard Business School since the 1920s (Christensen et al. 1983 and earlier versions). The approach provides the principal inspiration behind the most widely cited recent models of public-sector strategic planning (e.g., Olsen and Eadie 1982; Sorkin, Ferris, and Hudak 1984) (see Table 1).

The main purpose of the Harvard model is to help a firm develop the best "fit" between itself and its environment; that is, to develop the best strategy for the firm. As articulated by Andrews (1980), strategy is "a pattern of purposes and policies defining the company and its business." One discerns the best strategy by analyzing the internal strengths and weaknesses of the company and the values of senior management, then identifying the external threats and opportunities in the environment and the social obligations of the firm.

Effective use of the model presumes that agreement is possible among the members of a top management team about the firm's situation and the appropriate strategic response. Further, the model presumes the team has enough authority to enforce its decisions. A final important assumption of the model — common to all approaches to strategic planning — is that if the appropriate strategy is identified and implemented, the organization will be more effective.

The process presented in Figure 1 is strongly influenced by the Harvard model. Central to the process is attention to the internal strengths and weaknesses of the government or agency, to the values of key stakeholders (not just senior managers), and to the external threats, opportunities, and mandates (not just social obligations) affecting the government or agency.

In the business world, the Harvard model appears to be best applied at the level of the strategic business unit. A strategic business unit is a distinct business that has its own competitors and can be managed somewhat independently of other units within the organization (Rue and Holland 1986). The strategic business unit, in other words, provides an important yet bounded and manageable focus for the model. The public-sector equivalent of the strategic business unit is the strategic public planning unit, which typically would be an agency or department that addresses issues fundamentally similar in nature to one another (Montanari and Bracker 1986).

The Harvard model is also applicable at the higher and broader corporate level – in both private and public sectors – particularly if it is used with other approaches, such as the portfolio approaches to be discussed below. A portfolio approach is needed because a principal strategic concern at the corporate level is oversight of a portfolio of business in the private sector or a portfolio of agencies or departments in the public sector.

The systematic assessment of strengths, weaknesses, opportunities, and threats – or SWOT analysis – is the primary strength of the Harvard model. This element of the model appears to be applicable in the public sector to organizations, functions, and communities (Sorkin, Ferris, and Hudak 1984), although in the case of communities the distinction between inside and outside may be problematic. The main weakness of the Harvard model is that it does not offer specific advice on how to develop strategies, except to note that effective strategies will build on strengths, take advantage of opportunities, and overcome or minimize weaknesses and threats.

Strategic Planning Systems

Strategic planning is often conceived as a system whereby managers go about making, implementing, and controlling important decisions across functions and levels in the firm. Lorange (1980), for example, has argued that any strategic planning system must address four fundamental questions: (1) Where are we going? (mission); (2) How do we get there? (strategies); (3) What is our blueprint for action? (budgets); and (4) How do we know if we are on track? (control).

Strategic planning systems vary along several dimensions: the comprehensiveness of decision areas included, the formal rationality of the decision process, and the tightness of control exercised over implementation of the decisions (Armstrong 1982). The strength of these systems is their attempt to coordinate the various elements of an organization's

Table 1. Comparison and Applicability of Private Sector Approaches to Strategic Planning in the Public Sector

Approach	Key features	Assumptions	Strengths	Weaknesses	Applicability to the public sector
Harvard policy model (Andrews 1980; Christensen et al. 1983)	Primarily applicable at the strategic business unit level SWOT analysis Analysis of management's values and social obligations of the firm Attempts to develop the best "fit" between a firm and its environment; i.e., best strategy for the firm	Analysis of SWOTs, management values, and social obligations of firm will facilitate identification of the best strategy Agreement is possible within the top management team responsible for strategy formulation and implementation Team has the ability to implement its decisions Implementation of the best strategy will result in improved firm performance (an assumption held in common with all strategic planning approaches)	Systematic assessment of strengths and weaknesses of firm and opportunities and threats facing firm Attention to management values and social obligations of the firm Systematic attention to the "fit" between the firm and its environment Can be used in conjunction with other approaches	Does not offer specific advice on how to develop strategies Fails to consider many existing or potential stakeholder groups	Organizations: Yes, if a strategic public planning unit can be identified and additional stakeholder interests are considered, and if a management team can agree on what should be done and has the ability to implement its decisions Functions: SWOT analysis is applicable Communities: SWOT analysis is applicable if what is "inside" and "outside" can be specified

Approach	Description	Requirements	Coordination	Limitations	Applicability
Strategic planning systems (Lorange 1980; Lorange et al. 1986)	Systems for formulating and implementing important decisions across levels and functions in an organization Allocation and control of resources within a strategic framework and through rational decision making Attempts to comprehensively cover all key decision areas	Strategy formulation and implementation should be rational and anticipatory An organization's strategies should form an integrated whole The organization can control centrally all or most of its internal operations Goals, objectives, and performance indicators can be specified clearly Information on performance is available at reasonable cost	Coordination of strategy formulation and implementation across levels and functions Can be used in conjunction with other approaches	Excessive comprehensiveness, prescription, and control can drive out attention to mission, strategy, and organizational structure The information requirements of planning systems can exceed the participants' ability to comprehend the information	Organizations: Less comprehensive and rigorous forms of private-sector strategic planning systems are applicable to many public-sector organizations Functions: Necessary conditions for strategic planning systems to succeed are seldom met Communities: Unlikely

Table 1. (Continued)

Approach	Key features	Assumptions	Strengths	Weaknesses	Applicability to the public sector
Stakeholder management (Freeman 1984)	Identification of key stakeholders and the criteria they use to judge an organization's performance Development of strategies to deal with each stakeholder	An organization's survival and prosperity depend on the extent to which it satisfies its key stakeholders An organization's strategy will be successful only if it meets the needs of key stakeholders	Recognition that many claims, both complementary and competing, are placed on an organization Stakeholder analysis (i.e., a listing of key stakeholders and of the criteria they use to judge an organization's performance) Can be used in conjunction with other approaches	Absence of criteria with which to judge different claims Need for more advice on how to develop strategies to deal with divergent stakeholder claims	Organization: Yes, as long as agreement is possible among key decision makers over who the stakeholders are and what the organization's responses to them should be. Functions: Yes, with the same caveats Communities: Yes, with the same caveats

Content approaches

Portfolio methods (Henderson 1979; Wind and Mahajian 1981; MacMillan 1983)	A corporation's businesses are categorized into groups based on selected dimensions for comparison and development of corporate strategy in relation to each business Attempts to balance a corporation's business portfolio to meet corporate strategic objectives Aggregate assessment of a corporation's various businesses is important to the corporation's success Resources should be channeled into the different businesses to meet the corporation's cash flow and investment needs A few key dimensions of strategic importance can be identified against which to judge the performance of individual businesses A group exists that can make and implement decisions based on the portfolio analysis	Provides a method for evaluating a set of businesses against dimensions that are deemed to be of strategic importance to the corporation Provides a useful way of understanding some of the key economic and financial aspects of corporate strategy Can be used as part of a larger strategic planning process	Difficult to know what the relevant strategic dimensions are, what the relevant entities to be compared are, and how to classify entities against dimensions Unclear how to use the tool as part of a larger strategic planning process	Organizations: Yes, if economic, social, and political dimensions of comparison can be specified, entities to be compared can be identified, and a group exists that can make and implement decisions based on the portfolio analysis Functions: Yes, with the same caveats Communities: Yes, with the same caveats

Table 1. (Continued)

Approach	Key features	Assumptions	Strengths	Weaknesses	Applicability to the public sector
Competitive analysis (Porter 1980; 1985; Harrigan 1981)	Analysis of key forces that shape an industry, e.g., relative power of customers, relative power of suppliers, threat of substitute products, threat of new entrants, amount of rivalrous activity, exit barriers to firms in the industry	Predominance of competitive behavior on the part of firms within an industry. The stronger the forces that shape an industry, the lower the general level of returns in the industry. The stronger the forces affecting a firm, the lower the profits for the firm. Analysis of the forces will allow one to identify the best strategy whereby an industry can raise its general level of returns and whereby a firm within an industry can maximize its profits	Provides a systematic method of assessing the economic aspects of an industry and the strategic options facing the industry and specific firms within it. Gives relatively clear prescriptions for strategic action. Can be used as part of a larger strategic planning process	Sometimes difficult to identify what the relevant industry is. Excludes consideration of potentially relevant noneconomic factors. Tends to ignore the possibility that organizational success may turn on collaboration, not competition	Organizations: Yes, for organizations in identifiable industries (e.g., public hospitals, transit companies, recreation facilities) if a competitive analysis is coupled with a consideration of noneconomic factors and if the possibility of collaboration is also considered. Functions: Yes, if the function equates to an industry. Communities: No

| Strategic issues management (Ansoff 1980; King 1982; Pflaum and Delmont 1987) | Attention to the recognition and resolution of strategic issues | Strategic issues are issues that can have a major influence on the organization and must be managed if the organization is to meet its objectives

Strategic issues can be identified by the use of a variety of tools (e.g., SWOT analyses and environmental scanning methods)

Early identification of issues will result in more favorable resolution and greater likelihood of enhanced organizational performance

A group exists that is able to engage in the process and manage the issue | Ability to identify and respond quickly to issues

Has a "real time" orientation and is compatible with most organizations

Can be used in conjunction with other approaches | No specific advice is offered on how to frame issues other than to precede their identification with a situational analysis | Organizations: Yes, as long as there is a group able to engage in the process and manage the issue

Functions: Yes, with the same caveat

Communities: Yes, with the same caveat |

Table 1. (Continued)

Approach	Key features	Assumptions	Strengths	Weaknesses	Applicability to the public sector
Process strategies					
Strategic negotiations (Pettigrew 1982; Fisher and Ury 1981; Allison 1971)	Bargaining and negotiation among two or more players over the identification and resolution of strategic issues	Organizations are "shared power" settings in which groups must cooperate, bargain, and negotiate with each other in order to achieve their ends and assure organizational survival Strategy is created as part of a relatively constant struggle among competing groups in an organization Strategy is the emergent product of the partial resolution of organizational issues	Recognizes that there are many actors in the strategy formulation and implementation process and that they often do not share common goals Recognizes the desirability of bargaining and negotiation in order for groups to achieve their ends and to assure organizational survival Can be used in conjunction with other approaches	Little advice on how to ensure technical workability and democratic responsibility—as opposed to political acceptability—of results No assurance that overall organizational goals can or will be achieved; there may not be a whole equal to, let alone greater than, the sum of the parts	Organizations: Yes Functions: Yes Communities: Yes

Approach				
Logical incrementalism (Quinn 1980; Lindblom 1959)	Emphasizes the importance of small changes as part of developing and implementing organizational strategies Fuses strategy formulation and implementation	Strategy is a loosely linked group of decisions that are handled incrementally Decentralized decision making is both politically expedient and necessary Small, decentralized decisions can help identify and fulfill organizational purposes	Ability to handle complexity and change Attention to both formal and informal processes Political realism Emphasis on both minor and major decisions Can be used in conjunction with other approaches	No guarantee that the loosely linked, incremental decisions will add up to fulfillment of overall organizational purposes	Organizations: Yes, as long as overall organizational purposes can be identified to provide a framework for incremental decisions Functions: Yes, with the same caveat Communities: Yes, with the same caveat

Table 1. (Continued)

Approach	Key features	Assumptions	Strengths	Weaknesses	Applicability to the public sector
Framework for innovation (Taylor 1984; Pinchot 1985)	Emphasis on innovation as a strategy Reliance on many elements of the other approaches and specific management practices	Change is unavoidable, and continuous innovation to deal with change is necessary if the organization is to survive and prosper A "vision of success" is necessary to provide the organization with a common set of superordinate goals toward which to work Innovation as a strategy will not work without an entrepreneurial company culture to support it	Allows innovation and entrepreneurship while maintaining central control on a key outcomes Fosters a commitment to innovation Can be used in conjunction with other approaches	Costly mistakes usually are necessary as part of the process of innovation Decentralization and local control result in some loss of accountability	Organizations: Yes, but the public is unwilling to allow public organizations to make the mistakes necessary as part of the process and development of an overall framework within which to innovate and maintain central control over key outcomes is difficult Functions: Yes, but with the same caveats Communities: Yes, with same caveats

strategy across levels and functions. Their weakness is that excessive comprehensiveness, prescription, and control can drive out attention to mission, strategy, and organizational structure (Frederickson and Mitchell 1984; Frederickson 1984) and can exceed participants' ability to comprehend them (Bryson, Van de Ven, and Roering 1987).

Strategic planning systems are applicable to public-sector organizations, for regardless of the nature of the particular organization, it makes sense to coordinate decision making across levels and functions and to concentrate on whether the organization is implementing its strategies and accomplishing its mission. It is important to remember, however, that a strategic planning system characterized by substantial comprehensiveness, formal rationality in decision making, and tight control will work only in an organization that has a clear mission; clear goals and objectives; centralized authority; clear performance indicators; and information about actual performance available at reasonable cost (Stuart 1969; Galloway 1979). Few public-sector organizations — or functions or communities — operate under such conditions. As a result, public-sector strategic planning systems typically focus on a few areas of concern, rely on a decision process in which politics plays a major role, and control something other than program outcomes (e.g., budget expenditures) (Wildavsky 1979).

Bryson, Van de Ven, and Roering (1987) offer an example, based on the approach used by the 3M Corporation, of how such a control system might be implemented across levels in a government corporation or agency (see Figure 2). In the system's first cycle, there is "bottom-up" development of strategic plans within a framework established at the top, followed by reviews and reconciliations at each succeeding level. In the second cycle, operating plans are developed to implement the strategic plans.

A similar cyclic system is used by Hennepin County, Minnesota (the county that contains Minneapolis), to address 14 areas of strategic concern (e.g., finance, employment and economic development, transportation, program fragmentation, and coordination). The system includes three cycles: strategic issue identification, strategy development, and strategy implementation (Eckhert et al. 1986).

Stakeholder Management Approaches

Freeman (1984) has argued that corporate strategy can be understood as a corporation's mode of relating or building bridges to its stakeholders. A stakeholder is "any group or individual who is affected by or who can affect the future of the corporation"; for example, customers, employees, suppliers, owners, governments, financial institutions, and critics. Freeman argues that a corporate strategy will be effective only if it satisfies the needs of multiple groups. Traditional private-sector models of strategy

Figure 2. Annual Strategic Planning Process

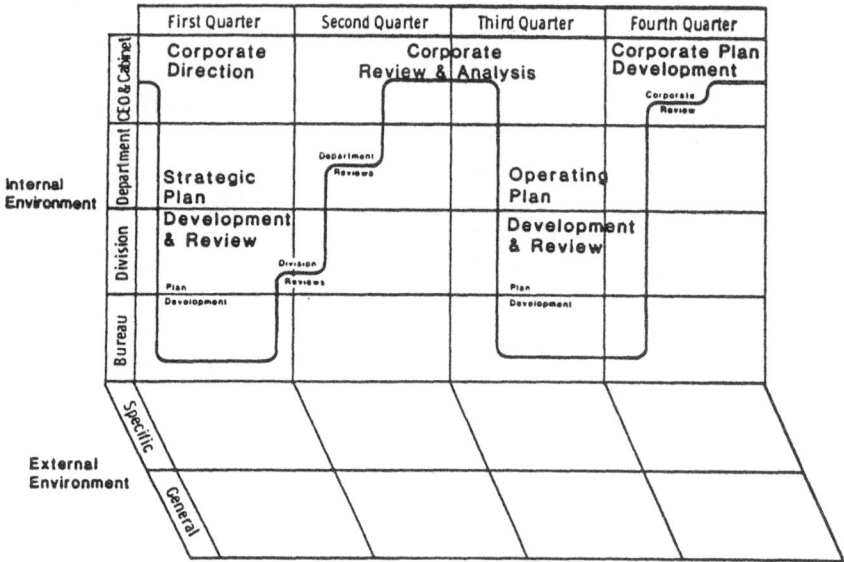

		First Quarter	Second Quarter	Third Quarter	Fourth Quarter
	CEO & Cabinet	Corporate Direction	Corporate Review & Analysis		Corporate Plan Development
					Corporate Review
Internal Environment	Department	Strategic Plan	Department Reviews	Operating Plan	
	Division	Development & Review	Division Reviews	Development & Review	
	Bureau	Plan Development		Plan Development	

External Environment — Specific / General

have focused only on economic actors, but Freeman argues that changes in the current business environment require that other political and social actors must be considered as well.

Because it integrates economic, political, and social concerns, the stakeholder model is one of the approaches most applicable to the public sector. Many interest groups have stakes in public organizations, functions, and communities. For example, local economic development planning typically involves government, developers, bankers, the chamber of commerce, actual or potential employers, neighborhood groups, environmentalists, and so on. Local economic development planners would be wise to identify key stakeholders, their interests, what they will support, and strategies and tactics that might work in dealing with them (Kaufman 1979).

Bryson, Freeman, and Roering (1986) argue that an organization's mission and values ought to be formulated in stakeholder terms. That is, an organization should figure out what its mission should be in relation to each stakeholder group; otherwise, it will not be able to differentiate its responses well enough to satisfy its key stakeholders. This advice to public organizations is matched by private-sector practice in several well-managed companies (O'Toole 1985). For example, the Dayton Hudson Corporation, a large retailer, identifies four key stakeholders — customers, employees, stockholders, and the communities in which they do business —

and specifies what its mission is in relation to each. Dayton Hudson assumes that if it performs well in the eyes of each of those stakeholders, its success is assured.

The strengths of the stakeholder model are its recognition of the many claims – both complementary and competing – placed on organizations by insiders and outsiders and its awareness of the need to satisfy at least the key stakeholders if the organization is to survive. The weaknesses of the model are the absence of criteria with which to judge competing claims and the need for more advice on how to develop strategies to deal with divergent stakeholder interests.

Freeman has applied the stakeholder concept primarily at the corporate and industry-wide levels in the private sector, but it seems applicable to all levels in the private and public sectors. Researchers have not yet made rigorous tests of the model's usefulness in the private or public sector, but there are several public-sector case studies that indicate stakeholder analyses are quite useful as part of a strategic planning effort – for example, the city government of St. Louis Park, Minnesota (Klumpp 1986) and the Ramsey County (Minnesota) Nursing Service (Allan 1985). If the model is to be used successfully, it must be possible to achieve reasonable agreement among key decision makers about who the key stakeholders are and what the response to their claims should be.

Content Approaches

The three approaches presented so far have to do more with process than with content. The process approaches do not prescribe answers, though good answers are presumed to emerge from appropriate application of them. In contrast, the tools to be discussed next – portfolio models and competitive analysis – have to do primarily with content and do yield answers. In fact, the models are antithetical to process when process concerns get in the way of developing the "right" answer.

Portfolio models. The idea of strategic planning as managing a portfolio of businesses is based on an analogy with investment practice. Just as an investor assembles a portfolio of stocks to manage risk and realize optimum returns, a corporate manager can think of the corporation as a portfolio of businesses with diverse potentials that can be balanced to manage return and cash flow. The intellectual history of portfolio theory in corporate strategy is complex (Wind and Mahajan 1981). For our purposes it is adequate to use as an example the portfolio model developed by the Boston Consulting Group: the famous "BCG Matrix" (Henderson 1979).

Bruce Henderson, founder of the Boston Consulting Group, argued that all business costs followed a well-known pattern: unit costs dropped by one-third every time volume (or turnover) doubled. Hence, he postulated a relationship, known as the *experience curve*, between unit costs and volume. This relationship leads to some generic strategic advice: gain market share, for if a firm gains market share, its unit costs will fall and profit potential will increase. Henderson argued that any business could be categorized into one of four types, depending on how its industry was growing and how large a share of the market it had: (1) high growth/high share businesses ("stars"), which generate substantial cash but also require large investments if their market share is to be maintained or increased; (2) low growth/high share businesses ("cash cows"), which generate large cash flows but require low investment and therefore generate profits that can be used elsewhere; (3) low growth/low share businesses ("dogs"), which produce little cash and offer little prospect of increased share; and (4) high growth/low share businesses ("question marks"), which would require substantial investment in order to become stars or cash cows (the question is whether the investment is worth it). Generic business strategies can be adopted to meet the whole corporation's cash flow and investment needs.

Although the applications of portfolio theory to the public sector may be less obvious than those of the three approaches described above, they are nonetheless just as powerful (MacMillan 1983). Many public-sector organizations consist of "multiple businesses" that are only marginally related. Often resources from a single source are committed to these unrelated businesses. That means public-sector managers must make portfolio decisions, though usually without the help of analytical portfolio models that frame those decisions strategically. The BCG approach, like most private-sector portfolio models, uses only economic criteria, not the political or social criteria that might be necessary for public-sector applications. Private-sector portfolio approaches, therefore, must be modified substantially for public-sector use.

The Philadelphia Investment Portfolio is a public-sector example of a portfolio approach applied at the community level (Center for Philadelphia Studies 1982a; 1982b). The portfolio consists of 56 investment options (i.e., investments of public and private time and resources) arranged according to the degree to which they take advantage of ongoing trends (their "position") and the degree to which they facilitate the strategic objectives of the Greater Philadelphia area (their "attractiveness"). (The judgments of position and attractiveness were formulated through the collaborative efforts of about 750 people in public, private, and nonprofit organizations who participated in the "Philadelphia: Past, Present and Future" project.) Each of the two dimensions consists of a set of economic, political, and social criteria. The creators of the portfolio view Greater Philadelphia as a community of interests and stakeholders; they strive to loosely coordinate the activities of disparate parties to achieve community goals by offering specific investment options that are attractive to specific organizations or coalitions. An organization or coalition would pursue an option because that option fit its needs and desires; but the city as a whole also would benefit from the organization's decision to invest.

The strength of portfolio approaches is that they provide a method for measuring entities of some sort (e.g., businesses, investment options, proposals, or problems) against dimensions that are deemed to be of strategic importance (e.g., share and growth or position and attractiveness) for purposes of analysis and recommendation. The weaknesses of such approaches include the difficulty of knowing what the appropriate strategic dimensions are; difficulties of classifying entities against dimensions; and the lack of clarity about how to use the tool as part of a larger strategic planning process.

If modified to include political and social factors, portfolio approaches can be used in the public sector to inform strategic decisions about organizations, functions, and communities. The approaches can be used in conjunction with process approaches, such as the one outlined in Figure 1, to provide useful information as part of an assessment of an organization, function, or community in relation to its environment. Unlike the process models, however, portfolio approaches provide an "answer" as to what the relationship should be once the dimensions of comparison and the entities to be compared are specified. The answer would be accepted only if a dominant coalition could be convinced that the answer was correct.

Competitive analysis. Another important content approach to assist with strategy selection has been developed by Michael Porter (1980, 1985) and his associates. Called competitive analysis, it assumes that by analyzing the forces that shape an industry, one can predict the general level of profits throughout the industry and the likely success of any particular strategy for a strategic business unit. Porter (1980) hypothesizes that five key forces shape an industry: relative power of customers, relative power of suppliers, threat of substitute products, threat of new entrants, and the amount of rivalrous activity among the players in the industry. Harrigan (1981) has argued that "exit barriers"—that is, the barriers that would prevent a company from leaving an industry—are a sixth force influencing success in some industries. There are two main propositions in the competitive analysis school: (1) the stronger the forces that shape an industry, the lower the general level of returns in the industry; and (2) the stronger the forces affecting a strategic business unit, the lower the profits for that unit.

For many public-sector organizations, there are equivalents to the forces that affect private industry. Client or customer power is often exercised in the public arena, and suppliers of services (e.g., organizations providing contract services and the government's or agency's own labor supply) also can exercise power. There are fewer new entrants, but recently the private sector has begun to compete more forcefully with public organizations. And governments and agencies also often compete with one another (e.g., public hospitals for patients, or states and localities for the General Motors Saturn plant). An effective organization in the public sector, therefore, must understand the forces at work in its "industry" in order to compete effectively. On another level, planning for a specific public-sector function (e.g., health care, transportation, and recreation) can benefit from competitive analysis if the function can be considered an industry. In addition, economic development agencies must understand the forces at work in given industries and on specific firms if they are to understand whether and how to nurture those industries and firms. Finally, although communities often compete with one another, competitive analysis does not apply at that level because communities are not industries in any meaningful sense.

The strength of competitive analysis is that it provides a systematic way of assessing industries and the strategic options facing strategic business units within those industries. For public-sector applications, the weaknesses of competitive analysis are that (1) it is often difficult to know what the "industry" is and what forces affect it and (2) the key to organizational success in the public sector is often collaboration instead of competition. Competitive analyses in the public sector, therefore, must be coupled with a consideration of social and political forces and the possibilities for collaboration.

Strategic Issue Management

We now leave content approaches to focus again on process approaches. Strategic issue management approaches are process components or pieces of the larger strategic planning process presented in Figure 1. Strategic issue management is primarily associated with Ansoff (1980) and focuses attention on the recognition and resolution of *strategic issues* — "forthcoming developments, either inside or outside the organization, which are likely to have an important impact on the ability of the enterprise to meet its objectives." The concept of strategic issues first emerged when practitioners of corporate strategic planning realized a step was missing between the SWOT analysis of the Harvard model and the development of strategies. That step was the identification of strategic issues. Many firms now include a strategic issue identification step as part of full-blown strategy revision exercises and also as part of less comprehensive annual strategic reviews (King 1982). Full-blown annual revision has proved impractical because strategy revision takes substantial management energy and attention, and most strategies take several years to implement anyway. Instead, most firms are undertaking comprehensive strategy revisions several years apart (typically five) and in the interim are focusing their annual strategic planning processes on the identification and resolution of a few key strategic issues that emerge from SWOT analyses, environmental scans (Hambrick 1982; Pflaum and Delmont 1987), and other analyses.

In recent years many firms have developed strategic issue management processes actually separated from their annual strategic planning processes. Many important issues emerge too quickly to be handled as part of an annual process. A separate, quick response is necessary. Typically task forces reporting directly to top management are used to develop responses to pressing issues that turn up unexpectedly.

Strategic issue management is clearly applicable to governments and agencies as well, since the agendas of these organizations consist of issues that should be managed strategically (Ring and Perry 1985). In other words, they should be managed based on a sense of mission and mandates and in the context of an environmental assessment. The strength of the approach is its ability to recognize and analyze key issues quickly. The weakness of the approach is that no specific advice is offered on exactly how to frame the issues other than to precede their identification with a situational analysis of some sort. The approach also applies to functions and places or communities, as long as some group, organization, or coalition is able to engage in the process and to manage the issue.

Process Strategies

The final three process approaches to be discussed are, in effect, strategies. They are strategic negotiations, logical incrementalism, and strategic planning as a framework for innovation.

Strategic negotiations. Several writers view corporate strategy as the partial resolution of organizational issues through a highly political process (Pettigrew 1977; Mintzberg and Waters 1985). As envisioned by Pettigrew (1977), strategic negotiations are very much contextually based, as strategy is viewed as the flow of actions and values embedded in a context.

The applicability of this view of strategy to the public sector is clear when one realizes that Allison's (1971) study of the Cuban Missile Crisis provided much of the stimulus for this line of private-sector work. Negotiation has become an increasingly important focus of planning research and practice (Susskind and Ozawa 1984). An example of planning-related strategic negotiations is the Negotiated Investment Strategy project of the Charles F. Kettering Foundation (1982), in which federal, state, and local agencies in several cities worked out a coordinated investment strategy designed to meet the strategic objectives of each.

The strength of a negotiation approach is that it recognizes that power is shared in most public situations; no one person, group, or organization is "in charge," and cooperation and negotiation with others is often necessary in order for people, groups, and organizations to achieve their ends (Bryson and Einsweiler 1986). The main weakness of negotiation approaches — as expounded, for example, by Fisher and Ury (1981) in *Getting to Yes* — is that although they can show planners how to reach politically acceptable results, they are not very helpful in assuring technical workability or democratic responsibility of results.

Logical incrementalism. Incremental approaches view strategy as a loosely linked group of decisions that are handled incrementally. Decisions are handled individually below the corporate level because such decentralization is politically expedient — corporate leaders should reserve their political clout for crucial decisions. Decentralization also is necessary — those closest to decisions are the only ones with enough information to make good decisions.

The incremental approach is identified principally with Quinn (1980), though the influence of Lindblom (1959) is apparent. Quinn developed the concept of *logical incrementalism* — or incrementalism in the service of overall corporate purposes — and as a result transformed incrementalism into a strategic approach. Logical incrementalism is a process approach that, in effect, fuses strategy formulation and implementation. The strengths of the approach are its ability to handle complexity and change, its emphasis on minor as well as major decisions, its attention to informal as well as formal processes, and its political realism. The major weakness of the approach is that it does not guarantee that the various loosely linked decisions will add up to fulfillment of corporate purposes. Logical incrementalism would appear to be very applicable to public-sector organizations, functions, and places or communities — the situations in which, and for which, Lindblom first developed the incremental model — as long as it is possible to establish some overarching set of strategic objectives to be served by the approach.

Strategic planning as a framework for innovation. Above we discussed strategic planning systems and noted that excessive comprehensiveness, prescription, and control could drive out attention to mission, strategy, and organizational structure. The systems, in other words, can become ends in themselves and drive out creativity, innovation, and new product and market development, without which most businesses would die (Schön 1971). Many businesses, therefore, have found it necessary to emphasize innovative strategies as a counterbalance to the excessive control orientation of many strategic planning systems. In other words, while one important reason for installing a strategic planning system is the need to exercise control across functions and levels, an equally important need for organizations is to design systems that promote creativity and entrepreneurship at the local level and prevent centralization and bureaucracy from stifling the wellsprings of business growth and change (Taylor 1984).

The framework-for-innovation approach to corporate strategic planning relies on many of the elements of the approaches discussed above, such as SWOT analyses and portfolio methods. This approach differs from earlier ones in that it emphasizes (1) innovation as a strategy, (2) specific management practices to support the strategy (e.g., project teams; venture groups; diversification, acquisition, and divestment task forces; research and development operations; new product and market groups; and a variety of organizational development techniques), (3) development of a "vision of success" that provides the decentralized and entrepreneurial parts of the organization with a common set of superordinate goals toward which to work, and (4) nurture of an entrepreneurial company culture (Pinchot 1985).

The strength of the approach is that it allows for innovation and entrepreneurship while maintaining central control. The weaknesses of the approach are that typically—and perhaps necessarily—a great many, often costly, mistakes are made as part of the innovation process and that there is a certain loss of accountability in very decentralized systems (Peters and Waterman 1982). Those weaknesses reduce the applicability of the approach to the public sector, in which mistakes are less acceptable and the pressures to be accountable for details (as opposed to results) are often greater (Ring and Perry 1985).

Nonetheless, the innovation approach would appear to be applicable to public-sector organizations when the management of innovation is needed (e.g., Zaltman, Florio, and Sikorski 1977), as in the redesign of a public service (e.g., Savas 1982). Innovation as a strategy also can and should be pursued for functions and communities. Too often a distressing equation has operated in the public sector: more money equals more service, less money equals less service. As public budgets have become increasingly strapped, there have not been enough innovation and public service redesign. The equation doesn't need to be destiny; it is possible that creative effort and innovation might actually result in *more* service for *less* money.

Conclusions

Our purpose in this paper has been to compare and contrast six approaches to corporate-style strategic planning, to discuss their applicability to the public sector, and to identify major contingencies governing their use. Several conclusions emerge from our review and analysis.

First, it should be clear that corporate strategic planning is not a single concept, procedure, or tool. In fact, it embraces a range of approaches that vary in their applicability to the public sector and in the conditions that govern their successful use. The public-sector strategic planning process outlined above provides a useful framework for review and critique of the private-sector approaches to strategic planning and their applicability to the public sector. The process comprises broad policy or direction setting, internal and external assessments, attention to key stakeholders, the identification of key issues, development of strategies to deal with each issue, decision making, action, and continuous monitoring of results. The process is applicable to organizations, functions, and places or communities. The private-sector approaches to corporate strategic planning, in contrast, emphasize different parts of this whole strategic planning process, and each is focused on a given organization.

Second, although the public-sector strategic planning process is a useful framework to guide thought and action, it must be applied with care to any given situation, as is true of any planning process (Bryson and Delbecq 1979; Galloway 1979; Christensen 1985). Because every planning process should be tailored to fit specific situations, every process in practice will be a hybrid. We have outlined a number of general assumptions and conditions governing successful use of the private-sector strategic planning approaches in the public sector in order to facilitate construction of such hybrids.

Third, we think familiarity with strategic planning should be a standard part of the intellectual and skill repertoire of all public planners. Given the dramatic changes in the environments of public organizations in recent years, we expect elected public officials, public managers, and planners to pay increased attention to the formulation and implementation of effective strategies to deal with the changes. When applied appropriately to public-sector conditions, strategic planning provides a set of concepts, procedures, and tools for doing just that. We suspect the most effective public planners are now — and will be increasingly in the future — the ones who are best at *strategic* planning.

Fourth, our assertion about the increased importance of strategic planning raises the question of the appropriate role of the strategic planner. In many ways this is an old debate in the planning literature. Should the planner be a technician, politician, or hybrid, i.e., both a technician and a politician (Howe and Kaufman 1979; Howe 1980)? Or should the planner not be a planner at all, at least formally, but instead be a line manager (Bryson, Van de Ven, and Roering 1987)? We believe the strategic planner can be solely a technician only when content approaches are used.

When all other approaches are used, the strategic planner should be a hybrid, so that there is some assurance that both political and technical concerns are addressed. Furthermore, since strategic planning tends to fuse planning and decision making, it is helpful to think of decision makers as strategic planners and to think of strategic planners as facilitators of strategic decision making across levels and functions in organizations and communities.

Finally, research must explore a number of theoretical and empirical issues in order to advance the knowledge and practice of public strategic planning. In particular, contingent models for public strategic planning must be developed and tested. These models should specify key situational factors governing use; provide specific advice on how to formulate and implement strategies in different situations; be explicitly political; indicate how to deal with plural, ambiguous, or conflicting goals or objectives; link content and process; indicate how collaboration as well as competition is to be handled; and specify roles for the strategic planner. Progress has been made on all those fronts (Checkoway 1986), but more is necessary if public-sector strategic planning is to help public organizations, functions, and communities fulfill their missions and serve their stakeholders effectively, efficiently, and responsibly.

References

Allan, J. H. 1985. A case study of the Ramsey County Nursing Service strategic planning process. Plan B paper. Minneapolis: School of Public Health, University of Minnesota.

Allison, G. T. 1971. *Essence of decision.* Boston: Little, Brown.

Andrews, K. 1980. *The concept of corporate strategy* (rev. ed.). Homewood, Ill.: R. D. Irwin.

Ansoff, I. 1980. Strategic issue management. *Strategic Management Journal,* 1, 2: 131–48.

Armstrong, J. S. 1982. The value of formal planning for strategic decisions: Review of empirical research. *Strategic Management Journal,* 3, 2: 197–211.

Bloom, C. 1986. Strategic planning in the public sector. *Journal of Planning Literature, 1,* 2: 253–59.

Bracker, J. 1980. The historical development of the strategic management concept. *Academy of Management Review,* 5, 2: 219–24.

Bryson, J. M. 1983. Representing and testing procedural planning methods. In *Evaluating Urban Planning Efforts* (Ian Masser, ed.) Hampshire, England: Gower.

_____, and A. L. Delbecq. 1979. A contingent approach to strategy and tactics in project planning. *Journal of the American Planning Association,* 45, 2: 167–79.

_____, and R. C. Einsweiler, eds. 1986. *Planning and decision making in a context of shared power.* Lanham, Md.: University Press of America.

_____, R. E. Freeman, and W. D. Roering. 1986. Strategic planning in the public sector: Approaches and direction. In *Strategic Perspectives on Planning Practice* (B. Checkoway, ed.) Lexington, Mass.: Lexington Books.

_____, A. H. Van de Ven, and W. D. Roering. 1987. Strategic planning and the revitalization of the public service. In *Toward a New Public Service,* (R. Denhardt and E. Jennings, eds.) Columbia: University of Missouri Press. Forthcoming.

Center for Philadelphia Studies. 1982a. *A Philadelphia prospectus.* Philadelphia: University of Pennsylvania.

_____. 1982b. *Philadelphia investment portfolio.* Philadelphia: University of Pennsylvania.

Charles F. Kettering Foundation. 1982. *Negotiated investment strategy.* Dayton, Ohio: Charles F. Kettering Foundation.

Checkoway, B., ed. 1986. *Strategic perspectives on planning practice.* Lexington, Mass.: Lexington Books.

Christensen, K. S. 1985. Coping with uncertainty in planning. *Journal of the American Planning Association, 51,* 1: 63–73.

Christensen, R., K. Andrews, J. Bower, R. Hammermesh, and M. Porter. 1983. *Business policy: Text and cases.* Homewood, Ill.: R. D. Irwin.

Eckhert, P., K. Korbelik, T. Delmont, and A. Pflaum. 1986. Strategic planning in Hennepin County, Minnesota: An issues management approach. Paper presented to the American Planning Association, National Planning Conference, Los Angeles. April.

Fisher, R., and W. Ury. 1981. *Getting to yes: Negotiating agreement without giving in.* New York: Penguin.

Frederickson, J. W. 1984. The comprehensiveness of strategic decision processes. *Academy of Management Journal, 27,* 2: 445–466.

_____, and T. R. Mitchell. 1984. Strategic decision processes: Comprehensiveness and performance in an industry with an unstable environment. *Academy of Management Journal, 27,* 2: 399–423.

Freeman, R. E. 1984. *Strategic management: A stakeholder approach.* Boston: Pitman.

Galloway, T. D. 1979. Comment on "Comparison of current planning theories: Counterparts and contradictions," by B. M. Hudson. *Journal of the American Planning Association, 45,* 4: 399–402.

Gilbert, D. R., and R. E. Freeman. 1985. Strategic management and responsibility: A game theoretic approach. Discussion paper 22. Minneapolis: Strategic Management Research Center, University of Minnesota.

Hambrick, D. C. 1982. Environmental scanning and organizational strategy. *Strategic Management Journal, 3,* 2: 159–74.

Harrigan, K. 1981. Barriers to entry and competitive strategies. *Strategic Management Journal, 2,* 4: 395–412.

Henderson, B. 1979. *Henderson on corporate strategy.* Cambridge, Mass.: Abt Books.

Howe, E. 1980. Role choices of urban planners. *Journal of the American Planning Association, 46,* 4: 398–409.

_____, and J. Kaufman. 1979. The ethics of contemporary American planners. *Journal of the American Planning Association, 45,* 3: 243–55.

Kaufman, J. L. 1979. The planner as interventionist in public policy issues. In *Planning Theory in the 1980s* (R. Burchel and G. Sternlieb, eds.) New Brunswick, N.J.: Center for Urban Policy Research, Rutgers University.

_____, and H. M. Jacobs. 1987. A public planning perspective on strategic planning. *Journal of the American Planning Association, 53,* 1: 21–31.

King, W. R. 1982. Using strategic issue analysis. *Long Range Planning, 15,* 4: 45–49.

Klumpp, S. 1986. *Strategic planning booklet for the city of St. Louis Park.* St. Louis Park, Minn.: City of St. Louis Park.

Lindblom, C. E. 1959. The science of muddling through. *Public Administration Review, 19* (Spring): 79–88.

Linneman, R. E., and H. E. Klein. 1983. The use of multiple scenarios by U.S. industrial companies: A comparison study, 1977–1981. *Long Range Planning, 16,* 6: 94–101.

Locke, E. A., K. W. Shaw, L. M. Saari, and G. P. Latham. 1981. Goal setting and task performance: 1969–1980. *Psychological Bulletin, 90,* 1: 125–52.

Lorange, P. 1980. *Corporate planning: An executive viewpoint.* Englewood Cliffs, N.J.: Prentice-Hall.

_____, M. F. S. Morton, and S. Ghoshal. 1986. *Strategic control.* St. Paul, Minn.: West.

MacMillan, I. 1983. Competitive strategies for not-for-profit agencies. *Advances in Strategic Management, 1:* 61–82.

McGowan, R. P., and J. M. Stevens. 1983. Local governments' initiatives in a climate of uncertainty. *Public Administration Review, 43,* 2: 127–36.

Mintzberg, H., and J. A. Waters. 1985. Of strategies, deliberate and emergent. *Strategic Management Journal, 6,* 3: 257–72.

Montanari, J. R., and J. S. Bracker. 1986. The strategic management process. *Strategic Management Journal, 7,* 3: 251–65.

Olsen, J. B., and D. C. Eadie. 1982. *The game plan: Governance with foresight.* Washington, D.C.: Council of State Planning Agencies.

O'Toole, J. 1985. *Vanguard management.* New York: Doubleday.

Ouchi, W. 1981. *Theory Z: How American business can meet the Japanese challenge.* Reading, Mass.: Addison-Wesley.

Peters, T. J., and R. H. Waterman, Jr. 1982. *In search of excellence: Lessons from America's best-run companies.* New York: Harper & Row.

Pettigrew, A. M. 1977. Strategy formulation as a political process. *International Studies in Management and Organization, 7,* 2: 78–87.

Pfeffer, J., and G. R. Salancik. 1978. *The external control of organizations: A resource dependence perspective.* New York: Harper & Row.

Pflaum, A., and T. Delmont. 1987. External scanning—A tool for planners. *Journal of American Planning Association, 53,* 1: 56–67.

Pinchot, G., III. 1985. *Intrapreneuring.* New York: Harper & Row.

Porter, M. 1980. *Competitive strategy.* New York: Free Press.

————. 1985. *Competitive advantage.* New York: Free Press.

Quinn, J. B. 1980. *Strategies for change: Logical incrementalism.* Homewood, Ill.: R. D. Irwin.

Ring, P. S., and J. L. Perry. 1985. Strategic management in public and private organizations: Implications of distinctive contexts and constraints. *Academy of Management Review, 10,* 2: 276–86.

Rue, L. W., and P. G. Holland. 1986. *Strategic management: Concepts and experiences.* New York McGraw-Hill.

Savas, E. S. 1982. *Privatizing the public sector.* Chatham, N.J.: Chatham House.

Schön, D. A. 1971. *Beyond the stable state.* Lo Temple Smith.

Sorkin, D. L., N. B. Ferris, and J. Hudak. 1984. *Strategies for cities and counties: A strategic planning guide.* Washington, D.C.: Public Technology, Inc.

Stuart, D. G. 1969. Rational urban planning: Problems and prospects. *Urban Affairs Quarterly, 5,* (December): 151–82.

Susskind, L. E., and C. Ozawa. 1984. Mediated negotiation in the public sector: The planner as mediator. *Journal of Planning Education and Research, 4,* 1: 5–15.

Taylor, B. 1984. Strategic planning—Which style do you need? *Long Range Planning, 17,* 3: 51–62.

Thompson, J. D. 1967. *Organizations in action.* New York: McGraw-Hill.

Tomazinis, A. R. 1985. The logic and rationale of strategic planning. Paper presented at the 27th annual conference of the Association of Collegiate Schools of Planning, Atlanta. October.

Wildavsky, A. 1979. *The politics of the budgeting process* (3rd ed.). Boston: Little, Brown.

Wind, Y., and V. Mahajan. 1981. Designing product and business portfolios. *Harvard Business Review, 59,* 1: 155–65.

Zaltman, G., D. Florio, and L. Sikorski. 1977. *Dynamic educational change.* New York: Free Press.

Strategic Management in Local Government

John J. Gargan

Introduction

Like their private-sector counterparts, public managers, including those in city governments, have sought out new management approaches to deal with increasingly complex problems. Contributing to the problem complexity have been several developments of recent years. Population trends show that people continue to vote with their feet by migrating inter-regionally and, within metropolitan areas, by moving from larger to smaller places some distance from a central city. Economic change has been induced by the death of manufacturing firms, formation of new types of economic activities, and capital mobility. Demographic patterns have resulted in an emerging middle-aged cohort group of unprecedented size. Changes in sexual mores and job opportunities have increased the number of dependent and single-parent households, particularly among black Americans living in central cities. Each of the developments has altered conditions in specific places.

Sources of the developments are external to individual cities, and therefore beyond any meaningful control by local public or private decision makers. Yet the developments have reduced city government autonomy and made it more difficult for city governments to operate as viable political systems. The differences between contemporary and historic urban places are largely differences of degree rather than form. That is, city governments have always been subject to the impacts of nonlocal decisions and to the societal imperatives of demographic, technological, and economic trends (Banfield 1974).

Reprinted with permission from Jack Rabin, Gerald J. Miller, and W. Bartley Hildreth, Editors, Handbook of Strategic Management, *1989. Published by Marcel Dekker, Inc., New York, New York.*

Coping with the impacts of nonlocal decisions and societal imperatives has frequently led to reactive decision making in city government: city officials respond to the problems brought to them (Yates 1977). Reactive decision making has been functional for governing coalitions since it allows for adjustments in existing policies, with the magnitude of the adjustment dependent on the political influence of those seeking change. It has not been judged favorably by governmental reformers. During the past century they have made numerous proposals to increase proactive decision making by city governments. Strategic management is a recent manifestation of that reform mindset.

City Governments and Public Administration Paradigms

The material covered here relates to a long tradition of inquiry. The viability of American cities as governmental and political systems has been regularly covered by the popular media and assessed in scholarly analyses. In the coverage and assessments two themes have been highlighted. The first theme has been one of general pessimism about prevailing political and governmental practices and the likely negative long-term consequences of unabated trends. The second theme has been optimistic, that adverse circumstances could be ameliorated by consciously developed public policies or by adoption of new structural arrangements.

The search for the most appropriate combination of public policies and structural arrangements is perennial and involves normative, empirical, and applied topics. It is important to note at the outset that in focusing on strategic management, certain aspects of city government and politics are emphasized in this chapter and other aspects are ignored or only superficially examined. This is only to raise the obvious but critical point that any understanding of phenomena is a function of paradigms brought to analyses and changes occurring in the phenomena of interest. During the past century, dominant or competing paradigms have been used to interpret the city (Banfield 1974; Bish and Ostrom 1973; Elkin 1987; Gurr and King 1987, Lineberry and Masotti 1976; Shefter 1984; Smith 1979) primarily as:

A community of individuals with a shared interest to be maximized; or
An essential training ground for citizenship and political leadership training; or
A site of intense social, economic, and political conflict based on ethnic, racial, religious, and class cleavages; or

An administrative unit within which the economical and efficient delivery
of services is the paramount objective and responsibility of public
officials.

Variations in the interpretations have been matters of emphasis; rarely
has one variable or factor been stressed to the exclusion of all others. Emphasis is significant, nonetheless. For the process of deciding which community problems are to be addressed in what order, it makes a good deal
of difference whether one views city politics either as a zero-sum game between racial and ethnic groups or as a process of negotiation among civic
amateurs and administrative or functional professionals.

Procedural rationality, governing capacity, and strategic management are topics of concern for a dominant professional management
paradigm that has guided the work of theoreticians, academicians, practitioners, and students within the public administration community from its
earliest days. Urban America has made substantial contributions to the
evolution and development of both the dominant paradigm and the field
of public administration. Ideas applied initially to concrete problems of
city governments influenced subsequent developments in the entire field.
Notes Mosher (1975, p. 8), "public administration as practice, as field of
study and as self-conscious profession, began in the cities." Activists in the
Progressive and municipal reform movements heightened civic awareness
of the administration, management, and policies of larger cities. Training
at university-based programs was to the preparation of experts qualified
to deal with urban management issues (Stone and Stone 1975). The intellectual and experiential bases brought by Charles Merriam, Louis
Brownlow, and Luther Gulick to the reorganization of the presidency in
the 1930s were the result of professional careers spent on theoretical and
applied issues of municipal government and administration (Karl 1963).

The specific details of urban management attended to by the public
administration community have varied through time and across cities. On
occasion, attention to one type of detail has preceded attention to others.
In the early days of the New York Bureau of Municipal Research, for example, considerable staff energy was expended gathering simple factual
data; recommendations for improved performance by New York City
government were contingent on basic information. At other times, a crisis
or an accretion of pressures has precipitated action on new management
and administrative concerns; innovations in budgeting and financial
management have been adopted because of dissatisfaction with existing
routines or episodic fiscal stress (Shefter 1987). Contributions to public
management generally and urban management specifically have been
derived from the models and ideologies of other fields; for its infatuation
with scientific management and its enduring support for the city manager

plan, the public administration community is indebted to the seminal work of Frederick W. Taylor on industrial management technology (Nelson 1980) and to organizing models provided by the private-sector corporation (Downs and Larkey 1986).

It is development within the prevailing dominant paradigm that leads to some level of professional consensus on significant concerns, exemplary practices, and appropriate professional behavior. During the 1930s a consensus of sorts was achieved on the meaning of a "science of administration" and its underlying principles. These principles provided frameworks and guidance for structuring the "major duties of the chief executive," planning, organizing, staffing, directing, coordinating, reporting, and budgeting (POSDCORB) (Gulick 1937, p. 13).

In retrospect, the consensus on the science and principles of public administration was short-lived. Inconsistencies in the principles were pointed out. New Deal and World War II experiences suggested to professors the futility of attempting to separate politics from administration. New graduate students were shown by their recently experienced faculty the incompleteness, if not quaintness, of POSDCORB as a summary of the multi-faceted nature of executive leadership.

While the criticisms were well placed, a caveat was, and is, in order. Other things being equal, as a general rule city governments in which executives give high priority to planning, organizing, staffing, directing, coordinating, reporting, and budgeting activities will perform more effectively than city governments in which such matters are not of high priority to executives. Fiscal stress encountered by cities since the mid–1970s has been best dealt with in cities with well-developed financial management practices (Clark and Ferguson 1983; Levine, Rubin, and Wolohojian 1981). Since things are rarely equal, there will be exceptions to the general rule: charismatic leaders with few analytic or management skills reach major goals; meticulous managers are overwhelmed by the volume of demands on their offices. But in most cases most of the time, the general rule holds for city governments with hierarchical authority structures and extensive functional professionalism as well as for city governments with substantial structural decentralization and service delivery based on citizen participation and coproduction.

Even if it failed to capture the totality of the executive function, POSDCORB did illuminate those key activities and tasks of public management that — in the 1980s as in the 1930s — constitute a *"technical core* of analytic and management skill" (Lynn 1987, p. 183). Among the major accomplishments of the public administration community since the 1930s and 1940s have been those contributing to greater sophistication of the conceptual orientations, technologies, and professional training in the various POSDCORB fields. Quite aptly, for many scholars the POSDCORB fields continue to be a basis for gauging the management capacity of city governments (Honadle 1981).

Strategic Management as the New POSDCORB

Ideational underpinnings and exemplary practices of generic management have been altered. Indicated by the alterations is a recognition in the private and public sectors that more and more problems arise from turbulent environments. The turbulence of the environments is caused by the rate and intensity of change in interdependencies, technologies, and attitudes and expectations. The frustrations of executives and managers in dealing with new realities have implied a diminished efficacy of traditional management and have generated widespread interest in strategic management approaches to policy development and problem resolution.

Defining *strategic management* as a concept and in terms sufficiently broad to cover different settings is difficult. According to Steiss (1985, p. 9):

> Strategic management is concerned with deciding in advance what an organization should do in the future (planning), determining who will do it and how it will be done (resource management), and monitoring and enhancing ongoing operations (control and evaluation).

With regard to its application in the private sector, Godet (1987, pp. 102–3) notes:

> *The strategic management* of the company consists of providing a coordinated transformation of its four sets of resources (human, technical, commercial, and financial) leading to a desired future. To each resource, objectives, strategic tools (budget), and tactical resources (management accounting) can be assigned. . . .
> The objectives (technical, economic and social) are partly self-contradictory. And strategic management is primarily a means of arbitrating between divergent objectives in a turbulent environment.

In some respects, the terminology and acronyms of strategic management are new. Not so new are the primary activities: strategic management builds on the familiar — selecting a course of action after due consideration of options, developing organizational proficiency to implement the programmatic details of the options chosen, and allocating sufficient resources to achieve option objectives. In one form or another, these activities of selecting, developing, and allocating have undergirded proposals to increase rationality in private and public decision making.

Proponents of strategic management stress the importance of an overall orientation, a wholistic approach to problems and environments, and a heightened sophistication with regard to management practices. The heightened sophistication can be illustrated by a current example. In financial management important work is underway in city (and other) governments by accounting professionals who are attempting to integrate budgeting, auditing, and accounting subsystems in order to collect appropriate data, generate measures, and report on the efficiency and effectiveness of public-sector performance (Brown and Pyers 1988).

Construction of valid empirical measures of the efficiency and effectiveness of city services would represent a major development in public policy and urban administration. The level of management sophistication required to construct such measures is high. Even when budgeters, accountants, and auditors cooperate to produce the desired measures, the data-gathering tasks, data-reporting forms, and data-analysis skills called for are of a qualitatively different order than when the budget is used primarily as a control instrument, accounting is used to provide a paper trail of budget transactions, and auditing is carried out to check compliance with legal requirements. Of course, city governments must have the capacity to assure adequate performance of these basic financial management activities before they can integrate budgeting, accounting, and auditing on behalf of measures for assessing efficiency and effectiveness. Capacity building for strategic management suggests a dilemma. Sophisticated managerial accounting, for example, requires considerable attention at the outset to what is to be achieved at the end. This means that there must be real front-end investment of time and energy to the development of data gathering, accounting, and analysis systems. Required are considerable sophistication and in-place management capacity to begin management capacity building.

The Centrality of Strategic Planning to Strategic Management in City Governments

Differentiating strategic management from traditional management approaches is the centrality of the strategic planning role. While strategic planning may be considered innovative, planning per se is not new to city government. Indeed, the origins of public-sector planning in the United States were local; public planning done before World War II was modeled largely on experience with city planning from the late nineteenth and early twentieth centuries onward. For most of its history, city planning's main purpose has been guidance of the physical development of the city, encapsulated in a comprehensive plan formulated by professional planners. In city government the planning function typically has been administered by nonpartisan commissions to prevent, according to reformers, political or special-interest criteria from interfering with technical criteria and achievement of the best interests of the community as a whole.

The scope of city and regional planning changed fundamentally from the 1950s to the 1980s. City and regional planners became more policy-oriented and less comprehensive plan-oriented. Though physical development concerns continued to be significant in their work (since cities and regions are, whatever else, the sites of physical development), social and economic problems have a high priority. Pressures for change were from within and from outside the planning profession. Demographic, social, and economic transitions in metropolitan areas demonstrated the range of substantive issues, including but beyond the physical, to which the profession needed to be attentive. Political activation of minority and poverty populations and citizen participation requirements imposed by the federal government as one of many conditions of federal grants reminded city planners that their technical skills and neutral competence fashioned policy, equity, and advocacy outcomes.

It was in the late 1970s and early 1980s that strategic planning began to permeate the public sector. Though important changes in traditional planning practices, methodologies, and approaches had already been made by city planners (Burchell and Listokin 1978; Kaufman and Jacobs 1987, pp. 25–26), a fact often overlooked by critics, the benefits of the new strategic planning were widely proclaimed. Since the late 1950s, most of the theoretical and applied literature on strategic planning and management has been directed to the business corporation. Academics writing this literature have been based in schools of business administration and management and have introduced models covering topics like SWOT (strengths, weaknesses, opportunities, threats) analysis, stakeholder management, portfolio methods, logical incrementalism, etc. (Bryson and Roering 1987, pp. 11–14; Freeman 1984, Chap. 2). Until recently, work on strategic planning and management for public organizations drew on the models, approaches, and literature of those scholars.*

While substantial, the dependence of city officials and the public administration community on the private sector for new ideas should not be

---

*There is a sophisticated body of literature developing on public sector strategic planning and management. See especially the substance and citations in John M. Bryson's Strategic Planning for Public and Nonprofit Organizations (1988) and also the symposium on strategic planning in the Winter 1987 issue of Journal of the American Planning Association.

exaggerated. Much innovative thinking on public management was done by public administration researchers and practitioners. Strain on existing decision-making processes and arrangements was a stimulus for this thinking. One consequence of the expansion of the federal government's role in domestic policy was anxiety over the ability of local governments to perform as equal intergovernmental partners.

In an important article on the rationale and logic of local management capacity, Philip Burgess (1975) argued the importance of policy management, program management, and resource management, which "*together constitute the core elements of public management and administration.*" The three elements involve different participants, emphases, and skills. Policy management is the province of elected officials and high-level administrators and relates to the processes of choice making, priority setting, and "the *strategic functions* of guidance and leadership with respect to a jurisdictional or territorial arena." Program management includes functional specialists with substantive expertise, which gives them the "capacity to perform the *administrative functions* and tactical requirements of existing policy by undertaking programs, activities, or services." Resource management draws on those technical specialists in personnel, finance, information, etc. with the abilities "to carry out the administrative and organizational *support functions* and their management, which together constitute an organization's basic capabilities and bottom line assets." Through the early 1970s, more capable local policy, program, and resource management were assumed to be indispensable to the success of national programs. In many instances these programs marked governmental involvement in a substantive area for the first time, were carried out by new means and mechanisms of service delivery, and raised very serious coordination problems.

The work of Burgess and others provided a conceptual basis for federal and state programs to help local governments by way of administrative experiments, workshops, and training programs. The spurt of interest in local governing capacity was acknowledgment that successful implementation of national policy depended on local officials and, therefore, the strategic management and planning abilities of those officials and their employees. Interest was also stimulated by other developments. Rapid changes in the fiscal conditions of local governments pointed up the critical importance of effective financial management. Retrospectively, in a very brief period of time local officials were forced to shift the focus of their management concerns from arrays of federal funding provisions, regulations, and reporting requirements to program reductions or eliminations and increased productivity. For either the management of an expanding public sector or cutback management, Burgess's observation holds true: "policy management requirements include capacities to assess needs, to evaluate productivity and impacts across programs, to systematically explore trade-offs and opportunity costs, and to perform ... other tasks...."

Strategic planning operationalizes the Burgess framework and permits private and public decision makers to heed Drucker's (1964, p. 6) advice: "The pertinent question is not how to do things right, but how to find the right things to do, and to concentrate resources and efforts on them." By design, strategic planning is action and results oriented. The aim is continuation of a process directed to the resolution of problems and the accomplishment of objectives rather than the production of comprehensive documents. This process is iterative and focuses simultaneously on the policy direction in which an organization is moving and the capacity of the organization to move; "the strategies of public agencies and the way those strategies change over time result largely from the interaction of organizational intention and capacity with external environment" (Wechsler and Backoff, 1987, p. 34).

Acceptance of a strategy may necessitate reorientation of long-standing operating procedures and transformation of organizational culture from one emphasizing a reactive, competitive stance to one supporting an entrepreneurial stance (Ansoff, Declerck, and Hayes 1976). Similarly, experience with the implementation of specific tactics may lead to modifications in an accepted broader strategy. When successful, the process enables a community, local government, or organization to determine its own future by way of present decisions. Properly implemented, strategic planning serves as a powerful tool for chief executives, legislators, and administrators to control policy priorities and to integrate the activities of relatively independent units.

Whatever the particular setting in which it is carried out, the strategic planning process proceeds through several identifiable stages. Table 1 shows one of several ways of listing these stages.

The stages have much in common with comprehensive city planning, management by objectives, performance management, and planning, programming, and budgeting systems. Each assumes a desire on the part of officials to be rational, to deal with problems of policy substance, and to practice "behavior that is appropriate to specified goals in the context of a given situation" (Simon 1985, p. 294).

A crucial stage of the process is when strategic issues are identified and placed on the agenda for serious consideration. Strategic issues are "fundamental policy questions affecting the organization's mandates, mission, values, product or service level and mix, clients or users, cost financing, or management" (Bryson and Roering 1987, p. 11). A city, firm, or organization must deal with these issues if it is to progress. Bryson (1988, p. 56) explains that:

Table 1. Stages of the Strategic Planning Process

Stage 1: Historical context.
Identification of "trends and critical events, directions, and ideals that characterize the historical context of the organization."

Stage 2: Situational assessment.
Determination and ranking of "the organization's current strengths and weaknesses as well as its future opportunities and threats...."

Stage 3: The issue agenda.
Determination of difficulties and problems that have "a significant influence on the way the organization functions or on its ability to achieve a desired future, for which there is no agreed-on response."

Stage 4: Strategic options.
Consideration of "possible strategies for dealing with each issue on the agenda, beginning with the most important issue to be managed."

Stage 5: Feasibility assessment.
Undertake "stakeholder analysis" of "who will be affected by the new strategy and how other parties could affect successful implementation." Assess "what resources are required to implement the strategy."

Stage 6: Implementation.
Deal with "broad-scale concerns raised by a change in strategy" and devise programs "to monitor and evaluate stakeholders' predicted actions and to manage resource suppliers."

Source: Nutt and Backoff (1987).

> Strategic issues, virtually by definition, involve conflicts of one sort or another. The conflicts may involve ends (what); means (how); philosophy (why); location (where); timing (when); and the groups that might be advantaged or disadvantaged by different ways of resolving the issue (who). In order for the issues to be raised and resolved effectively, the organization must be prepared to deal with the almost inevitable conflicts that will occur.

The quotation is worth pondering. At the city government level, what Bryson defines as strategic issues—those involving questions of what, how, why, where, when, and who—are the substance and stuff of local politics. Local political power is exercised in the resolution of such issues. Those proposing strategic planning for city governments must proceed as if there were no doubt of the acceptability of the outlined process to those exercising local political power.

The Diffusion and Utilization of Strategic Planning

With the published material available, summarizing the logic of the strategic planning process is not especially challenging. However, summarizing the diffusion and use of the process by local governments is problematic. As is often the case with innovations in administration and management, there is no complete data base to provide an accurate account of practices used. And it is unlikely that the data base will be developed in the immediate future, given the universe of local governments and the variety of management practices employed.

Some evidence can be cited on the extent of diffusion and utilization of strategic planning in a single state. A mail questionnaire to mayors and managers of Ohio cities requested information on city planning activities.* In a section of the questionnaire stages of the strategic planning process were listed and the mayors and managers were asked if their cities had "used strategic planning, or some approach similar to it." The distributions of responses — total and by categories — are reported in Table 2.

According to responding mayors and managers, strategic planning or something akin to it has been used in a number of Ohio cities. Overall, better than 68 percent of respondents indicate use of strategic planning. Larger cities (over 50,000 population) were more likely and smaller cities (under 15,000) less likely to have used strategic planning. The overall distribution is maintained for both city-manager and mayor-council cities, though there is a clear distribution between cities with a separate planning department and those without.

The interactive effects of management and planning professionalism can be seen in the figures for combinations of city government form and presence of a separate planning department. Strategic planning experience is virtually universal (94.4 percent) in city-manager cities with planning departments and is claimed for over three-quarters of mayor-council cities with planning departments. In line with the tenets of the reform movement, city managers are generally supportive of approaches like strategic planning (Abney and Lauth 1986).

Conclusions from the Ohio data are tentative, and the impression from Table 2 of widespread use of strategic planning needs to be qualified. When respondents were asked about the use of specific process stages, the level of experience reported is much lower. Better than 70 percent

*The questionnaire was sent in May 1984 to mayors and city managers in 150 Ohio cities with a 1980 population of 10,000 or more. Completed questionnaires were received from 85 cities, a response rate of 57 percent. Financial support for the project which included the questionnaire was provided by the Interinstitutional Research Program of the Ohio Urban University Program. Appreciation for that support is gratefully acknowledged.

Table 2. Percentage of Respondents Indicating Use of Strategic Planning or Some Similar Approach

	Percent
Total, all cities	68.3
City size	
100,000+	80.0
50,000–99,999	75.0
10,000–14,999	59.3
Form of city government	
City manager	69.0
Mayor-council	67.9
Separate planning department	
Cities with	85.7
Cities without	50.0
City manager cities with separate planning departments	94.4
Mayor-council cities with separate planning departments	76.0

have been involved in the basics of goal formulation, objectives definition, and priority setting, undoubtedly reflecting executive experience with those components of conventional city planning and operations management which overlap with strategic planning.

Familiarity with other process stages was less evident. Over 40 percent of respondents claimed no experience with the development of specific strategies to move toward desired and agreed on priorities or with efforts to identify all factors that influence progress towards objectives. Respondents had least experience with the stages related to the actual implementation* of a strategic plan:

> Establishment of a strategic planning calendar which lists, in detail, who is to be responsible for doing what and by when.

> Formation of an information system to monitor and to evaluate progress on strategies.

Just under one-third (31.3 percent) of the respondents indicated they had used some kind of strategic planning calendar, and just over one-quarter

*Reference is to the stages of the strategic planning process listed in the Ohio mail questionnaire. The wording used in the questionnaire to describe the stages differed from that of Nutt and Backoff (1987) as summarized in Table 1.

(25.7 percent) indicated formation of an information system to monitor progress.

Aside from the Ohio data, evidence on the diffusion and utilization of the strategic planning process is fragmentary. Sorkin, Ferris, and Hudak (1984) in their strategic planning guide do provide illustrative material on each process stage from the experiences of communities in several regions of the country; they also list for 16 city and county "information resources," local contact persons who are sources of hands-on expertise and advice for would-be strategic planners. Metropolitan newspapers regularly carry stories on strategic efforts to improve communities and editorials in praise of the community-minded spirit of those involved. Such coverage was given by the *New York Times* to the completion of the 1987 report of the Commission on the Year 2000, "New York Ascendant" (1987). The business section of the Detroit Free Press carried a story in early 1988 that noted that Charles Fisher III, chief executive of NBD Bancorp, had been "named chairman of Detroit Renaissance Inc., the business-civic alliance charged with implementing Detroit's strategic plan" (Blossom 1988, p. 1C); the details of the Detroit plan had been announced in November 1987 (Detroit Strategic Planning Project 1987).

Similar topics are reported on by more specialized media. The San Francisco Chamber of Commerce initiated, sponsored, and supported a strategic plan for the city; the Chamber also gave extensive publicity to the planning product by way of its in-house publication (Morten 1983). Evidence of successful strategic planning can even be found in what some observers might consider unlikely places. With the active support of a new mayor, a strategic plan was completed for Albany, New York (Swanstrom 1986), a city whose government and politics had been dominated by an old-style political machine since the 1920s (Kennedy 1983; O'Leary 1984; Robinson 1973).

Factors Complicating the Strategic Planning Component of Strategic Management

From coverage in the academic, practitioner, and popular literature, it is clear that strategic planning has been attempted in a number of places, including most large cities and many smaller jurisdictions. That evidence of strategic planning activity can be found does not mean a transformation of local management capacity is at hand. The success of strategic management in city government will be determined by the ways in which local officials handle strategic planning questions, especially those of plan sponsorship and substance.

The Sponsorship Factor

It is by way of strategic planning that the direction of city, organizational, or system movement is determined. If that movement is to inappropriate or unattainable objectives, steps to improve other elements of strategic management or to alter values and cultures will be of little significance. Included under the rubric of strategic planning have been ventures that produced fully developed and subsequently implemented plans; also included have been ventures that were largely symbolic exercises. Whatever the end results, the ventures have taken place under several sponsorships — city government, private organization, or a combination of public and private.

There has been some tendency to group together all forms of strategic planning in cities, regardless of formal sponsorship, participants, or funding sources. This is understandable. Much of the early promotion of strategic planning as an approach for dealing with community problems emphasized the importance of partnerships and cooperative undertakings by city governments and the private sector, particularly the local business community.

Not all strategic plans have involved cooperative undertakings. The renowned San Francisco Strategic Plan was inaugurated by the business community, financed by the business community, formulated by Arthur Anderson and Company, and overseen by the Chamber of Commerce (Hartman 1984; Jacobs 1983; Morten 1983). The Albany strategic plan was a city government project, financed with CDBG funds, formulated by committees representative of major public and private interests, and supported throughout by a powerful mayor (O'Leary 1984; Swanstrom 1986). In 1984, New York City Mayor Edward Koch formed a commission to study city problems, appointed a governmental political ally as commission chair, arranged for information support from city departments, and provided for an annual commission budget of several hundred thousands of dollars (Findler 1987; LeMoyne 1984; Roberts 1987).

That different strategic plans may be initiated by different sponsors means that the strategic planning process may serve several political functions. At least for the short haul, encouragement of any kind of strategic planning initiatives has been functional. According to So (1984, p. 18) there were reasons for the attention directed to strategic planning in the early 1980s:

> In part, the interest in strategic planning is fueled by the realization that it is a way of involving the local business community in civic affairs. Thus, the desire to build public-private partnerships provides a strong incentive. Business people may feel more comfortable involving themselves

in a business-derived process and technique. And some planners and city managers, seeking to build greater credibility with the business community, feel that the use of the process will make them look good in the eyes of the bottom line people.

So also points up the benefits accruing to the business community for participating:

> From the business community's point of view, a strategic planning project, especially if it is conducted by the private sector, is a way of encouraging government to go in a particular policy direction. There's nothing new about this — it began with Burnham in Chicago.

The implications of sponsorship change as the strategic plan progresses from excellent idea to specific recommendations. For elected officials and public-sector professionals, the question of *whose* strategic plan is to be implemented is significant. When the plan is taken on by political leaders and the top management cadre of an agency to improve administrative performance, the matter of sponsorship is clear-cut. The environment to be scanned, the stakeholders involved, the number of strategic issues, and the range of options are identifiable and limited in number. Under such circumstances, real improvements in agency operations and approaches to problem solving can be achieved (Eadie and Steinbacher 1985; Levine 1985; Wechsler and Backoff 1986, 1987).

Difficulties arise for local officials, especially elected officials, when strategic plans are sponsored, initiated, or dominated by others — business organizations, civic groups, voluntary associations — in the name of the community. Those involved are praised for working to promote community interests and for addressing problems that political and governmental leaders have been unable or unwilling to address. These private efforts or public-private partnerships often encourage widespread participation to insure the expression of diverse viewpoints.

With the support of the local media, project recommendations may become high-visibility items on a community's public agenda. As a result, public officials are forced to deal with an agenda and decisions not of their making and not necessarily to their liking. However couched in the language of environmental scans, goals, and analytical techniques, strategic planning is essentially a political process. It ends in the ultimate political act of devoting money, personnel, time, and energy to some activities and not to others. By definition, not all local interests benefit equally from strategic decisions.

The Substance Factor

Public problems and the ability to deal with problems are contextually determined. Effective strategic planning must deal with changes in objective conditions and changes in expectations about governing capacity. Strategies directed to changing expectations may be more difficult to devise than strategies directed to changing objective conditions. Increasingly, mayors, members of the city councils, and city bureaucrats are judged by the ability, or the claimed ability, to solve newly discovered and multifaceted problems. Officials are expected "to do something about" issues of nurturing economic development rather than simply promoting economic growth, of sheltering the mentally incompetent rather than building housing for low and moderate income families, of promoting affirmative action in city police and fire departments rather than assuring minority representation on governmental boards and commissions.

While public problems and expectations are contextually determined, there are similarities in the sets of problems and strategic issues identified in local strategic plans. Strategic planners in San Francisco, New York, Albany, and Detroit all, or nearly all, cited the need for action on the local economic base and especially its central business district component, physical infrastructure, housing supply, and city government finances. Contextual realities in individual cities have forced attention to other problems. The Detroit plan, for example, emphasized the importance to the Detroit metropolitan area of strategies directed to the elimination of racism, renewal of economic opportunities in the central city, improvements in education, and substantial reductions in inner-city crime (Detroit Strategic Planning Project 1987). New York City's Commission on the Year 2000 (1987, pp. 7–8) concluded that:

> Changes are needed in a host of areas . . . but reform is particularly needed in the area of poverty. Without a response to the problem of poverty, the New York of the 21st century will be not just a city divided, not just a city excluding those at the bottom from the fullness of opportunity, but a city in which peace and social harmony may not be possible. There is no more important issue for city government, no more important test for New York.

The probability of strategic plan success is in no small measure determined by the substance of the strategic plan. Substance derives from the selection of strategies that maximize opportunities and minimize risks in relevant environments. Presently, city officials do use their legal powers and entrepreneurial talents to protect the city's interests, form, and structure and to leverage future investments. Entertainment districts are established to draw middle-class suburbanites to the central business district. Tax abatements, land use controls, and health regulations have been used to encourage certain kinds of physical development downtown and to discourage undesirable conditions in residential neighborhoods. Capital facilities plans for the widening of city streets and installing of water and sewer lines are sometimes adopted before the completion of housing subdivisions. Choices can be made from an array of combinations for the production and provision of city services. Managers meet with their councils in a retreat setting to educate council members on the general fund and to decide priority objectives for the upcoming year. All of these are appropriate local strategic management initiatives to influence the local future.

Local strategies will probably prove faint or irrelevant in the face of environmental trends that have been centuries in the making or that are truly global in their effects. The fabric of social and political life in New York City is strained by poverty and associated pathologies. Participants in the Detroit Strategic Planning Project accurately read the environments of the Detroit area. Profound central city-suburban disparities are a consequence of conscious and unconscious racism and high levels of minority-group unemployment. At the same time, experiences of the past two decades in the United States and in other nations suggest that many racial problems are only minimally susceptible to public-sector action. As the problems become increasingly class-based and intertwined with high rates of school drop out, violent crime, and drug abuse, their susceptibility to public action, and certainly to city-level action, is lessened. Racism and the loss of central-city-based manufacturing jobs are not unique to Detroit. They are examples of societal problems for which causal understanding is inadequate and for which feasible and acceptable policies are unavailable (Banfield 1974; Jacob 1985). Inproving the quality of life for all and life chances for the underclass requires more than will and commitment: it also requires knowledge of what is to be done.

Shifts in economic bases from manufacturing to services to information processing are due to changes in the determinants of comparative advantage (Hanson 1983; Kasarda 1988). Since the changing determinants have favored some regions of the country over others, the economic well being of individual communities has been conditioned, to a considerable degree, by regional location. Recognition by city officials in all regions of the critical importance of retaining and attracting above average taxpayers to their communities (Peterson 1981) has increased the importance of economic development in local strategic planning (Bingham and Blair 1984). For officials in many cities, strategic planning and economic development are nearly synonymous terms.*

The mail questionnaire to Ohio mayors and city managers included an item: "If additional money and staff were available, on what three problems would you like to see more planning done?" Sixty-five percent of those who responded to the question designated economic development as one of the three problems to which additional planning would be directed.

Identifying patterns of change in economic and other conditions is basic to the development of strategies. The earlier the patterns are recognized and strategies developed, the greater the likelihood of appropriate actions. Care needs to be taken, however, not to overstate the wherewithal of strategic planning and management to shape the future. Existing city conditions are the product of an aggregate of private and public decisions and policies. These include decisions by individuals and families about housing arrangements and lifestyle preferences. Aspects of present conditions are a result of public policies of decades past; incorporation of suburban municipalities in the 1920s and 1930s precludes annexation as a central-city growth strategy in the 1990s (Jackson 1985). And present conditions are the result of more recent public strategies adopted with the best of intentions — urban renewal, public housing, highway construction, mortgage guarantees, tax credits, etc.

Strategic plan sponsorship and substance have political consequences for public officials accountable to city electorates. Rarely did the conditions the officials seek to change develop randomly. More often, the conditions have been shaped by public and private decisions of individuals and institutions protecting and promoting thier particularistic interests (Fainstein et al. 1986). To mayors trying to calculate their own optimal strategies, the implications of Smith's (1979, p. 27) comments on private planning could be equally applied to plans and policies of state and national governments:

> Today the reality of private planning is even more evident. The advanced capitalist city and its surrounding suburbs are by and large the result of private planning — the private planning of industrial corporations; the highway planning of the auto-industrial complex and its government allies; the "investment planning" (also known as "redlining") of savings institutions; the development planning of local, regional, national, and multinational possessors of investment capital. . . . The question is not planning or no planning but planning by whom, how, and at whose expense.

Conclusion

This chapter has provided an overview of strategic management in city government. Because it is difficult to detail the state of the art in management practices in any comprehensive way, the choice of material for inclusion in the overview has been eclectic. Part of the difficulty is definitional: to discuss strategic management is to discuss all of city government. Since careerists and academicians segment the broader field into subfields — budgeting, personnel, planning — and into functional

specialities — law enforcement, community development, public works —
describing management practices entails a major task of data gathering
and literature review.

One important source of information on city management practices
is the work of Poister and McGowan (1984). In a mail questionnaire they
asked city executives about the use of specific management techniques:
program budgeting, management information systems, performance monitoring, productivity improvement, management by objectives, management incentive program, zero or target-base budgeting, and productivity
bargaining.

Poister and McGowan found extensive usage by local managers of
relatively sophisticated management techniques, especially those that
could be labeled strategic management oriented. On either a city-wide
basis or in selected departments or policy areas, over two-thirds of
respondents indicated use of four of the seven techniques (program
budgeting, management information systems, performance monitoring,
and productivity improvement); nearly three-fifths of the respondents
noted use of management by objectives. According to Poister and Mc-
Gowan (1984, p. 217), of the seven management tools listed in the questionnaire, "more than half of the cities report using four or more of these
tools." Comparing their findings with those of a 1976 survey by the International City Management Association (ICMA), Poister and McGowan
concluded that more cities were using the management practices and "to
the extent that increased utilization of more sophisticated management approaches leads to increased capabilities, it would appear that local governments' management capacity has increased substantially since the mid
1970s" (1984, p. 217).

There is additional evidence that progress has been made by local
government in adopting and utilizing strategic management-oriented
techniques. The evidence is at varying levels of inclusiveness: some relates
to individual cities, other evidence to a few cities, and still other evidence
to cities from a single state or of a particular size. Brecher and Hartman
(1984) show that, since the fiscal crisis of the mid–1970s, New York City
officials have improved financial management processes for financial
analysis, revenue and expenditure projections, and accounting and reporting. In a number of cities (New Orleans, Kansas City, Shreveport, San
Antonio, etc.) use is made of carefully developed models, procedures, and
information systems to generate multiyear revenue and expenditure forecasts (Bahl and Schroeder 1984). Budget documents and budget instruction
manuals from 123 cities were used by Usher and Cornia (1981) to determine
the extent to which city budgets were based on agency goals and objectives
and performance assessments. Usher and Cornia found that in over half
the cities studied agencies were required to state goals or objectives and

that most cities "employ measures of effort in assessing agency activity" (p. 233). Greater attention has been given in recent years to the relationship between capital spending and economic development; among those cities responding to Doss's (1987) survey, at least half have developed a separate capital budget and do capital improvement planning. Though numerous other studies and examples of management innovations could be referred to, they would only confirm that significant progress has been made in the adaptation of management practices to public settings.

Whether adoption of sophisticated practices is evidence of strategic management is an empirical question. Again, strategic management presumes more than recognition of the importance of doing specifics well. To manage strategically is to integrate management activities rather than simply to keep operations moving in some desired direction, with managers carrying out assigned tasks in relative independence (Ansoff, Declerck, and Hayes 1976; Godet 1987). When a city government (or any organization or system) is managed strategically, its managers think, plan, and act strategically. The managers consistently seek to "read" environments, to process information and signals on opportunities and threats in those environments, to assess strengths and weaknesses of their organizations, to formulate strategies that maximize the opportunities and minimize the threats, and to modify strategies as required.

City officials have evidenced creativity in formulating strategic approaches to problems. Their creativity has been facilitated by the diffusion and adoption of tested management techniques and the development of a decision-making technology. With the aid of sophisticated computer programs, the quality of group decision making can be dramatically improved. A group can now examine a large number of items (proposed budget reductions, projects in a capital budget, sequence of strategic operations, etc.), decide its preferences on the basis of simple paired comparisons of the items, store the decisions in a matrix, and extract from the matrix a value hierarchy, the structure of the group's preference orderings (Gargan and Moore 1984; Saaty 1982; Saaty and Kearns 1985; Warfield 1976).

On the planning component of strategic management, Bryson and Einsweiler (1987, p. 6) point out:

> Strategic planning is being used by key governmental decision makers precisely because the drastic changes in the public sector are forcing them to think strategically about what government *ought* to be doing. Decision makers, in other words, now are asking themselves what effective private-sector executives always ask: What business *should* we be in?

Bryson and Einsweiler are, of course, correct. Effective private managers periodically ask the most fundamental questions about a firm's business. By extension, public managers need to ask about agency, organization, system, and governmental purposes. Thus, in recent years students and practitioners of public administration owe much to the public choice school for raising questions of purpose and for suggesting alternative ways of thinking about types of public goods and their production and delivery (Savas 1987). This does not necessarily mean that a generic approach to management will fit both public and private settings. Elemental differences between the sectors mean that the "criteria of evaluation of public management differ markedly from those of private sector management" (Ring and Perry 1985, p. 276). Separation of powers, diversity of constituencies, civil service protection of employees, vagueness of goals, time horizons of office tenure (Ring and Perry 1985), and other factors do impede strategic public management.

Pragmatically, for officials working in the trenches of city government and politics the question of "What business *should* we be in?" is easily answered. City governments are in whatever business state law and city charters say they are in. As Zimmerman (1983) has so carefully documented, in state-local relations the state government can inhibit, facilitate, or initiate local governmental activities. State law and city charters detail mandated service levels, which local governments are empowered to do what, and specification of activities that can be started at the discretion of local officials. There are differences across the states regarding these details and within states among classifications or types of local governments. Allowing for the interstate differences, city governments generally are concerned with the management of conflict between competing interests and provision of services essential for the health, welfare, and safety of citizens and the maintenance of an urban society — water supply and waste removal, fire and police protection, public welfare, maintenance of city streets. These basic services are mandatory rather than discretionary and account for the lion's share of general revenues derived from the community's wealth.

The sheer press of events in the 1990s may make the most hidebound of bureaucrats receptive to strategic management proposals. Conversely, strategic planning by, and strategic management in, local governments may be constrained by several essentially political factors. Local decision making is differentiated from decision making at the state and national levels by the shortness of the feedback loop from decision to policy impacts to decision maker. As Lipsky (1976) and Yates (1977) have demonstrated, local government is about the delivery of services by street-level bureaucrats who interact directly and personally with service consumers; these services are divisible and are allocated to individuals and neighborhoods that vary in their needs. Local officials are therefore more likely than their counterparts at other levels to have an experiential base rooted in policy implementation realities and to have perceptions of program and agency effectiveness shaped by the views of their neighbors, the policy consumers. This proximity to program and organizational arrangements can inhibit long-range policy consideration or the kind of "what if" and unstructured intuitive thinking required of creative strategic planners.

The relevance of this elementary point should not be ignored. When existing approaches to service delivery are satisfactory to office holders, functional professionals, and clientele groups, the probability of success for any serious effort to devise new approaches is not great. Fundamental to any meaningful strategic planning is a willingness to examine the future from totally new perspectives. Serious attempts at strategic planning can disrupt existing political arrangements and strain the ability of civic activists to look beyond the present.

Also constraining the feasibility of strategic planning and management is the availability of resources. To engage the essential processes, at least minimal slack resources must be available. If all city employees are devoting all of their time and attention to day-to-day operations, a precondition of any strategic effort is expansion of available time. Time is but one example of basic resources. Money is another in such short supply in most city governments that revenue availability determines expenditures, and funding extant programs is the annual strategic objective to be achieved (Wildavsky 1986; Chap. 2). To time and money can be added knowledge, technical skills, and good will.

Availability of these resources is a necessary, but not sufficient, condition for the success of strategic planning or any other capacity initiative. In one early study of organizational innovation, Lawrence Mohr (1969, p. 114) hypothesized:

> Innovation is directly related to the motivation to innovate, inversely related to the strength of obstacles to innovation, and directly related to the availability of resources for overcoming such obstacles.

Availability of resources to innovate is a function of size. Though the correlation is not perfect, the relationship between organizational size and personnel specialization and staff professionalism is positive. Most of the actual governing in the United States is by local governments serving limited populations. Despite the attention to the problems of a small number of central cities and interdependencies among units within SMSAs, the modal local government is not large. As of 1980, 65.9 percent of the nation lived in places with 50,000 or fewer residents. In such places, governmental resources that can be allocated to worrying about the future are in short supply and will have to be skillfully marshalled.

Constraints of city size and resources acknowledged, strategic planning and management will undoubtedly continue to be promoted through the 1990s and into the early 2000s as means of improving the governance of cities. Strategic approaches advance the level of rationality brought to bear on issues. Equally salient, the approaches will prove politically appealing to middle-class constituencies susceptible to the imagery of "running city government like a business." As experience with the approaches broadens, academic researchers have a responsibility to inform their colleagues and fellow citizens as to what specific management/planning techniques are most effective in different contexts and, over time, whose and which political and community interests are advanced by strategic management.

References

Abney, G., and T. P. Lauth. 1986. *The politics of state and city administration.* Albany: State University of New York Press.

Ansoff, H. I., R. P. Declerck, and R. L. Hayes. 1976. From strategic planning to strategic management. *From strategic planning to strategic management* (H. I. Ansoff, R. P. Declerck, and R. L. Hayes, eds.). Wiley, New York, pp. 39–78.

Bahl, R., and L. Schroeder. 1984. The role of multi-year forecasting in the annual budgeting process for local governments. *Public Budgeting and Finance* 4: 3–13.

Banfield, E. C. 1974. *The unheavenly city revisited.* Boston: Little, Brown.

Bingham, R. D., and J. P. Blair, eds. 1984. *Urban economic development.* Beverly Hills, Calif.: Sage.

Bish, R. L., and V. Ostrom. 1973. *Understanding urban government: metropolitan reform reconsidered.* Washington, D.C.: American Enterprise Institute.

Blossom, T. 1988. Bancorp chief executive casts a line for Detroit Renaissance. *Detroit Free Press.* Feb. 1: 1C.

Brecher, C., and J. M. Hartman. 1984. Financial planning. *Setting Municipal Priorities: American Cities and the New York Experience* (C. Brecher and R. D. Horton, eds.). New York: New York University Press, pp. 198–240.

Brown, R. E., and J. B. Pyers. 1988. Putting teeth into the efficiency and effectiveness of public services. *Public Administration Review* 48: 735–42.

Bryson, J. M. 1988. *Strategic planning for public and nonprofit organizations.* Jossey Bass, San Francisco.

————, and R. C. Einsweiler. 1987. Introduction. *Journal of the American Planning Association* 53: 6–8.

————, and W. D. Roering. 1987. Applying private-sector strategic planning in the public sector. *Journal of the American Planning Association* 53: 9–22.

Burchell, R. W., and D. Listokin, eds. 1978. *Planning theory in the 1980s: A search for future directions.* New Brunswick, N.J.: The Center for Urban Policy Research, Rutgers University.

Burgess, P. M. 1975. Capacity building and the elements of public management. *Public Administration Review* 35: 705–16.

Clark, T. N., and L. C. Ferguson. 1983. *City money.* New York: Columbia University Press.

Commission on the Year 2000. 1987. *New York ascendant.* New York: Commission on the Year 2000.

Detroit Strategic Planning Project. 1987. *The report of the Detroit strategic planning project.* Detroit: The Publications Company.

Doss, C. B., Jr. 1987. The use of capital budgeting procedures in U.S. cities. *Public Budgeting and Finance* 7: 57–69.

Downs, G. W., and P. D. Larkey. 1986. *The search for government efficiency: From hubris to helplessness.* Philadelphia: Temple University Press.

Drucker, P. 1964. *Managing for results.* New York: Harper & Row.

Eadie, D. C., and R. Steinbacher. 1985. Strategic agenda management: A marriage of organizational development and strategic planning. *Public Administration Review* 45: 424–30.

Elkin, S. L. 1987. *City and regime in the American republic.* Chicago: The University of Chicago Press.

Fainstein, S., et al. 1986. *Restructuring the city: The political economy of urban redevelopment.* New York: Longman.

Findler, A. 1987. Guide to New York City's future recommends sweeping changes. *New York Times.* July 1, B4: 1.

Freeman, R. E. 1984. *Strategic management.* Boston: Pitman.

Gargan, J. J., and C. M. Moore. 1984. Enhancing local government capacity in budget decision making: The use of group process techniques. *Public Administration Review* 44: 504–11.

Godet, M. 1987. *Scenarios and strategic management.* London: Butterworths.

Gulick, L. 1937. Notes on the theory of organization. *Papers on the Science of Administration* (L. Gulick and L. Urwick, eds.), New York: Institute of Public Administration, pp. 1–45.

Gurr, T. R., and D. S. King. 1987. *The state and the city.* Chicago: The University of Chicago Press.

Hanson, R., ed. 1983. *Rethinking urban policy: Urban development in an advanced economy.* Washington, D.C.: National Academy Press.

Hartman, C. 1984. *The transformation of San Francisco.* Totowa, N.J.: Rowman and Allanheld.

Honadle, B. W. 1981. A capacity-building framework: A search for concept and purpose. *Public Administration Review* 41: 575–80.

Jackson, K. T. 1985. *Crabgrass frontier: The suburbanization of the United States.* New York: Oxford University Press.

Jacob, H. 1985. Policy responses to crime. *The New Urban Reality* (P. E. Peterson, ed.). Washington, D.C.: The Brookings Institution.

Jacobs, J. H. 1983. City: Sustaining greatness, San Francisco's strategic plan in action. *San Francisco Business*, February: 3.

Karl, B. D. 1963. *Executive reorganization and reform in the new deal.* Cambridge, Mass.: Harvard University Press.

Kasarda, J. D. 1988. Economic restructuring and America's urban dilemma. *The Metropolis Era.* Vol. 1 (M. Dogan and J. D. Kasarda, eds.). Newbury Park, Calif.: Sage.

Kaufman, J. L., and H. M. Jacobs. 1987. A public planning perspective on strategic planning. *Journal of the American Planning Association* 53: 23–33.

Kennedy, W. 1983. *O Albany!* New York: Penguin Books.

LeMoyne, J. 1984. Panel formed to study goals for city's growth. *New York Times*, Feb. 18: 27.

Levine, C. H. 1985. Police management in the 1980s: From decrementalism to strategic thinking. *Public Administration Review* 45: 691–700.

Levine, C. H., I. S. Rubin, and G. G. Wolohojian. 1981. *The politics of retrenchment.* Beverly Hills, Calif.: Sage.

Lineberry, R. L., and L. H. Masotti. 1976. The new urban politics. *The New Urban Politics* (L. H. Masotti and R. L. Lineberry, eds.). Cambridge, Mass.: Ballinger, pp. 1–15.

Lipsky, M. 1976. Toward a theory of street-level bureaucracy. *Theoretical Perspectives on Urban Politics* (W. D. Hawley, et al., eds.). Englewood Cliffs, N.J.: Prentice-Hall, pp. 196–213.

Lynn, L. E., Jr. 1987. Public management: What do we know? What should we know? And how will we know it? *Journal of Policy Analysis and Management* 7: 178–87.

Mohr, L. B. 1969. Determinants of innovation in organizations. *American Political Science Review* 63: 111–26.

Morten, R. 1983. Making a great city greater: The unveiling of the strategic plan's 19 key strategies for 1983. *San Francisco Business*, February: 16–21.

Mosher, F. C. 1975. Introduction: The American setting. *American Public Administration: Past, Present, Future* (F. C. Mosher, ed.). University, Ala.: The University of Alabama Press, pp. 1–10.

Nelson, D. 1980. *Frederick W. Taylor and the rise of scientific management.* Madison: The University of Wisconsin Press.

Nutt, P. C., and R. W. Backoff. 1987. A strategic management process for public and third-sector organizations. *Journal of the American Planning Association* 53: 44–57.

O'Leary, E. A. 1984. "Strategic planning in Albany: A study of political values and participation in decision-making," unpublished thesis for the Master of Regional Planning, Graduate School of Cornell University, New York, August.

Peterson, P. E. 1981. *City limits.* Chicago: University of Chicago Press.

Poister, T. H., and R. P. McGowan. 1984. The use of management tools in municipal government: A national survey. *Public Administration Review* 44: 215–23.

Ring, P. S., and J. I. Perry. 1985. Strategic management in public and private organizations: Implications of distinctive contexts and constraints. *Academy of Management Review* 10: 276–86.

Roberts, S. 1987. A Koch agenda may be born from study of ills. *New York Times*, June 29: B1.

Robinson, F. S. 1973. *Albany's O'Connell machine.* Albany, N.Y.: Washington Park Spirit.

Saaty, T. L. 1982. *Decision making for leaders: The analytical hierarchy process for decisions in a complex world.* Belmont, Calif.: Wadsworth.

———, and K. P. Kearns. 1985. *Analytical planning: The organization of systems.* Oxford: Pergamon.

Savas, E. S. 1987. *Privatization: The key to better government.* Chatham, N.J.: Chatham House.

Shefter, M. 1984. Images of the city in political science. *Cities of the Mind: Images and Themes of the City in the Social Sciences* (L. Rodwin and R. M. Hollister, eds.). New York: Plenum Press, pp. 55–82.

———. 1987. *Political crisis/fiscal crisis: The collapse and revival of New York City.* New York: Basic Books.

Simon, H. A. 1985. Human nature in politics: The dialogue of psychology with political science. *American Political Science Review* 79: 293–304.

Smith, M. P. 1979. *The city and social theory.* New York: St. Martin's Press.

So, F. S. 1984. Strategic planning: Reinventing the wheel? *Planning* 50: 16–21.

Sorkin, D. L., N. B. Ferris, and K. Hudak. 1984. *Strategies for cities and counties: A strategic planning guide and workbook.* Washington, D.C.: Public Technology, Inc.

Steiss, A. W. 1985. *Strategic management and organizational decision making.* Lexington, Mass.: Lexington Books.

Stone, A. B., and D. Stone. 1975. Early developments of education in public administration. *American Public Administration: Past, Present, Future* (F. C. Mosher, ed.). University, Ala.: University of Alabama Press, pp. 11–48.

Swanstrom, T. 1986. Strategic planning in a white collar city: The case of Albany. *Reindustrializing New York State: Strategies, Implications, Challenges* (M. Schoolman and A. Magid, eds.). Albany: State University of New York Press, pp. 117–29.

Usher, C. L., and G. C. Cornia. 1981. Goal setting and performance assessment in municipal budgeting. *Public Administration Review* 41: 229–35.

Warfield, J. N. 1976. *Societal systems.* New York: Wiley.

Wechsler, B., and R. W. Backoff. 1986. Policy making and administration in state agencies: Strategic management approaches. *Public Administration Review* 46: 321–27.

———, and ———. 1987. The dynamics of strategy in public organizations. *Journal of the American Planning Association* 53: 34–43.

Wildavsky, A. 1986. *Budgeting: A comparative theory of budgetary process,* 2nd ed. New Brunswick: Transaction Books.

Yates, D. 1977. *The ungovernable city.* Cambridge, Mass.: MIT Press.

Zimmerman, J. F. 1983. *State-local relations: A partnership approach.* New York: Praeger.

Strategic Management by Design

Douglas C. Eadie

Why do organizations so often encounter disappointment in their strategic management efforts? The reasons are many. The "quick fix" mentality is a common culprit, ensuring that insufficient resources are invested in strategic management efforts. Staff may not have the requisite time or skills to carry out a strategic management process. The political environment may militate against making strategic decisions. And in the realm of interinstitutional problem solving, it is difficult to build an organizational entity with the influence and resources necessary to implement an effective strategic management process that crosscuts political subdivisions.

The Design Answer

None of the familiar obstacles to effective strategic management need be insurmountable, and the key to overcoming them is *design*, the process by which generic strategic management techniques are tailored to a particular situation—to particular needs, particular capabilities, and particular circumstances. After a general description of strategic techniques, this article considers the design process in detail, drawing upon the recent experiences of some public organizations.

The Evolving Field of Strategic Management

While strategy is not a new idea, the systematic use of strategic techniques in business and government and the study of strategy in graduate

Reprinted with permission from National Civic Review, *Vol. 78, No. 1, January/ February 1989. Published by the National Civic League Press, Denver, Colorado.*

schools of management have appeared only in the past quarter century. Moreover, the field is evolving rapidly in the following broad directions:

- We now recognize that traditional long-range planning of the five and ten-year ilk, with its assumption of a predictable future and its generation of multi-point plans, is an unwieldy tool in this time of rapid environmental change. Indeed, the time spent writing, editing, and printing traditional long-range plans can actually make an organization strategically less capable by diverting attention from the changing environment and creating the illusion of control over events.
- We now understand that in the context of complex, changing environments and limited organizational time and resources, public organizations are well advised to take a more selective and action-oriented approach to strategic planning (i.e., identify and select a small number of strategic issues calling for immediate attention and formulate action plans to address them).
- We recognize that as much attention must be given to the implementation of strategy as to its formulation, and that if action is the objective, strategies must be practical and achievable rather than shopping lists of aspirations.
- Finally, we know that people are the critical factor in the formulation and implementation of strategies, making human resource development and team building matters of vital concern in strategic management-process design.

Strategic Management Techniques

The broad strategic planning logic involves the following major elements: 1) confirming the planning organization's mission and long-range goals; 2) scanning environmental trends and conditions that are pertinent to the mission; 3) identifying the strategic issues facing the organization—both the opportunities and the threats; 4) formulating strategies to address the issues; and 5) executing these strategies.

Before examining each of these elements, it is important to keep in mind that while the strategic management process described below is distinct from a public organization's annual operational planning and budget process, there are important linkages between the two. Also, the strategic management process is uniquely focused on the identification and management of organization-wide issues that transcend departments and their operational planning. However, departments themselves can utilize issue management throughout the budget process (for example), thereby making their own management more strategic. This will be discussed in greater detail after the following discussion of the elements of strategic management.

Mission/Goals

The mission of an organization is a statement of its basic purposes, often in terms of the broad outcomes that it is committed to achieving or the major functions it carries out. Mission statements come in all shapes and sizes — from pithy paragraphs to a page of prose — and occur at all organizational levels (bureaus, divisions, and departments have their own missions). An organization's long-range goals statement naturally follows from its mission statement, which might best be thought of as a summary of the long-range goals of the organization.

The mission/goals statement of an organization serves a number of important purposes. It inspires internal organizational commitment and is, therefore, an important organizational development tool. It communicates to the wider public and thus serves as a public information tool. The mission/goals statement also serves as a kind of "natural law" for an organization, setting boundaries for its activities and providing the "constitutional rules" for evaluating proposed new organizational functions and programs.

Because they should be enduring, mission statements are not normally revised annually. There are, however, certain times in an organization's history when detailed consideration of its mission/goals statement(s) makes good sense. For example, a rapidly growing suburban city recently had to focus on its mission when development proposals began to bog down in city council because consensus on the ends of development had eroded due to a "young turk-old guard" split. The solution was for the council and city manager to spend a day in a retreat hammering out a mission/goals statement in the area of development, against which development proposals could be measured.

With regard to the process of mission/goal development, two elements are critical: 1) the involvement of the policy body (board of directors, city council, county commission or legislature) and executive staff; and 2) the allocation of adequate time to the task.

Environmental Scan

The purpose of the "environmental" scan is to understand the external environment of an organization in terms that are relevant to its mission and goals. A local government, for example, will be interested in national and state legislative, programmatic, and funding trends, as well as local demographic, economic, and social trends and conditions. How has the population changed over the past ten years in terms of sex, age, race, and income? What kinds of businesses have moved in and out over the past decade, and why? What kinds of jobs do our residents have and where do they work?

The depth and breadth of an organization's environmental scan will depend on the staff and/or consultant time allocated to its production and other resources, such as financing for a citizen survey. However it is developed, the point of environmental scanning is not academic research. Rather, it is to raise questions about the organization's current strategies in light of its changing environment.

Strategic Issue Identification

Strategic issues are "change challenges" in the form of major opportunities and problems or threats. For example, the scan of a county's changing economy may indicate a slow but steady loss of jobs in a particular industrial sector (a possible threat) but at the same time significant growth in a particular kind of small business (a possible opportunity). Strong growth in the over-65 population of a county may represent a "change challenge" in a number of county government areas, including recreation and parks and public safety. In a strategic management process, the task of the policy body and executive staff is to select those issues which will receive intensive attention in the coming months through strategy formulation and implementation.

Consequences or *"costs"* are probably the most practical guide to the selection of strategic issues. For each possible change challenge, what will be the likely future cost to the organization (and those it serves) if it is not addressed now? Cost can be measured in direct and indirect ways: out-of-pocket payments (e.g., the cost of repairing neglected infrastructure), human pain and suffering (e.g., driving off a collapsed bridge), political capital (election defeat), and lost benefit (failure to capture a federal grant or promote growth in a promising entrepreneurial venture resulting in lost tax revenue).

Selection is critical because time and other organizational resources are both precious and finite. Only so many issues can be seriously addressed while also carrying out the day-to-day work of an organization. An overly inclusive shopping-list approach — so common in traditional long-range planning — will guarantee inaction.

Strategy Formulation

Strategies are action plans to achieve targets or objectives associated with major shared issues. These action plans are often formulated by interdepartmental staff task forces that go through the following process:

- Detailed analysis of the issue, breaking it down into the various sub-issues.
- Consideration of a number of change targets that might be chosen to address the various sub-issues.
- Evaluation of the change targets in terms of the benefits and costs to the organization.
- Formulation of action plans to achieve the targets that have been selected.

Implementation

Two factors are critical to the successful implementation of strategies. First, the policy body, chief executive officer, and executive staff of the organization must be firmly committed to implementation of the strategies. Most importantly, such commitment means the resources required to implement the strategies are actually allocated. Second, there must be a formal structure to manage implementation. This may involve establishment of a steering committee of senior managers and the appointment of a coordinator to manage the process day-to-day. The task forces that formulated the strategies may be kept in existence to manage implementation.

Strategic and Operational Management Agenda

As discussed earlier, the strategic management process described above may be thought of as a very special organizational management agenda distinct from other agenda (e.g., the management of day-to-day operations). The operational management agenda is developed and promoted through an organization's annual budget process, the preeminent comprehensive planning process of all public organizations. While obviously related, the strategic and operational agenda are distinct and must be managed separately. The strategic management process enables organizations to identify issues that cut across departments and functions, but cannot be left to departmental management.

Public organizations increasingly manage these two agenda in a sequential fashion, using organization-wide strategic management as a preface to the annual operational planning process, in which day-to-day issues are also identified and managed:

- Prior to the commencement of the annual operational planning/budget process, the organization conducts a comprehensive environmental scan, and identifies organization-wide, usually interdepartmental, strategic issues to be addressed through strategy formulation.
- Subsequently, the operational planning process commences with departmental scans and agreement at the executive level on the strategic issues that will receive special attention during budget preparation.
- Strategies to address both the organization-wide and the departmental issues are formulated concurrently during the budget preparation process — on the one hand through ad hoc interdepartmental task forces, and on the other hand through the normal departmental planning process.

Designing Specific Applications

The basic purpose of the design process is to ensure that an organization considering the application of strategic management techniques adopts an approach that it can implement and will achieve the results it wants. Design is a survival technique in light of the fact that there is no such thing as *the* strategic management process. Instead, there is a generic logic that can be applied in any number of ways, each involving different products, processes, and costs. Without design, there is a clear and present danger of buying one of the many vendors' preconceived notions of the "right" planning approach and having it break down mid-stream.

Through design, an organization deals with the three essential points of the strategic triangle: planning outcomes, planning structure and process, and organizational capability. The point is to ensure that 1) the structure and process will deliver the desired products, and 2) the organization is capable of implementing the process.

It is complex enough to deal effectively with strategic issues involving only one organization. When dealing with regional issues requiring interinstitutional cooperation, so much more complex the process and so much more important the design. A major cause of strategic process failure is the absence of a detailed design that takes into account outcomes, structure/process, and capability.

Outcomes

The first question with regard to the outcomes of a strategic management process is *who* should define them. The answer is those stakeholders whose support and/or participation in the strategic management process is deemed critical to its successful implementation. Typically, these will include an organization's governance or policy body—board, council, commission—and its senior managers (e.g., chief administrative officer and department heads). Depending on the scope of the anticipated strategic management effort, participation in identifying outcomes might be extended more widely—for example, to the directors of other organizations with a stake in the issues to be addressed or to prominent representatives of the business community.

When Bexar County (Texas) designed its approach to strategic management, the stakeholders involved were the Commissioners Court (the chief elected officials), the County Auditor (in charge of operational planning/budget preparation), and the Court administrative staff. The Executive Committee of the Board of the West Michigan Regional Planning Commission in Grand Rapids, Michigan—along with the Executive Director—identified the outcomes of its strategic management process. When the County Commissioners of Montcalm County, Michigan, received a substantial grant to engage in community-wide strategic management, they established an interinstitutional steering committee to identify outcomes. The Ohio Job Training Coordinating Council delegated the design task to its Planning Committee and the Committee staff.

Primary Outcomes

The term "primary" refers to outcomes that relate directly to the content of the strategy to be designed. In the recent past, several cities, such as San Francisco, have engaged in community-wide strategic management processes intended to set broad directions on issues such as housing, education, and economic development. These strategic directions *by design* require interorganizational cooperation and action to implement.

Montcalm County, *by design*, adopted as the primary outcome of its strategic management effort the generation of strategies to deal with community-wide, interorganizational issues. By contrast, the West Michigan Regional Planning Commission chose to focus on generating organizational growth strategies that could be implemented by the organization itself, without engaging in large-scale interinstitutional planning and implementation activities. The Bexar County Commissioners Court decided to focus strategic management on the annual budget process during its first cycle, which was designed to identify operational strategic issues in two test departments — Information Systems and Public Works. The Ohio Job Training Coordinating Council, responding to a gubernatorial charge to recommend ways to improve state job training programs, decided its first cycle of strategic management should be limited to the production of strategies to improve management coordination among job training departments, rather than tackle the content of training programs.

Indirect or Secondary Outcomes

A strategic management process can result in important outcomes that do not relate to the scope and content of strategy. In some cases, these indirect outcomes ultimately benefit the organizations more than the strategies themselves. Examples of indirect outcomes include the following:

- Strengthening the role of the policy body and the working relationship between the policy body and the CEO and top administrative team.
- Building community understanding and support.
- Upgrading the capability of executive and management staff.
- Building a more cohesive senior management team.
- Improving internal climate and staff morale.

Structure/Process

Both direct and indirect strategic management outcomes have structural and procedural implications. The following examples illustrate that the outcomes-structure/process linkage must be explicit and detailed if the strategic management process is to succeed.

West Michigan Process

The West Michigan Regional Planning Commission selected as the primary outcome of its first strategic management cycle the generation of growth strategies aimed at bolstering its tarnished reputation. The Commission's board had become frustrated at its passive leadership role, the board-staff working relationship, and the need to upgrade staff capacity. Accordingly, the Commission's design included the following major elements:

- The Commission's management staff, in preparing a comprehensive environmental trends and conditions briefing, were assisted by consultants so they would be left with the resident expertise to do scanning in the future. Different members of the management staff were involved throughout the scan-development process, strengthening team work and enhancing staff morale. The top four staff members, rather than the consultants, took the lead in presenting the scan to the board as an additional capacity-building tactic.

- The "make-or-break" factor in the West Michigan process was a two-day, professionally facilitated work session of the Commission board and its top staff members in a retreat setting. The first day was devoted to review of the environmental scan and brainstorming strategic issues in the Commission's three major functional areas (economic development, land use planning, and transportation) plus a fourth area, "emerging opportunities."

  To promote the board's active and creative involvement, board-staff working groups formulated lists of strategic issues in the four areas. The second day focused on the identification of more internal targets to upgrade board participation and the board-staff working relationship. For example, it was decided on the second day to restructure the regular business meetings of the board to make them more productive and policy oriented.

- In the months following the two-day work session, the working groups continued to refine the issues they had identified and formulate action strategies to address them. This approach assured follow-up to the session and continued active board involvement in the board-staff partnership.

Bexar County Process

The Bexar County Texas, design focused on one preeminent objective: to upgrade the strategic leadership role of the County's policy body, the Commissioners Court. The vehicle selected was the annual budget-preparation process, primarily because this critical leadership tool had been so obviously underutilized by the Court. The design provided for senior management teams from the two test departments to prepare, in addition to their normal financial budget requests, special first-time briefings for the Commissioners Court consisting of 1) a mission/goals statement, 2) a description of past accomplishments, 3) a scan of the department's environment, and 4) a description of the major issues likely to face the Court in the coming year.

The Court set aside a half day for each test department – in addition to the regular financial budget hearing – to review the foregoing briefing. Since staff capability building was a secondary outcome of the process, the senior managers of the two departments were actively involved in presentation and discussion; senior staff reviewed and critiqued presentation content and style.

Montcalm County Process

Since the primary outcome of the Montcalm County design was to deal with community-wide, interinstitutional strategic issues, the Montcalm structure and process were interinstitutional. The Steering Committee consisted of representatives of major local institutions such as the community college and regional health district. The environmental scan was developed by an interinstitutional task force, and strategic issues were identified in a "Community Forum" widely representative of the County's public and private sectors.

The Capability Question

Before committing to an outcomes-process combination, an organization must consider the capability factor in order to ensure the workability of its strategic management design. Although capability is hardly a precise concept, certain facets stand out as critical to strategic management applications.

First and foremost, the understanding and commitment of the principal stakeholders are essential to carrying out a strategic management design. Of course, stakeholder participation in developing the design is an obvious means of securing commitment. Most important in this regard is a detailed understanding of all costs associated with implementing the design — not just out-of-pocket costs for, say, consulting assistance, but also the required time contribution of the stakeholders. It is also important to understand the risks that might be incurred, such as public criticism of the cost of holding work sessions, etc.

Capability is also constrained by the political realities at work in the organization contemplating a strategic management application. The Bexar County Commissioners Court explicitly factored this into its design in choosing to deal during the first cycle with only two directly administered departments, rather than tackle one or more of the offices headed by semi-autonomous elected officials. The Court intended to incorporate these semi-independent offices into the process gradually.

Financial resources are another important factor. The dollars available for consultant and facilitation assistance, collection of trends/conditions information, display equipment, and meeting space will significantly impact the strategic management design.

Organizational capability can also be measured in terms of 1) skills and planning experience of the participants in the strategic management effort, 2) the internal climate of the organization, and 3) external demands upon the organization. An organization with little long-range planning experience, a recent history of failed strategic management efforts, poor morale, bad press, or weak financial management must move forward with strategic management more slowly than a healthy organization with substantial and successful planning experience. The outcomes-capability road runs in both directions: desired outcomes may be adjusted to existing capability and capability may be enhanced to achieve outcomes. An organization with little long-range planning experience can increase its capability with a training program in planning techniques prior to the strategic management process. The understanding and commitment of the key stakeholders can be enhanced through carefully structured participation in the design process. Morale problems can be addressed through team-building exercises, and inadequate financial resources can be supplemented by obtaining a third-party grant to support the strategic management effort.

Conclusion

Strategic management techniques have demonstrated their usefulness as a management tool in the business sector, and there is growing evidence of their successful application in the public and nonprofit sectors. But it is no easy matter to apply these complex, rapidly evolving techniques in the public sector, and for every success story told there is a sad tale of failed expectations. As policy boards and managers become more aware of the important design requisites of these processes, we may be encouraged that strategic management will be viewed increasingly as a powerful tool for addressing regional, interinstitutional issues.

Initiation of Strategic Planning by Local Governments

John M. Bryson and William D. Roering

Government leaders have become increasingly interested in strategic planning since the early 1970s as a result of the wrenching changes that have beset the public sector (Eadie 1983). The changes have stemmed from oil crises, demographic shifts, changing values, tax levy limits, tax indexing, tax cuts, reductions in federal grants and mandates, the devolution of responsibilities, and a volatile economy. The changes have brought into sharp relief the need for important policy choices and thus have highlighted the potential usefulness of strategic planning. Indeed, strategic planning may be defined as a disciplined effort to produce fundamental decisions and actions that define what an organization (or other entity) is, what it does, and why it does it (Bryson 1988; cf. Olsen and Eadie 1982, p. 4).

The deliberate attempt to produce change is probably the greatest strength and weakness of strategic planning as a process. Changes in organizations normally occur through disjointed incrementalism or "muddling through" (Lindblom 1959; Quinn 1980). Any process designed to force important changes, therefore, can be seen either as a highly desirable improvement on ordinary decision making or as action doomed to failure. Indeed, whatever the merits of strategic planning in the abstract, *normal expectations have to be that most efforts to produce fundamental decisions and actions in government through strategic planning will not succeed.* At the very least, strategic decision making in public organizations should be prone to involvements by numerous actors (especially through boards, committees, task forces, and teams), variability in information, extensive negotiations, and frequent delays. Further, because of pressures for public accountability, decisions ultimately are likely to be made at the highest

Reprinted with permission from Public Administration Review, *Vol. 48, No. 6, November/December 1988. Published by the American Society for Public Administration, Washington, D.C.*

levels (Hickson et al., 1986, pp. 117, 203), while political rationality dictates that top decision makers not make important decisions until forced to do so (Benveniste 1972, 1977; Quinn 1980).

The study reported here tracked the initiation of strategic planning by eight governmental units. All are located in the Twin Cities metropolitan area of Minnesota. Each used the same basic strategic planning process (Bryson, Freeman, and Roering 1986; Bryson and Roering 1987; Bryson, Van de Ven, and Roering 1987; Bryson 1988). The process consists of eight steps: an initial agreement or "plan for planning"; identification and clarification of mandates; mission formulation; external environmental assessment; internal environmental assessment; strategic issue identification; strategy development; and development of a description of the organization in the future—its "vision of success."

The study followed the units until they either discontinued their strategic planning efforts or completed a strategic plan. While at least some plan implementation efforts were underway during the study period, plan implementation was not the primary focus of this study. The overall effectiveness of the strategic planning process model, therefore, was not assessed. Instead the study tried: 1) to document what happens when units of government work through a strategic planning process (when that process represents an innovation for the units) and 2) to uncover the conditions necessary for successful initiation of a strategic planning process by governmental units.

The rest of this article is organized into three major sections. First, the sample and research methods are described. Second, the efforts of the eight units are reviewed and analyzed. Finally, conclusions are presented about the initiation of strategic planning by governments.

Study Sample and Research Methods

Eight governmental units participated in this study. Five were suburban city governments, one was a county government, and two were units of the same county government—the county executive director's office and the county's public health nursing service (Nursing Service). All units were located in the Twin Cities metropolitan area of Minnesota (see Table 1). The study spanned a two and one-half year period between August 1984 and February 1987, with a follow-up questionnaire administered in November 1987. One of the units, Nursing Service, participated the whole time, while the other units were involved for less time.

The authors served as consultants to the eight units as they worked through the process. Nursing Service went through the process independently from the other units. The other seven units were participants in a

Table 1. Characteristics of Governmental Units and Strategic Planning Process—1986

Government Unit	Population	Number of Full-Time Equivalent Employees	Annual Budget	Size of Team	Sponsor Present	Champion Present	Policy Board Support
City A	42,583	168	$8,977,013[a]	4	Y	Y	?
City B	9,842	35	$2,070,000[a]	10	Y	Y	?
City C	22,100	103	$7,302,926[a]	5	Y	Y	Some
City D	41,207	130	$7,212,612[a]	7	Y	Y	Some
City E	42,600	228	$12,201,433[a]	9	Y	Y	Some
County A	127,000	550	$66,783,000[b]	19	Y	Y	Y
County B Executive Director's Office	471,369	2,847[c]	$275,421,249[b]	5	Y	Y	Some
County B Nursing Service	471,369	104	$4,507,102[d]	22	Y	Y	Some

Key: Y=Yes
a=General Fund
b=Total Budget
c=Entire County Government Employment
d=½ from General Fund
?=not clear

series of strategic planning workshops sponsored by the government train-ing service that serves the metropolitan area.[1] These workshops introduced the units' strategic planning teams to the strategic planning process and helped them to work through the steps in the process.[2]

Several kinds of data were collected.[3] Of particular importance for purposes of this article were narratives that we prepared for accuracy with team leaders, and they are available from the authors. Because of the relative absence of quantifiable data, most of the description and analysis of what happened relies on the case narratives, the authors' observa-tions, and interviews with strategic planning team members. The authors met frequently over the course of the study to discuss what was happening in the units. We searched our memories and data files for patterns and themes across units. We self-consciously tried to engage in the kind of mental activity that experts usually pursue unconsciously — namely, the development and application of tentative diagnoses to individual cases and sets of cases (Johnson 1984). We were the "experts" on strategic plan-ning, but we had to be much more self-conscious about our expertise than we would have been had we not acted as researchers as well as consul-tants.[4]

Despite our efforts, however, we must emphasize the speculative nature of these analyses and the conclusions. We obviously were not totally detached observers. Quite the contrary, we were active participant observers who wanted the eight units to succeed with their strategic plan-ning efforts. We were active teachers, consultants, and advisors at various points throughout the units' efforts. Our role therefore gave us privileged access to the phenomena we were trying to study, on the one hand; but it makes our analyses and conclusions somewhat suspect, on the other hand (Sussman and Evered 1978).

A final serious limitation of the study is that the criteria used to measure success (embodied in the follow-up questionnaire to process champions) are the authors' criteria, not necessarily the units' criteria. At the beginning of the study we did not really know how success should be measured, other than to note whether or not units completed the strategic planning process. Toward the end of the study, we concluded that suc-cessful initiation of strategic planning ought to be assessed according to the extent that the process: 1) helped focus the attention of the strategic plan-ning team on what was important, 2) helped the team set priorities for ac-tion, 3) helped generate those actions, and 4) helped focus the attention of the organization's key decision makers (whose number might include peo-ple not on the strategic planning team) on what was important. The follow-up questionnaire solicited the team leaders' assessments of success according to these criteria.

Review and Analysis of the Eight Units' Strategic Planning Efforts

Results of the strategic planning efforts of the eight units are summarized in Tables 2 and 3. Table 2 shows that two units discontinued the process before they identified strategic issues. The other six units completed the formulation of strategies to deal with at least some of their strategic issues. For purposes of this research, a strategic plan consists of one or more recommended strategies to deal with one or more strategic issues. These six units, therefore, completed preparation of strategic plans, at least according to our minimalist criterion. In addition, three units developed descriptions of their organizations in the future, or their "visions of success."

The relevant decision bodies in all six units have adopted at least parts of the proposed strategic plans. Different parts of different strategies, of course, came within the purview of different decision-making bodies. Depending on the circumstances, one or more of the following individuals or groups was the relevant decision-making body: the strategic planning team, a single top administrator, a "cabinet" of top administrators, or an elected policy-making body (i.e., a city council or county board of commissioners).

Table 3 summarizes additional perceptions of team leaders of the success of the process (according to our criteria for success) for the six units that completed strategic plans. All felt that the process had helped "a good bit" or "very much so" to focus their strategic planning teams on what was important. There was more variability in the extent to which the champions felt that the process helped teams set priorities for action. One-third felt that the process helped do so "a moderate amount," "a good bit," and "very much so." The process was marginally less successful in generating priority actions. Half the units thought the process helped to generate those actions "a moderate amount," one unit felt it did so "a good bit," and two felt it helped greatly. Finally, the process was marginally even less successful in focusing the attention of key decision makers (who may not have been on the strategic planning team) on what was important. One unit felt it did so only "some," three units felt it did so "a moderate amount," one felt it helped "a good bit," and one felt it helped greatly.

The process was a clear success in only two of the six cases: County A and County B—Nursing Service. In the other cases success was much more mixed. The process obviously helped strategic planning teams focus on what was important, but in several cases it was less successful in setting priorities for team action and generating those actions. The process also was less helpful in focusing the attention of key decision makers on what

Table 2. Strategic Planning Process Steps Completed and Time Devoted to Process

Government Unit	Strategic Planning Process Steps*								Adoption	Months Devoted to Process
	1	2	3	4	5	6	7	8		
City A	Y	Y	Y	Y	Y	N	N	N	N	2
City B	Y	Y	Y	Y	Y	N	N	N	N	2
City C	Y	Y	Y	Y	Y	Y	Y	N	Partial	5
City D	Y	Y	Y	Y	Y	Y	Y	Y	Partial	5
City E	Y	Y	Y	Y	Y	Y	Y	N	Partial	24
County A	Y	Y	Y	Y	Y	Y	Y	Y	Y	12
County B Executive Director's Office	Y	Y	Y	Y	Y	Y	Y	N	Partial	7
County B Nursing Service	Y	Y	Y	Y	Y	Y	Y	Y	Y	30

*1 = Initial Agreement   5 = Internal Assessment
2 = Mandate Clarification   6 = Strategic Issue Identification
3 = Mission Development   7 = Strategy
4 = External Assessment   8 = Vision of Success

Y = Step Completed
N = Step Not Completed
Source: Follow-up Questionnaire

was important. The process did help, but not as much as we had hoped. Varied patterns occurred, as follows.

The Process Clearly Was Prone to Stoppage or Delay. In City A and City B the process stopped completely when their city managers (who were both sponsors and champions) left for other jobs. In County B's Executive Director's Office, the process terminated when the executive director was forced to resign and other key staff members left. In City E and Nursing Service, frequent and lengthy delays occurred. The planning teams for the remaining units — City C, City D, and County A — all feared a crisis would terminate their processes prior to completion. Indeed, two prior attempts at countywide strategic planning in County A had aborted because of crises, although two departments had been able to complete the process.

Table 3. Responses to Follow-Up
Questionnaire to Strategic Planning Team Leaders

	City A	City B	City C	City D	City E	County A	County B Executive Director's Office	County B Nursing Service
Q1	*	*	4	4	4	5	5	5
Q2	*	*	4	3	3	5	4	5
Q3	*	*	3	3	3	5	4	5
Q4	*	*	3	3	2	5	3	4

Key:
Q1 = Did the strategic planning process help focus the attention of the *strategic planning team* on what was important?
Q2 = Did the strategic planning process help set priorities for action by the *strategic planning team*?
Q3 = Did the strategic planning process help generate those actions?
Q4 = Did the strategic planning process help focus the attention of the organization's *key decision makers* on what was important? (Note: the organization's key decision makers may include a number of people not on the strategic planning team.)
* = No questionnaire sent because city dropped out early in the process.

5 = Very much so
4 = A good bit
3 = A moderate amount
2 = Some
1 = Not at all

In Each Case the Attempt to Initiate Strategic Planning Was Prone to Disintegration. In City A and City B the process disintegrated completely when a key actor departed. In each of the others the process often appeared to be on the verge of disintegration, but not because of the permanent departure of key actors (although such occurrences did threaten the continuity of the process). There was always the possibility that a crisis of some sort would destroy the process, since the units would not have enough slack, particularly staff attention, to deal with the crisis and plan strategically. The processes therefore were always prone to the temporary loss of key actors. Indeed, even without major crises, planning teams rarely operated with their full complement of members, and when two process champions left for maternity leaves, their units' processes came to temporary halts.

Beyond the loss of key staff, the process itself appears particularly susceptible to collapse during the strategic issue identification and strategy development steps. These two steps appear to have been difficult for three reasons.

First, as the number of potential strategic issues and strategies to deal with each issue multiplied, the teams had difficulty comprehending the volume of information and its implications, and they had difficulty deciding what their priorities ought to be and how to set them. During these steps, the process was divergent, and the teams had difficulty figuring out how to make it convergent (Van den Daele 1969).

Second, the problem of divergence was not just conceptual, but also political. Each issue and the associated strategies to deal with it often implied that a different decision set (Hickson et al. 1986) was needed to deal with the issue. The teams never incorporated the full range of possible decisions sets to deal with all the issues identified. The processes were only able to converge, therefore, on those issues and strategies (or parts of issues and strategies) that the team was able to do something about, or else the process itself expanded out laterally or shifted to a higher hierarchical level where more of the members of the necessary decision sets were represented. In City D, for example, the team was able to convince the city manager to form a "cabinet" in which more key decision makers would be represented, and in County B the county board undertook a strategic planning process that preempted the efforts of the Executive Director's Office and set the stage for dealing with some of the key issues identified by Nursing Service. It is possible, therefore, that strategic planning at lower levels can force strategic planning horizontally and at higher levels in addition to the more expected top-down progression. But when different units in the same system engage in strategic planning, each is likely to have to recycle through various parts of the process to take account of the strategic planning activities of other units. The fact that the strategic planning teams did not encompass the appropriate decision sets for many issues probably accounts in part for some of the results noted in Table 3. Recall that the team leaders felt that the process was successful in focusing the teams on what was important. The process did less to set priorities for team action, to generate those actions, and to focus the attention of the organization's key decision makers on what was important.

Third, the difficulties of divergence and partial convergence were hard enough to manage, but the partially cumulative nature of the processes added yet another problem (Van den Daele 1969). The processes were partially cumulative in that what happened in prior steps had to be taken into account in subsequent steps — but, once taken into account, what happened earlier might be changed or dropped. The cumulative nature of the process was most clearly illustrated by the teams' efforts to identify strategic issues. Strategic issues emerge from the conjunction of: the initial agreement about the purpose of the strategic planning effort and mandates, mission, strengths, weaknesses, opportunities and threats. The partially cumulative nature of the process is best illustrated by Nursing Service's decision, after the participants had identified their first set of strategic issues, to change their mission statement — whereupon they dropped their first set of issues and came up with a second. Each of the other unit's processes also were partially cumulative as well. Quite simply, more ideas and information were created in each step than could possibly be carried on to the next, so that there was only a partial cumulation from step to step. Also, the teams often could do nothing about ideas and information carried on to succeeding steps, so those items, too, were dropped. Further, the teams often had difficulty deciding what to keep and what to drop as step followed step or their thinking recycled through previous steps.

The Units Varied Widely in the Amount of Calendar Time Devoted to Their First Efforts at Strategic Planning. For the units that completed plans, the calendar time devoted to the process varied from 5 to 30 months. In several units a variety of stoppages, delays, and difficulties dragged out the process. This is consistent with Hickson et al.'s (1986) finding that strategic decision making in public sector organizations has a tendency to be interrupted and lengthy.

Successful Completion of the Process Depended on the Presence of a Powerful Sponsor to Legitimize the Process, Even If That Sponsor Was Not Especially Supportive. Also, Multiple Sponsorship Was the Rule, and It Was Constructive. In addition to legitimizing the process, sponsors were also able to make important decisions concerning the process and could push the process laterally and vertically to involve more actors and to facilitate decision making. Each unit had some sort of multiple sponsorship. Such sponsorship appears to be necessary to legitimize an effort aimed at framing and informing major decisions that are cross-departmental in scope. Again, the fact that most units' processes were not fully sponsored by most of the key decision makers probably partly accounts for the results presented in Tables 2 and 3. Only County A's process appeared to enjoy relatively complete sponsorship by the unit's key decision makers. Perhaps as a result, County A's process was the most successful of all the units' efforts. Nursing Service's process also enjoyed relatively complete sponsorship, at least ultimately, and that process was the second most successful. The other units had less complete sponsorship and also were less successful.

Successful Initiation of Strategic Planning in Governments Required a Strong Process Champion. A strong process champion was present in all six units that completed the process. Process champions were always the team leader or a co-team leader. The process champions appeared to believe that the strategic planning process would produce desirable outcomes.

The champions did not push personally favored issues and solutions, although they almost always entered these into team discussions for consideration along with everyone else's ideas. It is this belief in a process that distinguishes process champions from other champions, such as the more general idea champion (Kanter 1983, p. 296), *product champion* (Kotler 1976, p. 200), or *policy entrepreneur* (Roberts and King, forthcoming; Bardach 1987). A process champion is also different from being a facilitator, although it appears to help the process if the champion is also a good facilitator. (Not all champions in our sample were able facilitators, although all possessed at least some facilitation skills.) Facilitators believe in the importance of process, too, but they usually give participants much more choice about the kind of process they will follow. The process champions in our sample held firmly to the importance of the steps, or "checkpoints," outlined in Figure 1 (on page 32).

Process Champions Were Particularly Important During the Strategic Issue Identification and Strategy Development Steps — Precisely Those Steps When the Process Appeared Most Prone to Disintegration. During these steps in the process, strategic planning teams appeared to fall into serious "gumption traps" (Pirsig 1974). As the processes diverged, the teams appeared to feel the ground on which they stood was collapsing. They fell into traps in which the team's morale, enthusiasm, and commitment waned. Only the countervailing morale, enthusiasm, and commitment of the process champions appeared able to lead the team out of the traps, toward convergence on which issues to choose, how to frame them, and what strategies to pursue in dealing with them. Even process champions, however, could fall into gumption traps. At various times over the course of the process, the consultants served as cheerleaders for the champions, helping to keep their spirits up and encouraging them to push the process along. The consultants also provided advice to all six units that completed plans on what to keep, what to drop, and how to converge on particular issues and specific strategies. Indeed, without the presence of the process champions and consultants, it is likely that the scores presented in Table 3 would have been lower.

Each Unit Relied on a Strategic Planning Team to Work Through the Process and to Prepare a Strategic Plan. This finding is not surprising, since the consultants required formation of a team by each unit. But the use of a team would be expected anyway in uncertain, complex, and political situations in which a variety of sources of information are needed and in which decisions have cross-unit implications (Galbraith 1973; Hickson et al. 1986).

What Counted As a Strategic Plan Varied Widely Across Units. City E and Nursing Service prepared formal strategic plans with mission statements, situation assessments, discussions of strategic issues, and strategies. County B—Executive Director's Office ultimately addressed three strategic issues identified by the county board and prepared fairly typical governmental "decision packages" for county board consideration. The packages consisted of a discussion of the issues, strategies to deal with them, and recommendations for action. The other three units prepared much more informal plans that typically consisted of discussion papers, memoranda, and or decision packages that dealt with a single issue at a time.

Several reasons accounted for the wide variation in plans. First, throughout the process the consultants emphasized that strategic thought and action were what counted, not preparation of a formal strategic plan. The consultants argued that teams should focus on a few key issues and strategies to deal with them and should prepare only such "plans" as were necessary to build coalitions around issue definitions and strategies to resolve them.[5]

Second, the efforts at the initiation of strategic planning were almost always out of sequence with the units' normal planning and budgeting processes, so that it was difficult for most to integrate strategic planning with existent formal processes. Third, it was not necessary to integrate all, or even most, of the strategic planning efforts with normal planning and budgeting processes. The commitments recorded in formal plans and budgets were not required to deal with many strategic issues or parts of issues. Finally, the issues identified by any one unit typically were at different stages in the issue "life cycle" (Schön 1971). Separate plans for different issues, therefore, often seemed desirable.

Participants in the Process Conceptualized Time in Three Ways: As Chronos (Calendar Time), Kyros (Peak Experience), and Juncture (Actual Or Potential Event). Van de Ven and Poole (1988) have argued that chronos appears to be the basic metric in structural approaches to organizational change, while kyros is the basic metric in purposive approaches to human action. Time, as chronos, appeared to dominate participants' conception of time when the teams' efforts began. Early discussion centered on the "time commitment"—or calendar time required—for the effort and on the scheduling of workshops or meetings, so they could be marked in appointment books. Occasionally a kyros conception of time occurred, as when teams were pleased with their efforts at workshop sessions or a policy board adopted a team's recommendations. More typical, however, was the experience of City E's city manager, who, after waiting for a draft mission statement that would give him "goose bumps," finally had to settle for a statement that he thought might have given him "one bump." Indeed, while completion of some steps in the process marked important, and often historic "firsts" for each of the unit's teams, the occurrences were hardly "peak" experiences.

The more prevalent conception of time that came to dominate participants' perceptions was of time as actual or potential *junctures* when things had to come together (Jakobson, personal communication, 1987). Process champions, in particular, always seemed to think about what had *to join together* for successful team meetings (e.g., invitations, reminders, premeeting strategy sessions, background papers, room arrangements, supplies, and briefings for consultants), presentations to relevant policy boards (e.g., background papers, decision packages, graphic displays, and premeeting briefings and strategy sessions), or incorporation of the results of strategic planning into ongoing unit planning and budgeting efforts.

Process champions planned both for the expected and, to the extent they could, the unexpected events that would occur throughout the process. Process champions, sponsors, and team members were always aware that unexpected events or crises could torpedo their strategic planning efforts. The conception of time as juncture, therefore, included both the *planned* convergence of ideas, people, transactions, and context and the *unplanned* junctures of the "garbage can" (Cohen, March, and Olsen 1972). People realized that they had to be ready for both, that they could plan on some things happening in a reasonably predictable fashion, but that other things would not, particularly because the purpose of their strategic planning was *to create change* the likes of which had not happened in quite the same way before.

The consultants helped to push and facilitate acceptance of this junctural view of time. The workshops and meetings with consultants were junctures. Process champions and teams worked hard to get their homework done to prepare for these occasions. Champions also prepared for interviews arranged by the consultants. Probably the best example of how the consultants facilitated acceptance of the junctural view of time is the case of City E, in which the champion prepared the city's strategic plan in order to be ready for a presentation to the first author's two-day university executive seminar on strategic planning—an important juncture both for the author and the champion.

Participants Were Intent on Ensuring That Proposed Missions, Strategic Issues, and Strategies Were Technically Rational, Politically Acceptable, and Morally, Ethically, and Legally Defensible. All teams appeared to apply several informal criteria to the evaluation of every statement, document, or recommendation that they prepared. Discussions were never orderly in the sense of formally sequenced considerations of proposals against formally agreed upon criteria, but they did focus on the technical workability of proposals; which stakeholders would and would not support the proposals; and whether the proposals were morally, ethically, and legally defensible. The frame of reference often would shift back and forth among criteria until finally the participants developed a proposal that satisfied all criteria. A temporal sequencing of rationalities or argumentation thus occurred: first one kind (i.e., technical, political, or moral) would predominate and then another, before the group settled on a proposal that everyone could "live with" (Schön 1979; Meyer 1984; Boland and Pondy 1986). Strategic planning became a kind of planning by argumentation (Goldstein 1984).

Finally, Each Unit Clearly Adapted the Process to Its Own Situation. For example, units began the process for different reasons. Sponsors and champions of the process also varied in number, position, and influence. Units responded differently to the tendency for the process to disintegrate; some units discontinued the process altogether, while others found various ways to cope. Units varied in the time they devoted to the process. And what counted as a strategic plan varied widely among the units. Whether or not these adaptations were necessary or useful is not altogether clear, but in the concluding section some tentative speculations are offered on the subject.

Conclusions

A number of conclusions emerge from this study. First, the initiation of strategic planning primarily involves a series of three simple activities for many governmental units, namely, (1) the gathering of key actors (preferably key decision makers), (2) to work through a "strategic thinking and acting" process, (3) in order to focus on what is truly important for the unit, to set priorities for action and to generate those actions. While these activities may be conceptually simple, they are quite difficult to implement because the initiation of strategic planning is a process deliberately designed to produce change. It is this deliberately disruptive nature of the process that partly explains the difficulty of implementing it.

Organizations prefer to program, routinize, and systematize as much as they can (Thompson 1967; Van de Ven 1976); yet here is a process designed to question the organizing that has occurred along with all of the treaties that have been negotiated among stakeholders to form a coalition large enough and strong enough to govern the organization (Pfeffer 1978). Units, therefore, may be scared of the potential disruptions occasioned by strategic planning (as Nursing Service was), unable to pursue the disruptions they think should occur (as when City D's team was the wrong team for the city's water management issue), or unable to decide which disruptions to pursue and how (as when all teams had trouble deciding which issues and strategies to pursue). In short, it is apparently very difficult to initiate and manage a divergent, partly convergent, partly cumulative process.

Said differently, nothing in the results of this study leads us to change our initial expectation: that most efforts to produce fundamental decisions and policy changes in government through strategic planning will not succeed. We might conclude that six of these eight units successfully implemented strategic planning (although there clearly were variations in how successful they were). But it took a lot of effort by these units, plus the help of two consultants, the efforts of the government training service (for seven units), and two small foundation grants to achieve that success. Even then, two units aborted the process early on. Strategic planning obviously is no panacea.

Second, and paradoxically, governmental strategic planning is probably most needed where it is least likely to work. Governmental strategic planning would appear to work best in units that have effective policy-making boards, strong and supportive process sponsors, superb process champions, good strategic planning teams, enough slack to handle potentially disruptive crises, experience in coping with major disruptions, and a desire to address what is truly important for the organization. Any unit with those features probably already uses some sort of "strategic thinking and acting" process. Introducing such a unit to a formal strategic planning process probably would constitute minor tinkering with a "high-performance social system" (Vaill 1978).

Unfortunately, few governments (or organizations of any sort, for that matter) are high-performance social systems. Instead most organizations tend to "muddle through" in a disjointedly incremental way from one situation (often a crisis) to the next. The introduction of strategic planning to such organizations may be doomed to failure. At the very least, the efforts of strategic planners in such situations should focus in part on how to create the conditions outlined in the previous paragraph that would make strategic planning more likely to succeed. One of the process champions in this study captured "the paradox of strategic planning" with the following analogy: "Effective strategic planning is like a quilt. You need all of the pieces before you can stitch together an interesting pattern. But what do you do when you're missing some of the pieces?"

Third, if a government unit wants to initiate strategic planning, this study indicates that the following pieces of the quilt, at a minimum, should be in hand: (1) a powerful process sponsor, (2) an effective process champion, (3) a strategic planning team, (4) an expectation of disruptions and delays, (5) a willingness to be flexible concerning what constitutes a strategic plan, (6) an ability to think of junctures as a key temporal metric, and (7) a willingness to construct and consider arguments geared to many different evaluative criteria.

Fourth, a governmental unit must think carefully about what aspects of strategic planning it might wish to institutionalize. This study seems to indicate that at least the following elements of a strategic planning system (Lorange 1980; Lorange et al. 1986) can be institutionalized: (1) a formal or informal "cabinet," (2) mission statements, (3) "policy objectives" that emerge from the sense of purpose embodied in mission, mandates, and prior decisions (Eckhert et al. 1988) or that characterize the goals of adopted strategies, (4) periodic situation analyses, (5) periodic strategic issue identification exercises, (6) strategic issue management practices (e.g., appointment of issue managers and task forces, strategy development exercises, development of decision packages, and issue monitoring processes) (Eadie 1986; Bryson and Roering 1987), and (7) more formal multicriteria proposal evaluation procedures.

For a number of reasons, we think that these elements can be institutionalized. All of the units that completed strategic plans prepared mission statements. Several prepared policy objectives (either before, during, or after the process) to detail desired performance in key policy areas related to the mission; moreover, preparation of lists of goals and objectives is common practice in most governments. All units performed situation audits and found the exercise relatively simple, not too time consuming, and useful. All of the units identified strategic issues and developed strategies to deal with the most important issues. All of the units in effect adopted an issues management approach (Delmont and Pflaum 1983; Eadie 1986). This was because they realized that different issues were on different time frames and at different stages of development, that different teams were required to handle them, and that different decision sets were needed to resolve them. Finally, all of the units used informal, multicriteria proposal evaluation procedures. These seven aspects of strategic planning, therefore, seem most amenable to institutionalization by governments.

A unit should be cautious about how it institutionalizes strategic planning. After all, strategic planning systems have been known to drive out strategic thinking (*Business Week* 1984; Bryson, Van de Ven, and Roering 1987). What is important about strategic planning is the extent to which it facilitates strategic thinking and acting on the part of key decision makers. If any strategic planning system gets in the way of helping key decision makers think and act strategically, the system should be scrapped — not the strategic thought and action.

Fifth, governmental strategic planning probably should be judged by different standards than private-sector, corporate strategic planning. The nature of the public sector militates against exact duplication of private sector practice (Ring and Perry 1985; Crow and Bozeman 1988). The more numerous stakeholders, the conflicting criteria they often use to judge governmental performance, the pressures for public accountability, and the idea that the public sector is meant to do what the private sector cannot or will not do, all militate against holding governmental strategic planning practice to private-sector standards. The experience of the units in this study justifies this conclusion. None was able to follow the linear, sequential strategic planning models of the business policy textbooks, and none was able to prepare a public sector equivalent of the slick corporate strategic plan. Nonetheless, each unit that completed a plan was able to identify important strategic issues and was able to formulate strategies — plans — to deal with them.

Perhaps, with practice, a more formal, routine process might result, along with public-sector equivalents of private-sector strategic plans. But perhaps a more linear, sequential process and slicker strategic plans are neither necessary nor desirable in the public sector. As noted above, strategic planning systems in the private sector have been known to drive out strategic thinking. Until governmental units gain more experience with strategic planning, it seems best to judge governmental strategic planning according to the extent to which it: (1) focuses the attention of strategic planning teams and key decision makers on what is important for their organizations, (2) helps set priorities for action, and (3) generates those actions.

Sixth, a number of topics clearly should be subjects of future research. Our discovery of the importance of the role of *process champions* is one. The role seems to be crucial to the successful initiation of strategic planning. Are these process champions really different from other kinds of champions, and, if so, how? Can more be found out about exactly what they do to help the process along? Are there ways in which the champions' adherence to a particular process, or set of checkpoints, is dysfunctional? And can people be trained to be effective process champions?

Another subject that should be explored further is the exact nature of the strategic planning process in practice. Our discovery that it seems to be a *divergent, partially convergent, partially cumulative process* is one of this study's most interesting findings. More needs to be known about the nature of such processes and about how they can be managed.

Also, the specific ways in which strategic planning could or should be adapted to different situations should be explored further. A number of authors have suggested that the appropriate choice of planning strategy and tactics should depend on the situation (Bryson and Delbecq 1979; Christensen 1985), but exactly what that means for strategic planning is not clear.

Finally, it must be emphasized that this study concerned the *initiation* of strategic planning by governments. What was not studied was the effectiveness of the strategic planning process itself. That is, we studied the process through the development of strategic plans; we did not study the merits of the plans themselves or the effectiveness of efforts to implement those plans. To the authors' knowledge, no careful study of the effectiveness of governmental strategic planning has been done. Each of the teams that completed plans felt that their strategic planning efforts had been worthwhile. But obviously a great deal more study is necessary before it will be possible to say exactly what does and does not work, under what circumstances, and why, when it comes to strategic planning by governments.

Notes

1. The government training service is operated under a "joint powers" agreement of metropolitan area governments.

2. Workshop #1 consisted of an introduction to strategic planning and stakeholder analysis exercise. Workshop #2 focused on mission statement development and external and internal environmental assessments. Workshop #3 involved the identification of strategic issues. The remaining four workshops were consultations with individual strategic planning teams on an as-needed basis (i.e., Workshop #4, Cities C, D, and E; Workshop #5, Cities C and D; Workshop #6, Countries A and B; and Workshop #7, City E). Consultants' fees for services to all eight units were covered by small grants from two metropolitan area foundations.

3. The following data were collected: (1) Some basic background data was collected for each unit (i.e., budgetary and demographic data). (2) The applications from the seven units requesting participation in the government training service-sponsored exercise were reviewed. (3) Detailed process histories were prepared for City E and Nursing Service by students of the first author. (4) Periodic interviews were conducted with team leaders and each strategic planning team as long as the team continued to participate. Our notes from interviews of teams and team leaders are uneven in quality: some are quite detailed, while others are sketchy. (5) Baseline Minnesota Innovation Research Program (Van de Ven and Chu 1989 forthcoming) questionnaire data was collected for all units (the research was conducted as part of that program). (6) Time 2, Time 3, and Time 4 Minnesota Innovation Research Program questionnaire data, however, are available only for City E and Nursing Service. At Time 2 the other strategic planning teams either had dropped out of the program (City A), had completed the process and did not want to be bothered with questionnaires (City D), refused to fill out questionnaires deemed "too academic" (City B), or else filled out too few questionnaires, too incompletely to yield useful data (City C, County A, and County B — Executive Director's Office). (7) A follow-up questionnaire was filled out by the heads of the strategic planning teams of units that completed the process. This questionnaire measured the success of the strategic planning efforts according to the authors' criteria. (8) Finally, a brief narrative of each unit's experience was prepared. Verification occurred through one of two methods. First, our accounts of what happened in the two units that dropped out of the process early were checked against newspaper accounts and in telephone interviews with the government training service contact person. The accounts of what happened in the six units that completed the process were checked for accuracy with the appropriate team leaders. Copies of the narratives are available from the authors.

4. Further, Johnson and his colleagues indicate that while experts are quick to recognize patterns in their areas of expertise, they also are prone to recognize the "wrong" pattern. They frequently "jump to conclusions" based on limited data. In other words, being an expert simply may allow a person to make mistakes faster than a lay person (Johnson 1984). Once committed to a wrong diagnosis, an expert may remain committed to that diagnosis in the face of contradictory evidence (Salancik 1977).

5. We did, however, continuously urge each team to write up the results of their discussions and analyses so that they had adequate background materials to inform preparation of plans.

References

Primary source materials for this paper are contained in separate files for each of the governmental units. These files are in the possession of the first author and are available for inspection — with the caveat that the names of all governmental units and study participants are to remain anonymous.

Bardach, Eugene. 1987. October 29–31. "The policy entrepreneur amidst the flux," paper presented at the Annual Conference of the Association for Public Policy Analysis and Management, Washington, D.C.

Benveniste, Guy. 1972. *The politics of expertise.* Berkeley, Calif.: Glendessary.

_____. 1977. *Bureaucracy.* Berkeley, Calif.: Glendessary.

Boland, J. Richard, Jr., and Louis R. Pondy. August 1986. "The micro dynamics of a budget cutting process: Modes, models, and structure," *Accounting, Organizations and Society,* vol. 11, pp. 403–22.

Bryson, John M. 1988. *Strategic planning for public and nonprofit organizations.* San Francisco, Calif.: Jossey-Bass.

_____, and Andre L. Delbecq. April 1979. "A contingent approach to strategy and tactics in project planning." *Journal of the American Planning Association,* vol. 45, pp. 167–79.

_____, and William D. Roering. January 1987. "Applying private-strategic planning in the public sector." *Journal of the American Planning Association,* vol. 53, pp. 9–20.

_____, Andrew H. Van de Ven, and William D. Roering. 1987. "Strategic planning and the revitalization of the public service," in *Toward a New Public Service* (Robert Denhardt and Edward Jennings, Jr., eds.) Columbia, Mo.: University of Missouri, Extension Publications, pp. 55–75.

_____, R. Edward Freeman, and William D. Roering. 1986. "Strategic planning in the public sector: Approaches and future directions," in *Strategic Approaches to Planning Practice* (Barry Checkoway, ed.) Lexington, Mass.: Lexington Books, pp. 65–85.

Business Week. September 1984. "The new breed of strategic planner," vol. 17, pp. 62–68.

Christensen, Karen S. 1985. "Coping with uncertainty in planning." *Journal of the American Planning Association,* vol. 51, pp. 63–73.

Cohen, Michael D., James G. March, and Johan P. Olsen. 1972. "A garbage can model of organizational choice." *Administrative Science Quarterly,* vol. 17, pp. 1–25.

Crow, Michael, and Barry Bozeman. 1988. "Strategic public management," in *Strategic Planning — Threats and Opportunities for Planners* (John M. Bryson and Robert C. Einsweiler, eds.) Washington, D.C. and Chicago, Ill.: Planners Press, pp. 51–68.

Delmont, Timothy J., and Ann M. Pflaum. October 1983. "External scanning and issues management: New planning techniques for colleges and universities," a paper presented at the annual conference of the Association for Institutional Research.

Eadie, Douglas C. 1983. "Putting a powerful tool to practical use: The application of strategic planning in the public sector." *Public Administration Review,* vol. 43, pp. 447–52.

_____. 1986. "Strategic issue management: Improving the council-manager relationship," ICMA MIS Report, vol. 18, pp. 2–12.

Eckhert, Philip C., Kathleen Haines, Timothy J. Delmont, and Ann M. Pflaum. 1988. "Strategic planning in Hennepin County, Minnesota: An issues management approach," in *Strategic Planning — Threats and Opportunities for Planners* (John M. Bryson and Robert C. Einsweiler, eds.) Washington, D.C. and Chicago, Ill.: Planners Press, pp. 172–83.

Galbraith, Jay. 1973. *Designing complex organizations.* Reading, Mass.: Addison-Wesley.

Goldstein, Harvey. 1984. "Planning as argumentation." *Environment and Planning B,* vol. 11, pp. 297–312.

Hickson, David J., Richard J. Butler, David Cray, Geoffrey R. Mallory, and David C. Wilson. 1986. *Top decisions: Strategic decision-making in organizations.* Oxford, England: Basil Blackwell.

Jakobson, Leo. 1987. Personal communication.

Johnson, Paul E. 1984. "The expert mind: A new challenge for the information scientist," in

M. A. Bemelmans, ed., *Beyond Productivity: Information System Development for Organizational Effectiveness*. North Holland: Elsevier Science.

Kanter, Rosabeth Moss. 1983. *The changemasters*. New York: Simon and Schuster.

Kotler, Philip. 1976. *Marketing management*. Englewood Cliffs, N.J.: Prentice-Hall.

Lindblom, Charles. 1959. "The science of muddling through." *Public Administration Review*, vol. 19, pp. 79–88.

Lorange, P. 1980. *Corporate planning: An executive viewpoint*. Englewood Cliffs, N.J.: Prentice-Hall, 1980.

————, M. F. S. Morton, and S. Ghoshal. 1986. *Strategic control*. St. Paul, Minn.: West.

Meyer, Alan D. January 1984. "Mingling decision-making metaphors." *Academy of Management Review*, vol. 9, pp. 6–17.

Pfeffer, Jeffrey. 1978. *Organizational design*. Arlington Heights, Ill.: AHM.

Pirsig, Robert. 1974. *Zen and the art of motorcycle maintenance*. New York: Basic Books.

Quinn, James B. 1980. *Logical incrementalism*. Homewood, Ill.: Richard D. Irwin.

Ring, Peter S., and James L. Perry. 1985. "Strategic management in public and private organizations: Implications of distinctive contexts and constraints." *Academy of Management Review*, vol. 10, pp. 276–86.

Roberts, Nancy, and Paula King. 1989. "Roles of policy entrepreneurs in galvanizing innovation coalitions and networks," in *Research in the Management of Innovation* (A. H. Van de Ven, H. Angle, and M. S. Poole, eds.) Cambridge, Mass.: Ballinger, forthcoming.

Salancik, Gerald R. 1977. "Commitment and the control of organizational behavior and belief," in Barry M. Staw and Salancik, eds., *New Directions in Organizational Behavior*. Chicago, Ill.: St. Clair Press.

Schon, D. A. 1971. *Beyond the stable state*. London: Temple Smith.

————. 1979. "Generative metaphors," in Andrew Ortony, ed., *Metaphor and Thought*. Cambridge, Mass.: Cambridge University Press.

Sussman, Gerald, and Robert Evered. 1978. "An assessment of the scientific merits of action research." *Administrative Science Quarterly*, vol. 23, pp. 582–603.

Thompson, James D. 1967. *Organizations in Action*. New York: McGraw-Hill.

Vaill, Peter. 1978. "High performance social systems," in R. McCall and M. Lombardo, eds., *Leadership — Where Else Do We Go?* Durham, NC: Duke University Press.

Van de Ven, Andrew H. January 1976. "A framework for organizational assessment." *Academy of Management Review*, vol. 1, pp. 64–78.

————, and Scott Poole. 1988. "Paradoxical requirements for a theory of organizational change," in *Paradox and Transformation, Toward a Theory of Changing Organization and Management* (R. E. Quinn and K. S. Cameron, eds.) Cambridge, Mass.: Ballinger, forthcoming.

————, and Yunhan Chu. 1989. "A psychometric assessment of the Minnesota innovation survey," in *Research in the Management of Innovation* (A. H. Van de Ven, H. Angle and M. S. Poole, eds.) Cambridge, Mass.: Ballinger, forthcoming.

PART TWO

The Application

The Bellingham 2000 Project — An Experiment in Mid-Sized Community Planning

Skip Everitt

As a member of the governor's State-Wide Task Force for Alternatives for Washington, the author became increasingly concerned about the future of the local area in Northern Puget Sound and, in particular, the City of Bellingham. Bellingham is a beautiful place with a lot to lose by not planning for the future. As a result of informal conversations with a member of the city council, we explored with the city's Planning and Development Commission the possibility of a local Year 2000 program. Armed with their tentative approval, we submitted a proposal in the spring of 1974 to the State Office of Community Development of the State of Washington to fund a citizen-based long-range goal setting program. The result was a program that spanned over two years in time, involved over 1,100 local citizens, and produced goals and policy guidelines for both the short and long-range future of the city.

Bellingham 2000 attempted to incorporate three important assumptions about citizen involvement in planning into its process.

Assumption 1. That the idea of anticipatory democracy ("going to the people") should be a functional part of a community's decision-making process.

Assumption 2. That citizens can be vested with some degree of real authority in making political decisions, and that citizens need not be confined to advisory roles.

Assumption 3. That each citizen can attain a high level of "civic literacy," and thus be more effective in decision-making as an individual *and* as a member of a group.

Reprinted with permission from World Future Society Bulletin, *Vol. XII, No. 1, January/February 1978. Published by the World Future Society, Bethesda, Maryland.*

Bellingham: A City at the Crossroads

For even the casual traveler, there is an obvious uniqueness about Bellingham, Washington. While its economic health depends upon a large pulp mill, food processing and packing, and retail sales, it is best known for its setting, reasonable cost of living, and proximity to recreation of all sorts. In many ways, it appears to be an ideal place to live, work, and play. Located on Northern Puget Sound, 90 miles north of Seattle, it is within two hours of three major winter sports areas, minutes away from the San Juan Island, and less than two hours distant from major trailheads leading into the North Cascades National Park and Glacier Peak Wilderness. Seventy per cent of the total land area of Bellingham's parent county (Whatcom) is publicly owned as national forest, national park, county park, or national recreation area. With a population of less than 45,000, the city retains many small town features, and affords each citizen a variety of recreational and cultural opportunities.

Bellingham's location and natural setting is its greatest blessing and — at the same time — represents its greatest threat. In terms of the future, Bellingham is truly at a crossroads. Presently, neither the city nor county have permanent comprehensive plans, and development continues to occur in a more or less random fashion. As parts of the city experience aging and decay, there is a rush by developers to convert vacant land to commercial or multi-family use. Recently two older neighborhoods have successfully resisted this decay and turnover with assistance from the U.S. Department of Housing and Urban Development, and with effective citizen pressure to preserve low density zoning in each area. Unfortunately many areas of Bellingham are being transformed at a rate that takes local residents by surprise, and citizen protest is frequently "too little, and too late."

Citizen Participation in Bellingham

Until 1974, citizen involvement in planning in Bellingham was confined to membership on advisory boards such as the Planning Commission, to special advisory groups typified by the select Mayor's Advisory Committee, and to "reactive" bodies such as the Board of Adjustment and Board of Equalization.

In 1973, the county appointed a 50-person group to steer the progress of the new county land use ordinances. This group, called the Land Use Code Committee (LUCC) was established to work with professional planners to create a set of land use "zones" for future development in the county. No counterpart to this LUCC was developed by the city and, except on a case-by-case basis, citizens were not included in the planning process in

Bellingham. There was a growing frustration among many citizens who recognized new or rapidly growing land use, housing, and social service problems but had little or no voice in decisions about the future.

Therefore, despite its geographic and physical uniqueness, Bellingham was, and still is to a degree, a very typical town with regard to citizen involvement in planning or decision making. Bellingham 2000 was not a full solution to Bellingham's typical exclusion of citizens from the planning process. It was a beginning, and a signal to leaders that far more people were ready, able, and willing to assist in speculation and participation in the city's long-range future.

A Brief Historical Outline of Goals for Bellingham

In the early spring of 1974, a councilman and the members of the Planning and Development Commission held a number of informal discussions about citizen involvement in the planning process. Most agreed that a mechanism, or program, of citizen involvement would greatly assist the commission in formulating goals and policies for both the short- and long-term future of Bellingham. The councilman suggested that he, and others, seek state funding for such a program. He approached the author, then an assistant professor at Huxley College, whom he knew to have an interest in both citizen participation and long-range planning. Together we drafted a proposal for a "Civic Partnership" program and submitted this proposal to the State Office of Community Development. This "partnership" included the establishment of a citizen involvement program called "Bellingham 2000." Basically, the intent of Bellingham 2000 was to provide citizens with a variety of opportunities to tell their leaders about the "desirable futures" for the city. The grant for $12,000 was funded under Title I of the Higher Education Act of 1964, through the State of Washington Office of Community Development.

In the summer of 1974, the author met several times with the Planning and Development Commission to plan for the organization of the program. It was decided that the first step should be the establishment of an advisory group to serve as a steering committee. After careful deliberation, the Planning and Development Commission chose ten citizens that represented a wide range of perspectives and lifestyles. Later that summer, this advisory group met to define its role and began assisting the author with program planning.

The first task for the advisory group was to recruit a 30–40 person task force to conduct a series of neighborhood workshops. From a list of over 100 nominees carefully selected to represent a cross-section of the Bellingham community, 30 agreed to serve on the task force.

In September 1974, the contributor selected a free-lance educator as associate director for the program. The Director of Community Development, City of Bellingham, was designated as city hall liaison to the program. Together, we conducted a six-hour training workshop for task force members. The workshop dealt with the purposes of Goals for Bellingham and each member received instructions on how to conduct neighborhood meetings. Each task force member agreed to conduct two meetings, and a schedule was finalized by mid–October. By this time, four student interns had joined the staff. Two of these students served as staff assistants, a third assumed responsibilities for publicity, and the fourth agreed to design and conduct a comprehensive evaluation of the program. Publicity was kicked off with the mailing of 6,000 brochures and a full-page newspaper ad in the *Bellingham Herald.* The program also contracted with McGraw-Hill Films to rent a series of futuristic films that were shown to the public in November.

In early October, the Mayor and city council issued a joint resolution officially endorsing the program. With this resolution and the verbal support of the Planning and Development Commission, the task force proceeded to the business of conducting neighborhood meetings. The process for conducting neighborhood meetings was a modified version of the "Invent the Future" process developed by Warren Ziegler and John Osman. (A summary of this process appears in an article entitled "Civic Literacy," by Warren L. Ziegler, Grace M. Healy and Jill H. Ellsworth, in the collection *Methods and Materials in Continuing Education,* Chester Klevins, editor [New York: Klevins Publishing, 1976], pages 130–149.)

During November, December and January, the task force held approximately 55 meetings and collected over 400 recommendations from citizens regarding goals, objectives, and other statements about the future of Bellingham. Citizens were invited to neighborhood meetings by the Mayor in a letter enclosed with water bills, as well as in letters from task force members to their neighbors, radio and TV spots, newspaper articles and advertising, and via a telephone committee organized by a citizen active in community affairs.

The most effective publicity techniques appeared to be: (1) letters from the Mayor enclosed in utility bills and (2) the telephone committee. In the later stages of the program, a local radio talk show was effective in stimulating reactions to the policy team reports. The least effective means of soliciting participation was newspaper advertising. Some participation was also gained by speeches to civic clubs and community organizations.

After the completion of the neighborhood meetings, the task force reconvened to sort the 400 goals and recommendations into groups that would become the special area concerns of different policy teams. After discussing the general topic areas of the policy teams with the advisory group, Planning Department, and city council, a new publicity campaign was launched to recruit working members for these teams.

At this point (January 1975), a public hearing was held to solicit comments about the neighborhood meetings and to ask for participation by the public in the policy team phase. About 100 people attended this hearing.

The policy teams began meeting in early February and were to formulate a preliminary document by May. During the first week of policy team meetings, members of the teams were briefed by a city planner; the project associate director; a dean of Huxley College; and the director of Community Development, who explained the mechanics of transplanting neighborhood goals into objectives and policy guidelines. The staff also explained the fundamentals of the comprehensive plan process. During the four months of policy team meetings, a media presentation was shown to civic clubs, service and church groups, and educational organizations in an effort to further stimulate interest in Goals for Bellingham on the part of the community. Special emphasis was placed by the staff on involving the business-industrial community in the process, a segment of the population that was sparsely represented on the policy teams.

The policy teams completed a preliminary draft document for submission to the advisory group and Planning and Development Commission in late May 1975. At this time, reports were submitted on education, social services, pollution control, economic base, leisure activities, shorelines, citizen participation, housing, and transportation.

About this time, the entire program came under attack from two main sources: (1) the planning director and (2) the business community. The planning director had viewed Bellingham 2000 from the outset to the "interference" and "meddling" in the planning process. Her opposition was intensified when many citizen-generated goals implied that progress toward a comprehensive land use plan for the city had been negligible during her tenure.

The business community was approached by the staff well before the program's starting date. We briefed the chamber of commerce, the local Realtors Association, Independent Insurance Agents Association, Rotary, Kiwanis, and several other groups to solicit support and active participation. After the first round of neighborhood meetings the list of attendees included approximately 18 percent who were members of local business or industry. In conversations with several of these people they explained that most businessmen considered a Year 2000 program (especially one coordinated by a college) to be an academic exercise and not worthy of their time and effort. However, within two months this apathy turned to active opposition with the publication of the completed neighborhood goals document. The document — a verbatim summary of goals written by attendees of the neighborhood meetings — reflected a preference among a large number of attendees for slowed growth, both economically and population-wise, for Bellingham, and industrial diversification to deemphasize heavy industry while encouraging "clean" industry such as tourism, warehousing, shipping, cottage trades and crafts, and services. The business leaders in Bellingham felt threatened by any suggestion of a different form of economy and reacted in one case by terming the program as "subversive."

In early June 1975, the Planning Commission and advisory group met and decided to withhold public dissemination of the preliminary draft while they conducted a thorough evaluation of the program. The evaluation revealed that the program had met the objectives set forth in the original grant proposal. Furthermore, it was clear that any delays in the program had been caused by the planning director's refusal to commit her time and resources to the project.

Later in June, a second grant of $8,500 was awarded to provide money for producing four multi-media programs. These multi-media programs were developed by two graduate students in the master of environmental planning program at Huxley College. The total cost of the four programs was $1600. These programs presented summaries of the policy team reports and were distributed for viewing by community groups during the fall and winter of 1975-76.

Also in the summer of 1975, the city staff designed a questionnaire intended to solicit public opinion about the results of the policy teams. (The full results of this survey may be obtained by writing City Hall, Bellingham, Washington 98225.)

In the spring of 1976, the results of the policy team meetings, and preliminary results of the city-wide survey went to the Mayor, city council, and Planning Commission. In June 1976, a group of former policy team members met with the staff and decided to officially conclude the Goals for Bellingham program with presentations to the council and the Planning Commission. This group further decided to reconvene as an ad-hoc citizens' group in order to analyze the possibilities for implementing many of the policy statements contained in the policy team document.

Epilogue: The Future of the Future in Bellingham

In June 1976, the Goals for Bellingham program was officially completed. Many citizens sighed with relief as they looked forward to sailing, hiking, gardening, and "business as usual" without periodially receiving notices or calls to attend policy team meetings or hearings. After two years, over 1,100 concerned people had written goals, served on committees or policy teams, filled out surveys, viewed media presentations, or had offered advice to elected and appointed officials about Bellingham's future.

Among members of the community there are some very good and some very bad feelings about Goals for Bellingham. Generally, the government (city council, Mayor, Planning Commission, and Planning Department) remains strongly in support of the intent of the program. On the other hand, business and industry remain skeptical about Goals for Bellingham, and will probably continue to view it as a potential inhibitor to economic development.

As for those citizens who dedicated many hours to the program, a few pledged to carry on the spirit of Goals of Bellingham through an action-oriented lobbying effort. In the fall of 1976, this group of ex–policy team members met to analyze the policy team report from a cost-benefit perspective and recommended programs, plans, and legislation to the appropriate agencies for consideration.

A Practitioner's Guide to Community Futuristics

DO obtain the support of political leaders before starting or early in the program. In the case of Bellingham 2000, an elected official was the co-designer of the program and lent consistent support during good and bad times.

DO spend considerable time planning the mechanics of the program. Then, be prepared to back away from the tight agendas, deadlines, and "behavior outcomes" that you have set. Be flexible and sensitive to the fact that your program will be competing for people's time with other family and community activities.

DO strive for objectivity from yourself and your staff. Any opinionated, emotional rhetoric on your part will surely alienate *someone . . .* Assume that community year 2000 programs truly seek alternative scenarios — even if these scenarios are not "desirable" by your personal standards.

DO identify those who will resist or oppose the program. Then *don't* spend much energy trying to neutralize their opposition. Push the strengths of your program. Avoid mud-slinging. As in politics, avoid spending energy trying to make converts. Instead, cultivate your supporters and send them after the "undecideds."

DON'T expect volunteers to give and give and give their time and efforts. Try to cycle people in and out. Avoid the "burned-out volunteer" syndrome.

DON'T expect everyone to think rationally or systematically about the future of their community. Don't assume that everyone knows about "synergy," "steady state economics," or "trends analysis." As a futurist/educator, I advise you to move slowly as you introduce new vocabulary and ways of thinking to communities.

DON'T attempt to replicate other models for year 2000 programs without substantial modification. Enlist the advice of a wide spectrum of local citizens to assist you in planning the program. The nature of your particular community should determine the ways and means to conduct a successful program.

While this represents an overt attempt by citizens to "finish the process, several other results of Goals for Bellingham have surfaced since June 1976:

• The Mayor has instituted a system of neighborhood organizations to advise him on future planning issues. He credits the goals program with providing a precedent for his system and has recruited a former member of the citizen participation policy team to implement the system.

Other accomplishments:

• The County Parks Department has incorporated the report of the leisure activities policy team into its new long-range plan.
• The Planning and Development Commission, in a letter to the Goals for Bellingham staff voted unanimously "to accept the Goals for Bellingham final document as input for the upcoming comprehensive plan."

Intuitively, we believe that people in Bellingham now feel closer to their government. Internally, the city appears to have officials who are responsive to citizen participation. Given time, both the city and county appear to have the necessary human resources to plan and implement a variety of desirable "alternative futures."

However, it is the factor of *time* that leaves us feeling far from secure about Bellingham's future. Externally, the Northern Puget Sound region is growing quite rapidly. As future needs for food processing, energy supplies, and recreational space increase, so will the pressures on Whatcom County and Bellingham to provide these goods and services. Historically, we have made some tragic mistakes in similar situations, i.e., the Green River Valley near Seattle, the coast of New Jersey and Delaware, the offshore area of Southern California, and the back country areas of the Smokies, Sierras and Rockies. These are, for the most part, mistakes caused by *no* planning rather than poor planning. In these cases, we have followed short-run economic "instincts" and now lament the consequences of our "progress."

Even with the marvelous human talent that resides in this mid-sized city, the task ahead will be extremely difficult and complex. There is little time to waste and a great deal to lose by "letting history take its course."

The Charlotte-Mecklenburg 2005 Plan — Managing Through Strategic Planning

Martin R. Cramton, Jr. and Carol Stealey Morris

Many local governments are seeking to manage development and change through strategic planning. Not long ago, the limelight focused on techniques for limiting growth: the Petaluma, Boulder, and Boca Raton growth limit programs, among others, received great attention. Efforts to limit growth, however, have failed to gain a foothold in most communities. In fact, local public agendas on growth issues in the 1980s are dominated by the following considerations:

• Adequate infrastructure to support growth;
• Citizen involvement and mediation mechanisms; and
• Planning approaches that address issues of both growth and decline.

Interest in the narrowly focused growth limits techniques of the 1970s and in growth management systems relying on complicated phasing formulas has diminished. An increasing number of cities like Phoenix, Austin, and Charlotte, North Carolina, are adopting strategic planning techniques to facilitate growth management.

Attempts to apply techniques to restrict growth have often proven problematic. The use of population and building permit caps seems limited to smaller communities, and experience indicates that adequate public facilities ordinances are prone to offer more than can be delivered. The moral is that growth management techniques should be viewed simply as means to an end and not as ends in themselves. They must also be based upon

Reprinted with permission from Urban Land, *Vol. 45, No. 4, April 1986. Published by the Urban Land Institute, Washington, D.C.*

a clear definition of the public interest and incorporated within an across-the-board planning program.

Strategic Planning

Effective strategic planning aims to define appropriate long-term directions for change in a community, and a short-term operating framework for addressing such change. In communities on the forefront of growth management, this process is being carried out in accordance with the broader political and public consciousness.

As *Strategies for Cities and Counties* (U.S. Department of Housing and Urban Development and Public Technology, 1984) notes, strategic planning is a focused process that:

- Concentrates on a few issues;
- Explicitly considers resources available;
- Assesses both strengths and weaknesses;
- Defines major events and changes acting on the community from the outside that create problems and opportunities; and
- Is implementation-oriented.

It provides a tool for dealing with changes occurring as a result of either decline or growth. It avoids the weaknesses of narrow growth management approaches. And it revitalizes local planning by supplying a framework for mediation and by incorporating an inclusive definition of public objectives.

Deciding to Plan for Growth Management

"Strategic planning" has become a familiar term in the city of Charlotte and county of Mecklenburg. For the past few years area leaders have been working to create a land use plan aimed at effectively managing the rapid growth that might otherwise overwhelm the area.

By 1980, only four years after a *Comprehensive Plan 1995* had been adopted, community leaders and the local planning commission realized that Charlotte-Mecklenburg was changing more rapidly than had been expected. Charlotte was becoming the center of an expanding regional economy. Its population had been increasing steadily, major firms had relocated to the area, and significant development proposals were being announced regularly. Growth was bringing new opportunities to Charlotte-Mecklenburg, yet it was also threatening the very qualities that were attracting this growth: the area's livability and economic vitality.

Traffic congestion, water shortages, and a lack of adequate open space posed immediate problems. The ominous prospect emerged of a weakened economy over the long run, because of the spilling over of jobs, households, and tax revenues into adjacent jurisdictions.

It became evident that the community was not in a strong position to seize the opportunities and minimize the threats of rapid urbanization, due to the limitations of its existing comprehensive plan and zoning system. These were attuned to the land use philosophy of the 1960s, and had a rural-suburban outlook. Consequently, the planning commission was directed in early 1984 to draft a plan that would enable the region to cope with these pressing issues and that could be implemented with the available resources. A strategic approach was decided upon. The effort culminated in the adoption of *2005: A Generalized Land Plan for Charlotte-Mecklenburg.*

The *2005 Plan* was completed in a relatively short period—a little more than a year and a half. In a community and a history of fiercely competing interests and values, this in itself constituted a feat. The key to keeping the process moving and to reaching a consensus was to involve the public, interest groups, and various government agencies every step of the way.

A Process of Involvement

The first priority was to achieve consensus on the issues. In February 1984, the planning commission released *A Working Document of the Generalized Land Plan,* compiling the objectives, policies, and strategies contained in various approved plans such as the *Comprehensive Plan 1995* and the *1990 Transportation Plan.* The *Working Document* was intended to clarify the community's current official position on growth issues. It was emphatically only a starting point for discussion.

Stating the "old" position in the context of a new planning effort stirred up old controversies among various interest groups. In March, more than 700 citizens came together in workshops to review the *Working Document.* Business, development, and neighborhood leaders were among the participants. This review resulted in the release in April of a second document, an *Issues Report,* which summarized the workshop participants' comments on each of the objectives, policies, and strategies detailed in the *Working Document.* The issues causing the most public concern and debate began to come into focus.

On May 1, 1984, a day-long miniconference entitled "Urban Renaissance: Planning for a Livable Community" was attended by more than 600 citizens. Developers, neighborhood leaders, and civic leaders participated in panel discussions. Fresh perspectives were contributed by visiting planning professionals. A *Proceedings Document* was published soon after the conference, detailing the day's events. This document included the results of a questionnaire completed by the participants regarding issues that surfaced most often. Opposing views were expressed throughout the conference, but as Mayor Harvey Gantt commented, "If we keep before us the things we can agree on, we have the basis for a rational decision."

It was critical that public participation not end with these early steps, but that it remain at the heart of the process. A *2005* citizens' task force was therefore appointed by city and county officials to monitor the drafting of the plan and to provide a forum for further public discussion. Business, development, and neighborhood leaders were called upon to serve on this 12-member group. By the plan's completion, the task force had met more than 60 times.

Several interest groups also monitored the planning process. These included the local realtor and homebuilding associations, the chamber of commerce, and the Community Issues Council, a neighborhoods coalition. A technical coordinating committee, consisting of city and county department heads and officials, was also formed to coordinate with the planning staff.

A monthly *2005 Update* newsletter was distributed to keep communications flowing. It proved an effective means to disseminate information to interested citizens. The local media reported as well on meetings and the plan's progress through the course of the 18-month program.

Defining Critical Issues

A key element of the process was to obtain more detailed information on Charlotte-Mecklenburg's growth. A professional research team was hired to address the question: How much would the region grow? The team made projections through the year 2005 based upon current trends in population, households, and jobs. It also projected the strong and weak market areas for the seven planning districts.

Although not officially completed until December 1984, these "growth assumptions" were sufficiently gelled by the end of the summer to yield a realistic picture of Charlotte-Mecklenburg's future development. In addition, the planning commission staff conducted a "regional reconnaissance." They met with officials from neighboring town and county governments to discuss zoning policies, growth trends, existing and planned utility systems, and attitudes toward planning in general. This process proved beneficial in understanding the potential effects of development in the surrounding area on Charlotte-Mecklenburg's growth, and also in initiating a working rapport for future planning efforts.

Having combined growth assumptions with citizen input, the planning staff identified eight critical issues that needed to be addressed in the *2005 Plan*. These were growth assumptions; environment; public services and facilities; development; neighborhoods; citizen involvement; urban design; and local government. By exploring these essential issues, complex as they were, the community would be in a much better position to conserve its essential strengths and address significant weaknesses.

In September 1984, the first phase of the process wound down. There was agreement on the issues. Public meetings were held that month to review the issues and to explain the next phase.

Setting Directions and Choosing Actions

Theme. The next step was to establish a clear vision of the kind of future Charlotte-Mecklenburg would like to achieve. The theme that the best way to grow is to provide opportunities for economic mobility for all segments of the population was then translated into three broad goals:

* A more balanced growth pattern;
* An increasingly urban land use pattern; and
* A stronger urban design consciousness.

Objectives. How would this ambitious vision be achieved? Specific objectives were set within the structure of the eight critical issues that had been identified. For example, an objective addressing the growth assumptions and geographically balanced development issues is to "stimulate new development and redevelopment in the weaker market areas." Target figures have been set for population, households, and jobs for each of the seven planning districts. Another objective addressing the development issue is to revise existing zoning policies and districts.

Tools. Selecting an action plan was the next step. Since resources were limited, the implementation tools were narrowed into five categories: continued planning; regulations; public investment; organization; and legislation.

Incorporating strategic planning into all land use planning activities, monitoring the *2005 Plan* every five years, developing enterprise areas as a growth redirection strategy for weak market locations, and completing area plans for defined regions are examples of the tools that were suggested for continued planning. Some recommended regulatory tools are to revise the zoning, subdivision, and sign ordinances into joint city/county codes and to prepare policy guides for farmland preservation and stormwater management. Specific to the zoning revisions is a suggestion to consider phasing rezonings based on the availability of infrastructure, and to build a set of design standards into the ordinance.

Under the public investment category, a suggested implementation tool is a city/county capital investment program covering five- and 10-year periods. Among the possibilities for organizational changes are the implementation of a structure for citizens' involvement based on geographic areas, the sponsorship of community conferences on planning, and more effective coordination of an economic development program. Finally, recommended legislation tools include developing revenue options and evaluating the potential for a general countywide impact fee system.

All these objectives, policies, and tools were combined with the issues and growth assumptions into a single working-draft document that was released in March 1985. Two community meetings were held in April to discuss this report, and various groups that had been monitoring the planning effort, including the planning commission, also reviewed it. In June, a revised *Goals, Tools, and Objectives Document* was released, incorporating the comments of the citizens and the planning commission.

Refining the Plan

The planning staff had already begun work on the plan's third phase: application of the objectives and tools to the county's planning districts. A senior planner was assigned to each of the seven districts to design broad land use strategies and to specify infrastructure policies for achieving each district's vision for growth. For those parts of the county that were identified as strong markets, the emphasis was on accommodation of growth, while the emphasis in the weak market areas was on developing strategies that would attract jobs and people. Weak market areas were determined to be priority areas for providing infrastructure to stimulate private sector investment.

Key strategies addressing livability were also outlined for such countywide issues as infill development, reinvestment in declining areas, and the transit system.

The planning commission developed cost estimates for each of the recommended strategies and a schedule of priorities within different time frames: short range (5 years), medium range (10 years), and long range (20 years). The total estimated cost for implementing the strategies comes to $2.1 billion.

Presentations of the planning commission's strategies and priorities were made to all the monitoring groups and city and county officials throughout July and August of 1985. In September, the staff draft of the

2005 Plan was released. Public meetings, attended by more than 900 citizens, were held that month in each of the seven planning districts. The plan was then reexamined by the planning commission in the context of all the additional comments that had been heard. The commission, the 2005 Citizens Task Force, and the chamber of commerce all prepared reports critiquing the draft plan. Significantly, there were few adjustments necessary; the framework for developing the plan had worked, and the many parties involved had reached a general agreement on the direction Charlotte-Mecklenburg should take. As the chamber of commerce report put it: "The involvement of the *2005 Plan* has been a time-consuming, painstaking, and, we assume, sometimes frustrating job. . . . This endeavor is probably the most significant thing of its kind that has ever been undertaken by this community. It will set the stage for things to come. . . . In our judgment, the document has benefited greatly from the ongoing study, review, and comments by diverse groups that have spanned more than a year and a half."

In October, another public hearing brought out about 200 people, and finally on November 25, 1985, the *2005 Plan* was adopted unanimously by the city council and county commission with only minor modifications. A *Charlotte Observer* November 29, 1985, editorial noted: "The plan, as finally adopted, represents many months of intense discussion and patient, painstaking compromise on the part of elected officials, the appointed City-County Planning Commission and its professional staff, neighborhood leaders, land developers, and other interested citizens."

The outcome now rests with the ability of elected officials to continue planning efforts in accordance with the plan's priorities and to allocate the always limited resources in accordance with the plan's direction. A joint city/county five-year capital improvements program and 10-year capital needs assessment are currently in progress. Zoning, subdivision, and sign ordinance revisions are also underway. These are positive signs of a strong implementation commitment. As Mayor Gantt commented, "We passed it today, but how serious we are about implementing it will make this community special. The task is up to us, future councils, and county commissions."

Lessons

Back in early 1984, tensions had run high as Charlotte-Mecklenburg began preparation of a growth management plan. A developer then lamented, "We've gotten to the point where nobody but developers believe what developers say, nobody but neighborhoods believe what the neighborhoods say. I think the politicians are confused. . . . There should be some leadership to quell the tensions." In fact, city and county elected officials did exercise leadership. They used the strategic planning process to effect a truce in the battle over growth management.

The early decision to use and support a strategic approach to growth issues rather than an ad hoc approach provided the key to Charlotte-Mecklenburg's new-found ability to cope intelligently with development problems and to seize the opportunities the future offered.

Charlotte-Mecklenburg's 2005 planning experience illustrates a number of important principles of strategic planning for communities:

- The process should be well-organized and must involve the private sector. It must specify budgets, scheduling, participants and responsibilities, and products. A make-it-up-as-you-proceed approach will not be productive.
- The basis for setting the public agenda should be an integrated assessment of current conditions and future prospects. The alternative — simply responding to interest group evaluations and pressures — will doom the planning effort.
- The focus must remain on the critical issues, allowing precise statements of objectives and actions. Too broad a focus results in promising more than is possible at the action stage or, worse, no action at all.
- A variety of links to the citizenry must be established, including provision for participation by interest groups, the general public, and different government agencies.
- Emphasis must be placed on creative approaches to specific, immediate issues. Simply copying solutions from other communities will not work.
- The first step must be education. Education is needed to develop mutual understanding and trust among divergent interests. Without a level of trust and understanding, it is impossible to sustain the process through the tough mediation phases.

Planning for growth management is best understood as an ongoing process, the essential elements of which are a clear definition of issues, direct communication among divergent interests, and a commitment to action.

Putting Strategic Planning to Practical Use in Cleveland Heights

Richard V. Robinson and Douglas C. Eadie

Strategic planning is the new game in town, and no self-respecting manager wants to be left out of the action. Although it has been developed and applied principally in the for-profit sector over the past quarter-century, strategic planning has recently become the object of considerable attention in the public sector, among both practitioners and academicians. This growing interest is understandable, in light of the tremendous pressure on local government to maintain or enhance services while revenues are shrinking. Traditional planning techniques are not powerful enough to meet today's and tomorrow's public management needs, and strategic planning appears to fill a significant planning vacuum.

Making practical use of strategic planning in government will be no easy task, however. The field is new, rapidly developing, and until recently largely a matter of private sector practice. The literature documenting private sector practice is slim, and hardly exists for government. We only imperfectly understand the factors influencing the successful use of strategic planning in business, and know even less about its applicability in government. All of this is to say that governmental strategic planning is frontier territory — the trails yet to be blazed, and the risks many.

And as if the technical barriers were not enough, public managers must contend with an apparent tendency in the public sector to expect significant short-term results from new management techniques at little cost. Is strategic planning to become in the next few years a powerful tool for enhancing the quality of governmental management, or will it be another oversold panacea, doomed to fade away, the victim of overexpec-

Reprinted with permission from Cities & Villages, *Vol. XXXI, No. 10, October 1983. Published by the Ohio Municipal League, Columbus, Ohio.*

tation and underinvestment? The history of public planning reform should temper our optimism in this regard. Who can forget the sad tale of Planning/Programming/Budgeting? Introduced with tremendous hoopla, aggressively sold by consultants, PPB's day in the sun was all too brief. If the projected benefits were impressive, the costs — largely in human time and effort — were awesome. The result of failure to assess and pay these costs was predictable. Not only were the desired planning outcomes not achieved, but, perhaps worse, the debacle left countless disillusioned managers in its wake.

Over the past year, Cleveland Heights has experimented with the application of strategic planning. Starting with a strong sense of the barriers to successful application and of the risks involved in such trailblazing, we have proceeded at a measured pace within what we perceive to be our resource limits. The results to-date are encouraging and appear to be worth sharing with other local governments searching for more effective approaches to planning. This article describes the Cleveland Heights experience, with focus on those factors that appear to be critical to successful application. Three "golden rules" have emerged from our experience, and will receive considerable attention in the following pages:

- Strategic planning consists of a variety of complex techniques which can be applied in a variety of ways, depending on the needs and circumstances of particular governments. There is no such thing as a standard strategic planning process or system which can simply be installed. Therefore, the government which intends to make serious use of strategic planning will engage in a detailed tailoring process, determining what it wants to get out of strategic planning and utilizing the techniques so as to achieve these results, within its resource limits.
- Strategic planning is not merely an updated, sexier version of traditional umbrella-like master planning, within which (so it is said) "operational" planning is to be done. It is one of several important planning vehicles aimed at achieving particular kinds of planning outcomes, and these planning processes or vehicles do not fit neatly into a unified "system" or hierarchical structure. Strategic planning is likely to be most productive when it is done in the context of an overall planning improvement program addressing the various needed outcomes.
- Strategic planning techniques are highly complex, and cannot be mastered quickly. One of the significant implementation costs is staff training, and considerable practice is required as part of capability-building. This is to say that it's likely to make sense for a government to proceed with application in an incremental fashion, expanding the use of strategic planning as capability is built.

An Introduction to the Field

Strategic planning developed in the for-profit sector in response to the rapidly increasing rate of environmental change during the post–World War Two period. Businesses found that traditional long-range planning techniques — with their heavily internal focus and assumption of stability in the environment — were leaving them highly vulnerable and constantly off-guard. The basic idea of strategic planning is to enable an organization to maintain a balance with its environment which makes the fullest use of organizational resources in responding to opportunities for new business.

Strategic planning as it has developed, then, is oriented toward an organization's wider environment. Also, it has become a conscious tool for large-scale innovation, as contrasted with the control orientation of traditional long-range planning. In practice in the business sector, it is frequently applied in making significant investment decisions, and complex techniques such as portfolio analysis — highly quantitative and financially-focused — have been developed to aid the decision-making process.

Strategies come in all shapes and sizes. There are global, organization-wide strategies describing the basic businesses of an organization; organizational subdivisions can formulate their own strategies within the global framework; and strategies can be developed for particular functions, such as marketing. The process of producing strategies involves the following basic activities:

- Environmental scanning involves identifying pertinent features of an organization's environment — demographic, cultural, social, economic, political, technological, etc. — studying them to determine any trends and implications for the organization, and monitoring changes over time.
- The resource base of the organization — its human, financial, and technological resources — must be inventoried and assessed as a critical element in determining the organization's responses to environmental change. Whether an environmental trend or condition represents an opportunity for an organization obviously depends to a great extent on its resource base. Particular strategies may not be feasible because of inability to secure capital financing or to afford the amount of management training required.
- In practice, a continuous scanning process surfaces possible opportunities (and problems to be averted), and this "intelligence" is evaluated in the context of the organization's resources. Out of this comparative process emerge change targets or objectives and the strategies to implement them. An implementation strategy sets forth the major activities,

accountabilities, schedule, and costs involved in achieving the change target.

As the foregoing capsule description of the process indicates, strategic planning is not a once-a-year, cyclical process that results in a weighty master plan-like tome. The environment changes constantly and just will not oblige us by fitting into a cycle for decision-making purposes. The field appears to be moving away from formality and elaborate documentation and toward informality and flexibility, as a means to facilitate rapid organizational response to environmental change. This is not to say that strategic planning cannot be useful as a point-in-time planning tool; however, its power is likely to be most fully realized through continuous intelligence gathering and highly responsive strategy formulation and adjustment.

The Cleveland Heights Context

Cleveland Heights is a medium-sized city of some 56,000 residents, located in Cleveland's eastern suburbs in Cuyahoga County. A general fund budget of approximately $15 million supports some 450 full-time city employees. A council-manager city with a strong commitment to modern management, Cleveland Heights has twice been designated an All America City — in 1976 and 1978.

In common with most other local governments, annual budget preparation serves as the city's basic planning vehicle. The planning content of budget preparation consists of each department's projecting performance for the coming year along certain key indicators. Also, each department head submits with his or her annual budget request an "annual report" setting forth the major accomplishments for the current year.

Cleveland Heights has not utilized formal long-range planning across the board, but does follow a long-range capital maintenance plan. The Planning and Development Department has focused its efforts largely on the city's physical development, administering the CDBG program, managing several key construction projects, and supporting the work of the Board of Zoning Appeals and Planning Commission.

The city council consists of seven members who traditionally participate very actively in the six standing committees, giving considerable time to the examination of such issues as the construction of two new, state-of-the-art fire stations and the dramatically new Top of the Hill condominium/commercial development. In terms of the planning function, council has participated largely on an issue-by-issue basis, with the exception of the adoption of the annual budget, where council has traditionally focused on review of major expenditure objects after preparation of the budget request. No systematic council attention has been paid to the formulation of long-range goals or priorities, as a framework for operational planning in the city.

Cleveland Heights may be unique in the extent of citizen interest in public issues and participation in community associations. Probably the result of the large proportion of the population engaged in the professions and possessing a college education, this active interest in the affairs of government ensures an openness in the governance process that is surely rare. And, of course, it promotes a high degree of government respon-siveness. Indeed, city employees pride themselves on the closeness of the government to its citizenry.

In general, Cleveland Heights has been a well-managed city, with a commitment to sound planning and management. Its careful fiscal plan-ning has ensured a balanced budget without traumatic cutbacks, and long-range capital planning has resulted in significant infrastructure improve-ments and a timely maintenance program.

The Cleveland Heights
Application of Strategic Planning

In light of the pleasant picture painted above of a well-managed, fiscally sound city, what incentive was there to tackle city planning prac-tices as a serious issue over the past year? We see four main factors com-bining to force explicit attention to strategic planning:

- Significant environmental change certainly signaled the need for externally-oriented planning. Serious economic decline in Cleveland proper combined with a decrease in county population during the 1970s raised serious questions about economic and demographic stability over the long run in Cleveland Heights. More directly, the 1970s saw dramatic demographic change within Cleveland Heights itself. It was during this period that Cleveland Heights became an integrated com-munity which presently has stabilized with a population ratio of 75 per-cent white, 25 percent non-white.
- In November 1982, the report of a City Manager Community Evalua-tion Committee, while generally giving the city government high marks for performance, noted the absence of longer-range planning and the heavy reliance on short-range operational planning and specific issue analysis.
- Council had begun to raise serious questions about its role in city plan-ning, basically expressing dissatisfaction with its limited perspective on issues and its preoccupation with short-range planning. A particular concern was council's tail-end role in annual budget decision-making.

- Finally, the city manager, planning director and other executive staff had themselves reached the conclusion that the future demanded new approaches to planning and had begun to explore the potential of strategic planning.

Emergence of the Cleveland Heights Planning and Management Improvement Program

The city's Planning and Management Improvement Program took shape between January and July 1983. The first major step was the city's entering into an agreement with one of the authors of this article to assist the city manager and his staff in the design and implementation of a strategic planning process for the city. It was originally intended that the January through June period would be devoted to orientation and training for management staff, research on current planning practices of the city, and the development of a design for application of strategic planning, which would be implemented between July and January 1984. It was agreed at the onset that strategic planning would be applied in a highly selective fashion and not as an across-the-board kind of master planning — at least for the first year or so as the city gained practical experience in applying the techniques.

The city's strategic planning consultant conducted several full-day orientation sessions for executive and management staff on the techniques of strategic planning, and in a March session with city council gained council adherence to the basic step-by-step approach to application. That March council meeting represents a milestone in the development of the Planning and Management Improvement Program, in that council members decided that their role in strategic direction setting and long-range goals formulation was inadequately understood, and that until they had clarified their planning role, standing committees could not be fully effective. It was decided that council would participate in a two-day planning retreat with executive staff for the purpose of exploring the planning and policy-making roles and, if possible, reaching agreement on issues meriting the application of strategic planning.

Two basic outcomes of the April 30–May 1 council retreat were: (1) agreement that the council role in annual budget preparation should be stronger, basically through priority-setting and issue identification at the beginning of the process; and (2) the identification of two strategic issues which appeared to merit the immediate application of strategic planning — economic development and the maintenance of an integrated community. Through the use of an external facilitator, the retreat was also an effective forum for working through several other important day-to-day management issues, including communication between council and administration, and the participation of administrators in council deliberations.

During May, the city manager and executive staff, with the assistance of the city's strategic planning consultant, reached agreement on the three major components of what was now formally named the Planning and Management Program:

- Enhancement of city council participation in planning.
- Enhancement of operational planning/budget preparation.
- Application of strategic planning.

It was recognized that these three improvement areas are closely related, with considerable overlap, and that improvements in one of the areas would affect the other two. It was also recognized that a dynamic improvement program should be on-going and not a one-shot deal. This is to say that, even though improvements are to be implemented during the current year in each of the three areas, every succeeding year should see the formulation of an improvements agenda aimed at tailoring the city's planning activities to its needs and circumstances.

The remainder of this article will focus on the implementation of phase-one strategic planning in Cleveland Heights as one of the three basic components of the overall Planning and Management Improvement Program, but first we want to say a final word about the other two areas. With regard to council planning, a highly successful trends and conditions briefing in May made clear the potential of council issue identification as a very important kick-off for annual budget preparation. This May session was, in effect, a pilot test for a full-scale council priority-setting meeting early in 1984 as the first major step in preparation of the city's 1985 budget. At this point, it was agreed that the council component of the overall Improvement Program would be addressed through the other two components since these are the vehicles through which planning took place.

The operational planning/budget preparation component became active in October 1983, when a staff task force was charged to develop recommendations for improvement in the process for preparing the 1985 city budget. The task force was asked to address in detail such issues as the council role, the enhancement of the planning content in budget requests, and the relationship of operational to strategic planning.

First-Phase Strategic Planning

In May and June, three major foundation stones were laid for the first-phase application of strategic planning: (1) issue identification; (2) structure/process definition; and (3) provision of adequate staff resources to support the effort. As was noted above, council's broad scan of the environment at the retreat had identified economic development and integration maintenance as critical issues to be addressed, and this was confirmed in the later trends and conditions meeting. In making the detailed plans for the first-phase application, the executive staff confirmed that the two issues identified by council were appropriate for the application of strategic planning. Each issue satisfied the rough criteria suggested by the city's consultant: important in terms of benefits (including the cost of not addressing it); a highly complex, changing environment; and the necessary involvement of several city departments, as well as outside organizations, in addressing it. In other words, it was determined that the issues were not only very important to the well-being of the city, but also that they could not be handled through the traditional annual operational planning/budget preparation process.

The strategic planning portfolio was clearly assigned to the Planning and Development Department, with the planning director designated as the officer-in-charge of both the overall Planning and Management Improvement Program and the strategic planning component. A briefly considered alternative was to house strategic planning in the manager's office, but it was agreed that this would impede the development of the planning function in the city. Indeed the planning director and his senior staff had enthusiastically supported the application of strategic planning since its earliest consideration by the city.

The strategic planning was to be done largely in-house, by two interdepartmental staff task forces of between 10 and 15 members, each headed by a senior executive. The strategic planning consultant was to provide ongoing technical assistance to each of the task forces, but not to do the actual planning. At key points in the process, the consultant has served as a facilitator at task force meetings.

The need for high level staff support for this very ambitious undertaking was resolved by the appointment of a strategic planning manager in the Planning and Development Department. In addition to the provision of research assistance, the manager is responsible for such staff support as the scheduling of task force meetings, preparation of task force agendas, and maintenance of a record of deliberations.

The two task forces devoted a half-day weekly during July and early August in laying the foundation for strategy formulation:

- The pertinent environmental factors in each strategic issue area were identified, considerable data collected for each factor, and implications for the city identified.
- A resource analysis was completed for each issue area, basically identifying all city government activity having a bearing on the issue.

- A beginning was made in the identification of issues — apparent problems or opportunities — which might become targets for "attack" through detailed strategy formulation.

The first week in September, each task force met for a full day, with the planning consultant serving as facilitator, in order to develop a firm list of strategic issues and targets. As this article was being written, subcommittees of the two task forces were engaged in detailed analysis of each of the targets and the formulation of implementation strategies for each target. Each task force met again for a full day in late September to review and revise the implementation strategies, after which they were reviewed with council in a retreat setting. Meanwhile, council was briefed in detail in late September on the environmental scan and resource analysis, and the strategic issues which have been identified were introduced. It was anticipated that council would share any major concerns it had at that point relative to the strategy formulation process and that it would agree to participate in the detailed strategy review process at a November or December retreat.

In Conclusion

While Cleveland Heights is in the midst of its first-phase test of strategic planning, and the final results are not yet in, substantial benefits have already been realized, and the prospects of a highly successful test are excellent. At this stage in the Planning and Management Improvement Program, we are convinced that we have a workable framework for making major practical improvements in the city's planning without engaging in grandiose and expensive efforts.

Through work on the two task forces, staff have a far stronger grasp of the issues involved in two areas of immense importance to the future of Cleveland Heights, not to speak of their grasp of a powerful set of planning techniques. And the emerging strategic dialogue at the council level has already both enhanced the council role in planning and improved council-administration relations.

Although there remain miles to go, what matters is that we have chosen the right road. Above all, our planning aims have been set in terms of what we can feasibly expect to do *ourselves* with only relatively modest use of external technical assistance. Regardless of the detailed outcomes of this initial effort, a foundation now exists for grappling with complex planning issues in the years to come.

Clifton Prepares for the 1990s — The Future Vision Project

Roger L. Kemp

Introduction

Back in November of 1988, Clifton's municipal council approved the city's participation in the Future Vision Project, sponsored by the International City Management Association (ICMA). The purpose of this project was to identify ways to track key trends impacting local governments, to select major issues facing a municipality, and to develop workable strategies to better plan for the future.

In order to develop sound projections and trends for the city, the resources of the Planning Association of North Jersey (based in Clifton) were called upon to assist the city in this future planning project. Key trends impacting the municipality were researched, documented, and projected for the coming decade. They included employment trends, business trends, housing trends, land use and zoning trends, and population trends. The facts upon which these projections were based were gathered from existing public documents available from the municipal, state, and federal governments.

The city's department managers were then asked to identify key trends and issues facing their respective service area for the 1990s. Each department manager was then asked to identify the single most important issue facing their department during the coming decade. The results of this research effort were subsequently assembled and published as the *Future Vision Report: Projections, Trends, and Issues Facing Clifton in the 1990s*.

This report was designed to serve three general purposes. One, to inform elected and appointed officials of the major projections, trends, and

Reprinted with permission from New Jersey Municipalities, *Vol. 69, No. 3, March 1991. Published by the New Jersey State League of Municipalities, Trenton, New Jersey.*

issues facing the city during the 1990s. Two, to provide information to assist them as they make major decisions impacting the city's future. Three, to serve as a starting point for future strategic planning efforts within Clifton. Once an agreement has been reached on the major issues facing the city, the issues will be delegated to the appropriate city boards, commissions, and departments, to develop and implement successful strategies to deal with those major issues facing the municipality during the coming decade.

The major projections and trends developed as a result of this planning process, the key departmental issues identified by department managers, and the significant city-wide issues impacting Clifton in the future, are highlighted below.

Projections and Trends

Employment Trends

- The composition of the city's workforce is changing from manufacturing to white-collar, reflecting new jobs in service industries such as insurance, real estate, and finance.
- With the decline in manufacturing jobs, an increasing number of citizens will have to seek employment outside the city in future years.
- There is an increasing number of females in the workforce. This will create a need for full-time childcare for pre-school children, and before and after school care for older children.
- The greater availability of public mass transit, and regional park-and-ride locations, will make it easier for citizens to work elsewhere in the future.

Business Trends

- The number of manufacturing jobs will continue to decline in the future. An additional 20 percent decline is expected by the year 2015.
- An increasing number of females in the workforce will place greater demands in the future for full-time childcare, and related domestic services.
- The greater number of females in the workforce will create more two-income families, creating additional family income and purchasing power per household.
- With more working families, additional services will be needed in the future to accommodate this trend, creating demands to expand services provided in the local economy.

- The local development community is increasingly being influenced by regional housing and financing trends.

Housing Trends

- The city has an aging housing stock. By the year 2000, 85 percent of the existing housing stock will be over 40 years old. The need for comprehensive code enforcement will increase in future years.
- Since the city is basically built-out residentially, there will be increased pressure for multiple-family dwelling units in the future, such as apartments, townhouses, and condominiums.
- The availability of affordable housing is decreasing, placing greater demands in the future for assistance to low and moderate income families.
- A high proportion of senior citizens will result in the turnover of the existing housing stock in the future to non-seniors. Smaller affordable residential units will let seniors remain in the city.
- Increased residential development pressures will place greater demands for "high-rise" type development. Stricter zoning standards may be needed in the future to maintain low-density development.

Land Use and Zoning Trends

- Older industrial zones are being changed to accommodate newer commercial and residential land uses. This trend will continue in the future.
- The city is primarily built-out, creating future residential development pressures to build on smaller sized lots and marginal properties.
- With increased development pressures, and a limited amount of available land, there will be a greater emphasis in the future on acquiring open space and recreational areas for the public.
- As pressure mounts to retrofit older industrial sites to more modern uses, additional creative development standards will be needed in the future.

Population Trends

- Almost all residentially zoned land in the city has been developed. This will place future restrictions on population growth in the future.
- Any significant population changes in the future will come from the expansion of existing household sizes (i.e., as "empty-nesters" are replaced by younger, growing families).
- While future population changes will be minor, they will reflect a greater number of younger children, placing greater demands on the public school system.

- The city can expect an increasing number of smaller households created by smaller family units and one person households.

Departmental Issues

Administration

- There will be fewer federal and state grants, leaving cities to solve their own problems and issues with local funding.
- Any new federal funds will be limited to programs that help achieve national goals, such as affordable housing, shelters for the homeless, etc.
- In order to decrease their reliance on the property tax, local governments will be forced to increase user fees and charges to cover their costs.
- The public, as well as special interest groups, will continue to demand more services, but be opposed to increased taxation.
- There will be a greater use of new technologies and labor-saving devices to help hold down operating costs.

Assessing

- The redevelopment of older industrial areas into residential uses will help bring in new ratables and place more demands on existing public services.
- A possible increase in mortgage rates will have a dampening impact on the real estate market, creating a possible decline in future real estate values.
- Continuing property tax increases will have a negative impact on fixed-income citizens. Some form of state-wide relief is needed for these taxpayers.
- More state laws are envisioned in the area of local assessment practices, further eroding the homerule powers of local governments.
- As county, municipal, and school budgets increase in the future, the number of appeals will escalate accordingly.

Community Development

- A greater emphasis will be placed on creating safer neighborhoods through the use of environmental design techniques, as opposed to hiring additional police officers.
- Both the number and funding for federal housing programs are decreasing, placing greater financial burden on cities to maintain these programs.

- The cost of complying with state and federal environmental laws will be passed along to consumers, adding to the already high cost of housing.
- The rezoning of industrial land to residential uses, due to escalating land values, will increasingly require residents to work outside of the city, placing additional burdens on existing roadways.
- As the housing stock continues to age, greater code enforcement demands will be placed on homeowners to maintain their properties.

Finance

- Regional job market conditions, and increasing unemployment, could have a negative impact on the ability of taxpayers to absorb rising property taxes.
- The impact of state-mandated programs, without state reimbursement, will place a greater financial burden on existing municipal budgets.
- Infrastructure requirements are escalating and, due to limited local funding, may hamper the development of future properties, decreasing ratables.
- The use of high technology items, such as microcomputers, will be required to hold down rising personnel costs.
- In order to save funds, local governments will increasingly pursue joint purchasing arrangements for common products and services.

Fire

- The number of fire incidents should decline due to new construction technologies, improved building codes, and more fire-safety inspections.
- Due to an aging population, fire personnel will increasingly become involved in ambulance and emergency medical services to better serve the community.
- The importance of hazardous waste planning and management will increase due to the escalating costs of disposing of such materials.
- As older industrial sites are redeveloped into multiple family dwelling units, this higher building density will impact services and the type of equipment used for fire suppression.
- Future budgetary constraints may require the consolidation of neighborhood fire stations and the reallocation of existing fire equipment.

Health

- State and federal funds for health services continue to decrease, placing a greater financial burden on local governments to perform these services.

- Higher levels of government continue to mandate health-related programs and services without reimbursement, which will raise municipal taxes.
- An aging population will create greater demands for more specialized health programs for senior citizens and disabled persons.
- Increased interdepartment coordination will be needed to control the health programs created by the illegal dumping and spills of hazardous materials.
- Due to limited revenues, it may be necessary to contract out certain health services to the private sector, decreasing our control over these programs.

Legal

- The state and federal government continues to enact more laws and regulations impacting the affairs of local government.
- Because of the increase in the number of laws inpacting cities, a greater amount of litigation can be expected.
- The field of municipal laws is becoming more specialized, which will require more advanced training in new areas of municipal law.
- Due to the complexity of labor agreements, and the greater number of labor-related cases and appeals, the workload in this area will increase.
- As society becomes more litigious in nature, a greater number of lawsuits can be expected against the city and its public officials.

Police

- In order to keep the city a safe place in which to live and work, more commercial areas and neighborhoods will request walking patrols.
- Due to the high cost of refuse disposal, increased litter and debris in public rights-of-way will require additional patrols to cite offenders.
- The computerization of police operations and records will reduce the need for additional clerical personnel in the future.
- In order to provide additional services, without more police officers, the department will have to acquire the latest police-related technology.
- Increases in the population, and more motor vehicles per household, will require additional traffic enforcement.

Public Works

- There will be a greater deterioration of the public infrastructure without adequate grant funds and other revenue sources to perform this work.

- The decrease in state and federal grants for infrastructure development will force cities to bond for these capital projects.
- The increase in refuse collection costs will require the city to explore other collection options, such as less frequent pickups and charging for other services.
- The "off-site" impacts of development will require new developer charges for such items as traffic control, and provisions for more sewer and water capacity.
- An increased workload, without additional staffing, will require the greater use of new technologies and other labor-saving equipment.

Recreation

- The trend towards a shorter work week in the private sector will create more leisure time, placing greater demands on existing parks and recreational facilities.
- The redevelopment of older industrial areas to residential uses will create a greater demand for additional recreational and park services.
- There will be an expansion of independent sports leagues in the city, placing a heavier burden on existing public parks and ballfields.
- The increased use of microcomputers will help the department to better serve the public by facilitating course scheduling and ballfield assignments.
- Greater innovations and creative ideas will be required to maintain services due to limited grant and private sector funding sources.

City-Wide Issues

Municipal Revenues

- Decreasing revenues from higher levels of government, and citizen opposition to increased taxes, will require the increased use of user fees and charges in the future to help finance services.

Aging Population

- An aging population will require the future expansion of emergency medical and ambulance services. Modern building technologies, and stricter codes, should make time available to expand these services.

Older Industrial Areas

- The redevelopment of older industrial areas will increase the population and place greater demands on services in the future. New revenue sources, outside of raising property taxes, should be sought to finance these services.

Health Services

- State and federal funds for health services have been substantially reduced. New revenue sources must be acquired in order to maintain high quality health services to the public in the future.

Hazardous Wastes

- Due to the problem of disposing of hazardous wastes, a greater number of illegal spills and dumpings will occur in the future. A comprehensive Hazardous Materials Enforcement Program will be needed to mitigate this situation.

Juvenile Services

- Greater interdepartmental coordination will be needed in the future (e.g., police, fire, health, housing, and recreation) to help combat substance abuse and related juvenile social problems.

Public Infrastructure

- There will be a greater deterioration of the infrastructure in the future without adequate funding sources for needed improvements. New funding sources will be necessary for this purpose.

Parks and Playgrounds

- Parks and playgrounds are aging and will be in need of major renovations and repairs in the future. A master plan will be required to guide park and playground development and renovations.

The Future

Too often, government planning is reactive, short range, staff oriented, and dominated by single (and typically organizational) issues.

New thinking is needed in times of fewer grant programs, complex and interrelated issues, rising expectations regarding services, and a greater public aversion to increased taxation. A longer planning timeframe will enable cities to optimize their human and financial resources. For these reasons, it is imperative that public officials provide a strategic vision for their community.

A shared understanding of issues and goals facing a community not only provides a vision of the future, but also helps mobilize all available resources to effectively manage change. One of the basic assumptions of any future planning effort is that the issues selected are unique to each individual community, and that ways to deal with these issues must be adapted to each community's local political environment and administrative structure. Such a community planning effort helps to restore the public's confidence in their local government — the level of government closest to the people.

Duarte's Resurgence — Strategic Planning for the Year 2007

Jesse H. Duff and John K. Parker

Can smaller cities benefit from using strategic planning approaches like those employed in larger cities? The city of Duarte, California, population 21,000, would answer with an emphatic "yes!"

Located in the heart of the San Gabriel Valley in the dynamic Los Angeles region, Duarte is largely a built-up city bounded by the mountains, the San Gabriel River, and the 210/605 freeways.

In the spring of 1987, the city had substantially completed a 10-year redevelopment program that demonstrated that visionary action could significantly improve the community. Duarte's city council and staff were convinced that long-range planning was necessary if the city was to continue to improve and prosper.

With council encouragement, the city manager presented a work plan for a strategic planning project titled "Duarte Resurgence," with the year 2007 chosen as the planning horizon. The council unanimously approved the work plan and a project budget of $15,000 to defray the costs of meetings, expert speakers, consulting facilitation, printing, and communications.

In approving the project, the council identified five major issue areas for attention: (1) municipal services and public safety; (2) education, culture, and recreation; (3) economic development; (4) environment and aesthetics; and (5) health and medical services.

Careful attention was given to the organization of the project. The city council served as the policy body, with a steering committee responsible to it for the conduct of the project. Steering committee membership included the project's general chairperson and vice-chairperson, a liaison

Reprinted with permission from Public Management, *Vol. 71, No. 3, March 1989. Published by the International City Management Association, Washington, D.C.*

149

member from the city council, the city manager, and the chairperson of each of the five task forces that were to address the major issues. Also participating as nonvoting members were the project coordinator (an assistant to the city manager), senior city staff members assigned to each task force, and the superintendent of schools.

Membership of the steering committee linked it not only to city government but also to other important community organizations. The president of the school board and the president of the chamber of commerce served as task force chairpersons and thus also served on the steering committee.

Duarte is strongly committed to effective citizen participation. To this end, the city mailed a flier to every household, describing the strategic planning process and inviting applications to serve on one of the five task forces. More than 70 citizens responded and were appointed by the council to serve on the task forces.

While task forces were being formed, the steering committee prepared mission statements to provide general guidance to each task force. It also held a public forum, attended by about 100 people, to solicit public views on specific issues to be addressed in the strategic planning process. The steering committee then developed the initial list of issues to be studied by each task force.

In January 1988, the city council sponsored a general orientation and "kickoff" meeting for all task force members and city staff. The entire process of strategic planning was explained at the meeting, roles and responsibilities were defined, and guest speakers gave presentations on successful strategic planning efforts in other cities.

Project participants were provided with an "environmental scan" prepared by city staff, which summarized trends that were shaping the city, including regional as well as local factors. Task forces, each with an average of 14 members, were given the environmental scan, a mission statement, and a list of initial issues to address. They were permitted to add specific issues as their work progressed.

Meeting frequently over a period of two months, task forces analyzed external factors that presented threats or opportunities to the community in their assigned issue areas and identified relevant community strengths and weaknesses. They then developed goals, which were reviewed by the steering committee for consistency among the task forces. The task forces proceeded to identify strategies for achieving the goals; for each of the strategic courses of action, they developed recommended initial actions to be taken by the city, the schools, the chamber of commerce, or other organizations.

Beginning in March 1988, the steering committee worked closely with the task forces to synthesize a draft report containing the external and internal analyses, goals, and strategies for each of the 34 issues important to Duarte's future.

The draft strategic plan was provided to the press and made available to the public prior to holding two public forums, or "town hall meetings," on the draft. More than 200 people attended the public forums and generally were highly supportive of the draft strategic plan. In several instances, citizens pointed out unintended conflicts and ambiguities in the draft.

The steering committee revised the draft plan on the basis of the public comments; it presented the final recommended strategic plan to the city council in June 1988, 11 months after the council had approved the project.

The recommendations in the strategic plan will serve as a policy guide to decisions of the city, the schools, and the chamber of commerce in the years ahead. Strategies address a wide variety of action areas, including improvements such as

- A comprehensive disaster preparedness program
- An improved street and transportation system
- Expanded child care
- An expanded parks program
- Modernization of school facilities
- A dropout prevention program
- Maximum joint use of city and school facilities
- Increased low-to-moderate-income housing
- Upgrading of deteriorated housing
- More retail establishments to serve residents
- Increased senior housing
- An expanded program of cultural events
- Reduced noise pollution
- A solid-waste recycling program
- An improved water supply
- A health resources referral system

The city council is committed to using the strategic plan as a guide over the years to come. It will be an important source of information and direction in the update of the city's general plan soon to take place and will be a starting point for future redevelopment projects in the city. The annual budget process of the city and the schools provides another important means of implementation action on the recommended strategies. The strong citizen participation, both on task forces and in the public forums, provides a substantial consensus and base of support for the vision and recommendations of Duarte Resurgence. At the same time, it is recognized that the passage of time and unexpected events may make certain strategies and recommended actions inappropriate. Thus, the city council and other policy bodies must use, as always, their best judgment in adapting the strategic plan to changing realities.

The strategic planning approach employed by the city of Duarte offers a straightforward model that can be easily adapted by other cities, both large and small. It provides for a high level of citizen participation, while allowing for necessary guidance and quality control through the careful organization of the steering committee, which coordinated the work of the task forces. The work plan that guided the project formed a sound basis for informing all participants of the process and their responsibilities.

The city of Duarte now has a vision and a plan to guide it over the coming years, so that it need not merely react to events but can be proactive in creating a more prosperous, beautiful, and humane community.

Strategic Planning in Hampton — Choices and Challenges

Sandy Weir

Hampton lives in a much more complex world today than the world of 1975. Ten years ago was before Proposition 13, before the recession of the late 1970s, and revenue to Hampton from federal resources was increasing. The trends set in the prosperous 1960s continued. The logical future of Hampton, determined by past and present conditions, was a bright future. Although city government participated in Hampton's development to some extent, Hampton would have been a prosperous community with very little local government control or intervention.

In 1975, there were more opportunities than constraints associated with Hampton's physical development. The maturing of the city from a suburban to an urban community was marked by the construction of two regional shopping malls and the city's first high-rise office building. Still, there was plenty of land available to build neighborhoods that were not threatened by highway noise or the risk of severe flooding.

Since 1975, the rules by which Hampton city government must operate have changed; not only are we subject to new economic and demographic trends, but we are caught in some fluctuating situations in which no trend is apparent. For example, Hampton has faced cuts in federal revenues and shifts in the economic impact of our federal installations. Many of our key facilities and businesses are not in the best locations with respect to our transportation network. In the middle of a housing construction boom more of our citizens than ever before cannot afford to buy their own homes.

Hampton lives in a competitive world. Other localities are electing to

Reprinted with permission from Planning in Virginia, *Vol. 2, No. 1, January 1986. Published by the Virginia Chapter, American Planning Association, Charlottesville, Virginia.*

compete with us, which compels us to respond to the competition in some way.

In 1985, we cannot assume that our logical future is a bright future, even though we have much reason for optimism. If we want to bring about a willed future, we must make the deliberate choices it requires. Strategic planning offers us the tools we need to describe and act upon our vision.

Background

American corporations have used formal strategic planning since the 1950s. The methods began to be borrowed by local governments in the late 1970s. Corporations have learned from their generation of experience with strategic planning and their methods have changed accordingly. Hampton has paid attention to both strategic planning theory and practice as we have created our process.

Hampton's commitment to strategic planning has its roots in city council's annual goals-setting process. In 1982, Hampton city council formerly solicited public opinion on appropriate citywide goals in a series of forums with three targeted groups of leaders in commerce, industry, and civic/social organizations. Six goals were selected in 1982 with the intent that programs be set in motion to achieve the goals over the next five years. Town meetings, held periodically, contribute to revising the goals. City council's process has been very similar to the goals-setting step in the strategic planning process. It was done, however, without benefit of some of the earlier phases of strategic planning whose importance should become clear below.

Many projects in Hampton have been pursued strategically without reference to a formalized process. The construction of the Hampton Coliseum in 1969 was an important example of the city as entrepreneur and risk-taker. Currently, Old Hampton waterfront development includes construction of a Radisson Hotel and other facilities: it is [a] joint venture between the public and private sectors. Other projects in Old Hampton include an office tower, luxury townhouses, five retail/office buildings, and two commercial malls.

Capturing such large-scale development all at the same time required the city to find the market sector appropriate for its waterfront, within the Hampton Roads Area's six urban waterfront areas. In addition, the timing of the project was crucial; Hampton anticipated the opening of a bridge to provide improved access from Interstate 64 into the area and had a coherent plan ready before fragmented development could occur.

The level of city commitment to strategic planning can be gauged by its location in the Hampton city organization. The city manager designated one of three assistant city managers to head the project team. A senior city planner and several support staff members are assigned to the project full-time.

The strategic planning concept is new to most Hamptonians within and outside City Hall, so the project manager frequently repeats this concise definition of strategic planning to staff members: The strategic planning process will define the city's identity, or the business that we are in. The strategic plan will then describe how to concentrate limited resources into a few selected areas, confronting threats and capitalizing on opportunities, in order to gain a competitive advantage.

A strategic plan done in a city can be a plan for the city government institution, a plan for the whole community (public and private sectors), or a blend. Hampton's product will be a plan for the whole community, with city government taking the lead role. The philosophy of the city as we seek community participation is described well by this summary of what entrepreneurial officials do: "[Officials are] bringing together an informed, committed and enthusiastic public with private leaders to accomplish both traditional and non-traditional results." (Duckworth)

Our background information on strategic planning is of two types. Our applied strategic planning literature includes plans from other cities, case studies of the process, articles about corporate strategic planning, and handbooks for public sector strategic planning. Formalized corporate strategic planning has been widespread since the 1950s, so its methods have evolved during that generation of experience. Some of the most important lessons are:

First, line managers must be involved throughout the process if they are to claim ownership of the plan. Second, there should be a limit to the amount of information gathered and its quantification, but however much time is necessary should be dedicated to understanding Hampton's current identity in a metropolitan and national context. Third, while it may seem more exciting to seek new, innovative actions for Hampton, it is just as important to exert control to keep strong areas strong and turn weak ones into strong ones. Fourth, the plan document should be short.

A focus on decision-making techniques is a vital part of strategic planning because we will make decisions at several points in the process; some decisions will allocate many of the city's resources to one project at the expense of another. While ultimate authority will rest with the city council, the strategic planning process includes decisions recommended by many participants.

The Strategic Plan Issues

The standard strategic planning model calls for an initial assessment of where the city is right now with respect to the outside world—how we compare with other places and how we are influenced by external actions. This environmental assessment should make problems obvious. While we are doing an environmental scan in Hampton, our background research, described above, has enabled us to predefine issue categories. These are:

> Economic Development
> Local Government Effectiveness
> Infrastructure and Urban Design
> Shifts in Revenue Sources
> Quality of Life
> Housing
> Transportation
> Demographics
> Land Use
> Education
> Technology
> Environmental Quality and Energy Conservation

The first five areas are similar to the subjects of city council goals. The next four are concerns of the Comprehensive Plan. The education category reflects the close working relationship between city government and the school division, which has undertaken its own goal-setting process. Finally, technology, environmental quality and energy conservation could be of strategic importance to Hampton. Predefining issue categories helps us to gather and filter much data about relatively few subjects. Of course, as the final handful of issues is selected, categories may shift.

An example of an issue within the quality of life category is defining the best uses for Hampton's waterfront. We are blessed with a large proportion of Virginia's Chesapeake Bay/Hampton Road shoreline, but its use is limited by factors ranging from jellyfish visitation to tourists' perceptions to limited transportation access for the more remote areas. Current advantages related to the issue are Hampton's reputation as a seafood capital, a sailing and powerboating center, the success of Hampton Bay Days festivals, and the fact that the waterfront is Hampton's most scenic resource.

In the category of housing, there are several problems. First, Hampton is receiving less than a proportionate regional share of high-valued housing. In our market, high-valued housing is generally very low density, single-family housing. If we should try to attract more of such housing, we need to consider its land use implications. Second, suddenly more than half of Hampton's housing stock is over twenty years old. Maintenance problems associated with an aging housing stock can be expected. We have much experience in housing rehabilitation programs so we are prepared to deal with the problem, but federal government support of housing rehabilitation is dwindling. Third, the general trend for new housing is to build at higher densities than existing housing. Our challenge is to make such housing acceptable to the single-family home neighborhoods that will surround it.

Comprehensive Planning and Strategic Planning

Hampton's current project is a combination of a comprehensive plan update and a strategic plan. The blend of processes and products should assure that the goals, strategies, and programs of each are compatible. The processes are, however, contradictory in some ways, so the blend is awkward at times.

The chart summarizes the difference between the processes; a few points merit expansion. The lack of time dependence in strategic planning means that, rather than setting out a schedule for implementation, we describe the correct timing of an action based upon certain conditions that must be present. We look for "windows of opportunity."

Contrasts Between Processes

Strategic Plan	Comprehensive Plan
1. Selective	1. Comprehensive
2. Any city issue eligible	2. Physical Development plan only
3. City within environmental context	3. City within its own boundaries
4. Not time dependent	4. 10 to 25 year time frame
5. Process follows through to specific actions	5. Process partly implemented by Capital Improvement Program, zoning actions; sometimes implementation set out clearly
6. Large participation city governmentwide and throughout community	6. Largely limited to Planning Department, Planning Commission, and public hearings

The comprehensiveness of comprehensive planning includes mapping the entire city for several purposes to indicate the locations of land uses, facilities, and so forth. Such mapping could be extraneous to the purposes of strategic planning — the mapping of the characteristics of a large residential neighborhood might illustrate no issue of strategic planning importance to the city.

The strategic planning process calls for specific actions to be described, with their funding requirements. Those people who must carry out the plan help write it and thus should identify with it. Both of these points should make it more likely that Hampton's combined plan will be a "living document" rather than a typical comprehensive plan.

But what happens when the two processes have clearly divergent objectives? We are going to consider the strategic plan as the focus of the project — as much as possible, those issues that come from the comprehensive plan tradition will be handled strategically. Sometimes, though, important information for legal and record-keeping purposes has appeared only in the comprehensive plan. We cannot afford to ignore this information, even if it is not of strategic importance. We will simply prepare an additional comprehensive plan document to contain such information.

Schedule

The city began the strategic planning process in September 1985 with a target completion month of October 1986. The sequence of steps follows:

First, environmental assessment and issue identification;

Second, broad goal setting and determination of critical success factors;

Third, external and internal analysis of strengths and weaknesses of the community and other entities with whom Hampton is closely associated;

Fourth, setting goals, objectives, and strategies;

Fifth, development of an action/implementation plan that harnesses the community's talents both inside and outside City Hall;

Sixth, adoption of the Strategic Plan.

Throughout the process and after adoption of the document, decision makers will view options whose selection will depend upon the situation. An one-time, single-minded plan would not reflect political realities and the need for a periodic review of strategies. Therefore, both the information base and the format of discussions will encourage the examination of questions such as:

What business is the city in? What should it be in? To whom does it provide services? Who is paying for it? Who should pay for it?

What would be the effects on the city of capturing many new start-up companies, versus headquarters of small corporations or regional offices of large corporations? In what ways should we compete with neighboring communities? In what ways should we cooperate?

How should city government be organized, if we are to concentrate on social services, recreation, or education?

How can the city best work with the major federal installations and Newport News Shipbuilding Company as the activities of these large institutions change?

In the fourth step and following it, potential strategies should be developed with these questions in mind:

- Is the strategy consistent with the findings of the environmental assessment?
- Does it facilitate concentrating the community's and organization's resources on a few critical issues?
- Is it consistent with the resources available and the competence of the organization?
- Will it have community support and satisfy community expectations?
- Is the chosen level of risk realistic?

Many small-group discussions of the plan will take place, in a variety of formats. A task force of key city employees will meet during each step of the process. They will review the core staff's work before it is forwarded to the city manager, to the Planning Commission, or to city council. Focus groups, one for each major issue, will meet during the fourth step with personnel from business, civic and neighborhood leadership as well as city staff.

The kickoff to public participation was the retrospective event that ended Hampton's year-long celebration of our 375th Anniversary.

A narrated slide presentation identified the strategic issues and summaries of problems, threats, and opportunities associated with them. The basis of the narration was a discussion among Hampton's elder statesmen — the Mayors and city managers who have served the city since 1960.

The dedicated city residents who had produced the 375th Anniversary celebration and other invited leaders in commerce, industry, and civic groups attended the event. Because of the anniversary, citizens had spent an extraordinary amount of time reviewing Hampton's heritage and were in a unique position to know the historical context from which we face the future. It was a fortunate coincidence to be able to introduce a strategic plan at such a time.

Conclusion

It was at a previous event of the 375th Anniversary, the "Celebration of the Spirit," that it became clear that the strategic planning process is especially well suited to selecting a course of action, tackling each of its components, and, finally, completing the mission. Many historical and religious readings stressed the importance of faith, diligence, and connectedness. A reading from the Koran commanded: "Whenever thou are free, prosecute diligently the task." Strategic planning helps the city see the extent of our freedom to choose, to then define our task, and to carry it out to create a better Hampton.

Strategic Planning in Hennepin County — An Issues Management Approach

Philip C. Eckhert, Kathleen Haines,
Timothy J. Delmont, and Ann M. Pflaum

Strategic planning has become an increasingly useful approach to public sector management. Elected and appointed government officials have adopted techniques of strategic planning from the private sector chiefly to better anticipate emerging public needs and "to govern with foresight" (Eadie and Olsen 1982; Foresight Task Force 1983; Nanus 1984).

While styles of strategic planning have differed (Taylor 1984; Bryson et al. 1986), one activity has become an essential component of nearly all approaches: the assessment of emerging trends and concomitant issues likely to influence future planning and management decision making (Wilson 1983; Renfro and Morrison 1983; Delmont and Pflaum 1985). The term *issues management* has been applied to an integrated, often sequential set of actions involving the monitoring, analysis, reporting, and preparation of action responses to critical issues and trends (Zentner 1981; Chase 1984; Ashley 1985). These issue management activities have been integrated into the strategic planning processes of selected organizations (Dutton et al. 1983; Lozier and Chittipeddi 1985).

In adopting an issues management form of strategic planning, Hennepin County, Minnesota, has developed a process to identify and resolve issues having broad, countywide significance over the next three to five years. This chapter offers a description and analysis of the county's

Reprinted with permission from John M. Bryson and Robert C. Einsweiler, Editors, Strategic Planning: Threats and Opportunities for Planners, *1988. Published by the Planners Press, American Planning Association, Chicago, Illinois.*

planning process, one which we believe is a significant initiative because it (1) involves the pragmatic application of an innovative form of strategic planning, (2) uses a planning approach that encourages professional managers as well as elected officials to collaborate in policy and decision-making processes, (3) presents a systematic approach for developing quality public services in an era of limited resource growth, and (4) provides an example of one of the few strategic planning efforts successfully introduced in a large-scale local government entity; that is, a strategic planning initiative covering all departments, all functions, and all levels of service. The county's present efforts offer possible lessons for the improvement of planning practice to professional managers, planners, and elected officials in many levels of government.

The issues management approach the county developed consisted of three major phases:

1. The identification of strategic issues.
2. The preparation and analysis of alternative strategies to address each issue.
3. The development of plans to carry out strategies.

This chapter deals with all phases of the planning process. Section one identifies the factors leading to the adoption of this strategic planning initiative. Section two describes the issues management approach in detail and the county's process of implementation from 1983 to 1986. Section three offers an analysis of the effectiveness of the issues management process. Section four presents conclusions to the study.

This case study methodology involved two procedures: (1) initial in-depth as well as follow-up interviews with a cross section of 14 county board members, managers, and planners who have been consistently involved in the planning effort, and (2) a comprehensive review of all pertinent planning documents and materials prepared in the process.

Factors Leading to Strategic Planning

Hennepin County, the most populous and urbanized county in Minnesota, serves nearly one million residents in a geographic area covering 611 square miles. Its FY 1986 budget of $681 million — the largest among local government agencies in the state — provides residents with a broad range of health, social service, court, corrections, educational, transportation, library, financial, and licensing services.

Hennepin County government grew rapidly in the 1960s and 1970s, its budget increasing in real terms an average of 6 percent per year. Growth of federal and state revenues as well as the local property tax base permitted the concurrent development of many new programs and the expansion of traditional services. Much of the county's emphasis during this period was on managing growth and planning and guiding development.

The 1980s have produced a clearly different environment for the county. Service needs and demands have continued to grow, while revenue increases have not matched the local rate of inflation. Federal and state funding have decreased dramatically but statutory mandates to provide services have not been reduced. Management's challenge has been to find creative ways to ensure the provision of quality services in an era characterized by continuing cost increases and stable or declining revenues. That task has been complicated further by the emergence of a growing number of complex issues which require multiyear planning and implementation schedules, often also involving the development of public/private sector partnerships (e.g., health care delivery systems, maintenance of water quality standards, long-term care for the elderly).

Because of this changing environment, in fall 1983 the county administrator and planning staff — the Office of Planning Development — developed a strategic planning process for application across county departments. While the county board did not formally endorse the proposed process at this time, many of its members encouraged the county administrator to introduce the process as quickly as possible. Among the reasons for doing so were the following:

1. To improve the effectiveness of county services by "doing more with less, doing things better."[1] Because of increasing complaints about local property tax rates, the county board and many top-level administrators felt the need to provide demonstrably cost-effective services to the county's constituents and taxpayers. Improved effectiveness, they reasoned, would follow from an assessment of future directions and service options.
2. To improve budget planning. The short-term focus of the annual budget cycle often precluded a careful examination of the long-range implications and consequences of funding decisions. Moreover, in retrenchment periods across-the-board rather than selective budget cuts associated with countywide priorities usually had been emphasized.
3. To develop a systematic approach for investigating alternative policy and program choices, many of which were growing more difficult and controversial as the county's external environment changed.
4. To anticipate and better understand significant issues that were

likely to affect county services and performance (e.g., as one respondent suggested, "To get a hold of issues before they became political issues."[2]).

5. To find a method for integrating planning and policymaking functions across county departments and programs. Many significant issues were interdepartmental in nature and needed to be addressed in an integrated and cooperative fashion.

6. To focus the attention of the board and top management on priority program and fiscal strategies that required formal board approval.

Implementation of the Issues Management Approach in Hennepin County

The county defined strategic issues as fundamental policy questions having long-term service and funding implications for county operations. For the most part, these issues were not current problems or crisis situations, nor were they simply or quickly resolved. (See Table 1.) Their effective resolution typically involved decisions "on the nature of the services provided, to whom, by which methods, at what cost, and how financed and managed."[3]

The strategic issues arose from conflicts among three essential factors:

1. County policy objectives (the things the county *wanted* to accomplish in terms of service, financial, or management objectives).

2. Service mandates (the things that *must* be done pursuant to statute and regulations).

3. Environmental trends (*real* and perceived changes in demographics, economic climate, social and political trends, service needs, etc.).

The relationship among these factors is represented in Figure 1.

To foresee and address these issues effectively, the county developed its three-phase issues management process. Phase 1, the identification of strategic issues, began in September 1983 and continued to September 1984. Phase 2, the preparation and selection of broad, alternative strategies for issue resolution, occurred from fall 1984 through fall 1986 and, with respect to most issues, is continuing. Phase 3, the identification of actions to carry out selected strategies, was implemented in 1986 for specific issues and will continue through 1987 and beyond for others. A description of the three phases of the planning process follows.

Table 1. Strategic Issues and Areas of Concern: Strategic Planning Process, Hennepin County, Minnesota

Areas of Strategic Concern	Issues
Finance	Erosion of county tax base
	Maximization of nonproperty tax resources
Changing health mission	Health care mission
	Financing county health care services
	Organizational relationships within the bureau of health
	Relationships with external health care providers
Employment and economic development	Employment and economic development
	Child day care
Services to the elderly	Elderly
Environmental quality	Hazardous waste
	Waste resources
	Solid waste
Transportation	County roadway system
	Light rail transit
Justice system overload	Justice system workload
	Driving while intoxicated (DWIs)
	Correctional services
Technology and information management	Opportunities through automation
Risk/liability management	County litigation and liabilities
	Workplace health hazards
Development and management of the work force	Employee development
	Affirmative action
	Comparable worth
	Management succession
	Merit system
	Performance evaluation and incentive systems
Capital resource management	Downtown property disposition
	Capital and operating project delivery systems
	Capital resource allocations
Service contracting policy	Service contracting policy
External relationships	Protection of parklands
	Overlapping park authority
	County as service provider
	Communications to the public
Program fragmentation and coordination	Energy
	Social services coordination
	Family violence
	Juvenile placements
	Special needs prisoners
	Delivery of economic assistance programs

Source: "Hennepin County Strategic Planning, Phase I: Management Report," Minneapolis, Minnesota, 1984, pp. i and ii.

Figure 1. Factors Influencing Strategic Issues

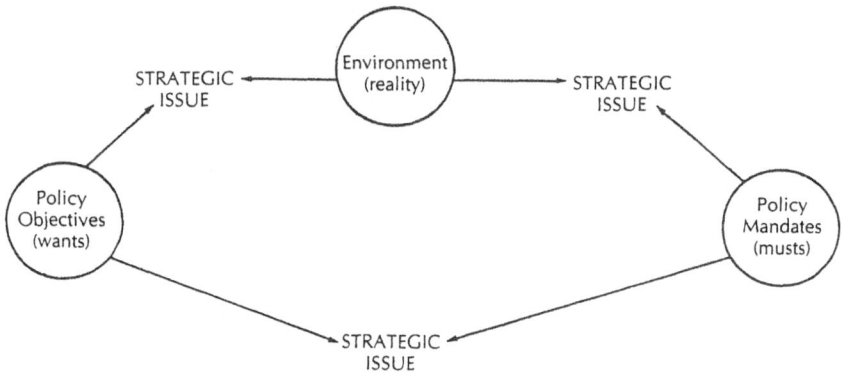

Phase 1

In the first four months of Phase 1, each of the county's 36 departments developed multiple issue statements as requested by the county administrator. These statements included a brief description of the external and internal environmental factors influencing the issue, applicable program or service mandates, county board policy objectives, and a statement of assumed consequences of failure to respond.[4]

Issue statements were prepared by departmental planning teams composed of top managers and staff. These teams were assisted by the Office of Planning and Development (OPD) which conducted initial workshops on strategic planning concepts, developed planning guidelines, prepared demographic and fiscal trends data, and offered staff support as needed.

To help department planning teams identify strategic issues and distinguish them from operational, short-term concerns, OPD prepared a set of evaluation questions titled "A Litmus Test for Strategic Issues." Among the most pertinent questions identified were: How broad an impact will the issue have on your department? What are the possible consequences of not addressing this issue? How sensitive or "charged" is the issue relative to community social, political, religious, and cultural values?

Much of the planning teams' issue identification work was intuitive in nature, involving brainstorming and unstructured group discussions. Some, but not all, of the teams used the demographic and fiscal data prepared by OPD to stimulate discussion. Assumptions about future trends and their likely impact on county service delivery were, for the most part, professional seat-of-the-pants judgments, varying according to the perspectives of department managers.[5]

County departments submitted 136 issues to the cabinet for review. From January 1984 to May 1984, the county cabinet and OPD staff discussed these issues, consolidating them into a set of 40 strategic issues. Some issues — the anticipated costs of civil liability insurance coverage or the nature of coordination of services for the elderly, for example — were relatively easily defined by the teams or the cabinet. Others, such as the slowdown in growth of the county's property tax base, took much longer to define, required more in-depth analysis, and did not lend themselves readily to easy solution. For these issues, Phase 1 work continued far beyond May.

Phase 2

Phase 2 involved a systematic exploration of strategies for issues resolution. A strategy was defined as a general approach used by an organization in achieving its objectives or in addressing critical issues; it was not defined in detailed terms nor limited to specific fiscal years or other short-term variables. Strategies provided general policy direction to guide detailed planning and management decisions over a multiyear period.[6]

In this phase, the county administrator assigned each strategic issue to a planning team composed of managers representing departments chiefly affected by the issue. A lead department — one most affected — coordinated team planning efforts. Teams identified alternative strategies for resolving the issue and estimated costs, staffing, capital requirements, and probable impact of each strategy developed.

Through 1986 these interdepartmental planning teams had developed strategies for 8 of the original 40 issues that were formally approved by the county administrator or the county board. On the issue of the county's capacity to control and maintain county highways, for example, new strategies included seeking legislative approval for changes in the county's bonding authority and highway funding formulas. With respect to the civil liability insurance issue, a strategy of reviewing insurance policies for departments most likely to face lawsuits was adopted.

The issues for which strategies were initially identified and approved were usually less complicated, better understood, and more amenable to action than other issues.[7] Strategy development for more complicated though no less critical issues required a lengthier period of time, with debate on many of these issues continuing into 1987. This has been the case often because each issue consisted of multiple subissues requiring separate attention by the planning teams. With respect to the issue of the slowdown in tax base growth, for example, the planning team has identified separate strategies for six related subissues. In effect, the total of all of these strategies has become a collective strategy for addressing this major critical issue.

In evaluating alternative strategies and establishing priorities among them, many planning teams used decision criteria developed for the process by OPD. These criteria included public acceptance, availability of financing, nature of capital expenditures, long-term impact, service impact, staff requirements, compatibility with department mission, relevance to strategic issues, cost effectiveness, flexibility, timing, client and user impact, and coordination/integration with other services or programs (see Table 2 for a definition of each of the 12 criteria).

Phase 3

In Phase 3 of the issues management process, many of the interdepartmental planning teams that developed strategies for issue resolution prepared action plans for their implementation. Through 1986, action plans — which chiefly involved changes in program budgets, personnel assignments, or policies — had been developed for strategies dealing with eight issues. For example, the county prepared specific pieces of legislation for submission to the 1987 Minnesota legislature that were designed to increase funding for county highway development and maintenance. To improve communication with constituents — another issue needing attention — the county has added a separate color-coded section for departmental telephone listings in the metropolitan Twin Cities phone directory.

Analysis of the Effectiveness
of the Issues Management Process

Much of the issues management process has been implemented as designed. However, problems also have developed with each major activity of the process. This section highlights the aspects of the activities that worked, the ones that did not, and their impact on the overall effectiveness of the planning initiative.

In the private sector, the issues management process has consisted typically of monitoring the social and political environment, analyzing and evaluating the impact of emerging issues, establishing priorities among these issues, and preparing responses to new developments in the environment.[8] As designed, the county's three-phase model of issues management incorporated these elements. The county specifically moved

Table 2. Criteria for Evaluating Alternative Strategies: Strategic Planning Process, Hennepin County, Minnesota

Public Acceptance: The resolution of some strategic issues will result in varying levels of public acceptance. The most desirable strategy is the one you perceive will have the greatest public acceptance.

Financing: If additional funding is required, is nonproperty-tax-derived funding available? A desirable strategy will identify alternative financing and/or will not require additional property taxes.

Capital Expenditures: A desirable strategy will better utilize existing county-owned or managed space and available equipment rather than require increased additional capital expenditure. However, in certain cases it may be financially and programmatically prudent to commit to an increased capital expenditure rather than utilize or attempt to upgrade existing assets of questionable value or benefit.

Long-Term Impact: The major thrust of strategic planning is to anticipate future issues that will confront the county and to respond effectively to those issues. The desirable strategy will offer long-term (more than five years) solutions to the issue and have a lasting positive effect.

Staff Requirements: A desirable strategy will allow the resolution of the issues by better utilizing existing county staff capabilities rather than hiring new employees.

Compatibility with Mission Statement: A desirable strategy is one that can be accomplished within or is appropriate to the department's mission statement.

Relevance to Strategic Issues: It is assumed that every strategy will respond to the issue; however, some strategies will better resolve the issue than others. The desirable strategy is the one you anticipate will best resolve the issue as a long-term solution with lasting effect.

Cost Effectiveness: A countywide policy objective is to provide cost-effective service delivery and management. A desirable strategy will improve or increase service and management within the existing budget parameters, or realize cost savings in the long term.

Flexibility: Flexibility in implementing a strategy is a desirable feature. A desirable strategy should lend itself to a trial or test before full implementation.

Timing: When implementing a strategy, timing is often critical. The desirable strategy should enable you to satisfactorily respond to the strategic issue within known time/response constraints.

Client or User Impact: If the delivery of client services is a part of the strategy being considered, a desirable strategy should have a positive effect on the client group.

Coordination/Integration with Other Services or Programs: A desirable strategy would allow for coordination and/or integration with services provided by other agencies.

Source: *Hennepin County Strategic Planning Manual*, Minneapolis, Minnesota, 1983, pp. 2–28 and 2–29.

beyond this private sector approach with its second phase — the identification of alternative strategies to address emerging issues — thereby linking
issues management with strategic planning (which many corporations
have not yet successfully accomplished).[9]

The conceptual simplicity of the county's three-phase model helped
county managers and board members understand the planning process
and, we believe, contributed to their acceptance of it as a credible,
workable planning approach. In politics as well as administrative operations, attention and response to significant issues is a characteristic role.[10]
The county's planning process mirrored this familiar activity rather than
requiring participation in an elaborate, wholly new endeavor.

The three-phase process was an effective mechanism for: (1) systematically investigating a broad array of policy issues likely to confront county
operations and (2) developing practical policy and program strategies to
address these issues. Prior to initiating the planning process, county personnel anticipated that the three phases would follow each other sequen-
tially, with all issues moving through the three-step process simultaneously.
The county has found however, that the length of each phase varied for
different issues depending on the complexity of the issue being examined.
Thus within planning teams, work on issues has often overlapped, as have
review efforts by top management. As a result, problems have been
created in the overall coordination and direction of the countywide planning effort and within individual teams (i.e., unexpected time demands on
participating managers and staff, priority setting in the work agenda, the
meeting of deadlines, etc.). This particular finding of the study is consistent with Halstead's observation that a key problem in the issues management process is the lack of coordination both within and between organizations.[11] In sum, however, the county's three-phase approach, while
difficult to manage over the nearly four years of the planning process, has
emerged as an useful, implementable format.

The county's decision to adopt a broad scope in its issues identification phase — to require county departments to address a multiple array of
issues simultaneously — further complicated the effective implementation
of the planning effort.

Among the positive accomplishments of the county's comprehensive
approach are: (1) the (often early) detection of issues before they became
crises (the erosion of the tax base, for example), (2) it helped managers with
policymaking responsibilities and, in some cases, county board members
to understand better the administrative and political implications of
strategic issues, and (3) in general, it resulted in the county's first comprehensive assessment of the quality and effectiveness of its public services.[12] The scope of the effort ensured that a fundamental review of the
purposes, activities, and costs of county programs was accomplished,

something not previously achieved in the county's attempts at program budgeting and management by objectives.

The scope of the effort, however — which resulted in the identification of 136 issues initially by planning teams and 40 following central review — helped create irritating although not insurmountable problems. These problems involved the length of time demands on planning teams, slowdown in the movement of issues through the three-phase process, significant reporting requirements, lack of systematic analysis and central review of issues and, most importantly, an inability to identify the selected issues which in an overall sense were most critical to the county. In this regard, the county's experience was consistent with what Halstead also has identified as key problems in issues management: The identification of too many issues as well as too little analysis of the issues.[13]

At the formal conclusion of the first phase in fall 1984, the county faced the formidable task of developing strategies and action plans for 40 issues, a challenge that was not successfully met during the 1984–86 period.

The effort by the county to decentralize the planning process — to create a bottom-up process through the use of multiple planning teams — has been, for the most part, successfully realized. Over the three-and-a-half-year planning period, departmental and interdepartmental planning teams have met consistently to identify significant issues, carefully define and analyze them, prepare detailed alternative strategies for many issues, and, with respect to eight of the issues, persuade the county administrator or county board of the need for action responses. Decentralization has led to more coordination and collaboration among managers and staff within and across departments — many of whom previously had had no knowledge of each other's needs and responsibilities. Thus communication and information sharing on issues of mutual concern was initially established or strengthened.

Collaboration on policymaking between top management and the board on selected issues and between the county administrator and department managers, many of whom headed planning teams, also has been improved. Most respondents further indicated that the team approach to planning has contributed to an increase in morale among managers and a lessening of the feeling of having been isolated from decision processes in this large (7,200-person) bureaucracy.[14]

The widespread use of planning teams also has had its drawbacks. Respondents indicated that the lack of outsiders on teams may have prevented the surfacing of divergent, critical points of view on issues; that foot-dragging on controversial issues — those with especially difficult political overtones — was evidenced; that planning progressed slowly on some teams where leadership was weak; and that information overload sometimes occurred for members and especially chairs of planning teams.

Staff assistance by the OPD has been essential to maintaining the momentum of planning and to the success enjoyed thus far. Staff helped design, skillfully facilitate, and publicize within and outside the county the strategic planning accomplishments of the planning teams and top management. In doing so, OPD has neither made strategic planning decisions nor developed a strategic plan for the county; that has remained the fundamental responsibility of the county's line managers. The scope and direction of the planning process has resulted, however, in the continuingly heavy, and as yet unmet, demand for staff time — the thinning of staff resources.[15]

Conclusion of the Study

The county's issues management approach to strategic planning may be successfully applied, we believe, to other units of local government. Our conclusions to the study address the potential benefits and pitfalls of adopting the Hennepin County model.

The first conclusion is that the county's use of an issues management approach helped integrate strategic planning and operational decision making. In an environment where, as one respondent suggested, "County departments have nothing in common except the property tax base,"[16] the issues management process has prompted the top management, many departmental planning teams, and, with respect to certain issues, the county board to assess complex issues systematically, to weigh long-range policy and program options, to select practical strategies and, in some cases, to implement action steps including budget request or allocation decisions. What is emerging is an attitude among county managers that issues management is "not a project but part of my job," that planning, in other words, is being perceived as an ongoing or recurring operational responsibility of line managers.[17]

A second conclusion is that the identification of a limited number of critical issues is essential to the effective implementation of the issues management approach. We concur with a recent decision of the county administrator that in the planning process county managers should address no more than 10 issues simultaneously; that, in effect, the team planning approach will be used selectively on major issues to be determined by the cabinet and county board.[18] The bottom-up process will become more of a top-down and bottom-up collaborative effort.

This emerging policy chiefly is a recognition that many complex and some controversial issues carrying potentially adverse political implications for board members may take a lengthy period to move through the planning process — until the timing for action steps is appropriate. A narrowing of the overall issues agenda will improve the management of the planning process by decreasing the number of functioning planning teams, reducing time spent in planning by the teams, easing the burden of coordination and direction of teams, reducing in-kind costs, and permitting a more effective scheduling of staff assistance.

A third conclusion is that the use of a broadly implemented, collaborative planning approach has increased expectations among county managers for organizational development and change. Managers have reported that they feel more ownership and commitment to the management of county services, more a part of a management team giving direction to county operations. In a climate where the raising of questions about the mission of the county, its policy and funding priorities, and the effectiveness of board leadership has been encouraged, improved morale among many managers has resulted.[19] Many planning teams also have experienced direct, positive response to their planning efforts as their proposed strategies and actions have met with board approval and have been implemented. As these initial changes have been made in the delivery of services, expectations among managers that additional changes will be forthcoming have increased.

Notes

1. Interview with Mark Andrew, Hennepin County Commissioner, September 13, 1985.
2. Interview with Bruce Kurtz, Hennepin County Deputy Administrator, August 8, 1985.
3. "Hennepin County Strategic Planning, Phase 1: Executive Report," 1984.
4. "Hennepin County Strategic Planning, Phase 1: Management Report," 1984.
5. Interview with Sue Zuidema, director, Hennepin County Community Health Department, August 3, 1985.
6. Eckert 1986.
7. Interview with Philip Eckert, director, Hennepin County Office of Planning and Development, November 24, 1986.
8. Zentner 1981.
9. Zentner 1981.
10. Crable and Vibbert 1985.
11. Halstead 1985.
12. Kurtz interview, 1985.
13. Halstead 1985.
14. Interview with Jan Smaby, director, Hennepin County Economic Assistance Department, August 13, 1985, and Zuidema interview, 1985.
15. Zuidema interview, 1985.
16. Interview with Dan McLaughlin, administrator, Hennepin County Medical Center, September 13, 1985.
17. Eckert interview, 1986.
18. Eckert interview, 1986.
19. Zuidema interview, 1985.

References

Ansoff, H. Igor. 1980. Strategic issue management. *Strategic Management Journal* 1, 2: 131–80.

Ashley, William. 1985. Issues management. A presentation at the Issues Management Seminar, Minneapolis Chamber of Commerce, Minneapolis, Minnesota. October.

Bryson, John M., Andrew H. Van de Ven, and and William D. Roering. 1986. Strategic planning and the revitalization of the public service. In *Toward a New Public Service*, edited by Robert Denhardt and Edward Jennings. Columbia, Mo.: University of Missouri Press.

_____, Bryson, John M., R. Edward Freeman, and William D. Roering. 1985. Strategic planning in the public sector: Approaches and future directions. In *Strategic Perspectives on Planning Practice*, edited by Barry Checkoway. Lexington, Mass.: Lexington Books.

Chase, W. Howard. 1984. *Issue management: Origins of the future*. Stanford, Conn.: Issues Action Publications, Inc.

Crable, Richard E. and Steven L. Vibbert. 1985. Managing issues and influencing public policy. *Public Relations Review* 7, 2: 3–16.

Delmont, Timothy J. and Ann M. Pflaum. 1985. External scanning in public and private organizations: Implications for strategic management in higher education. Paper presented at the 25th Forum of the Association of Institutional Research, Portland, Oregon. April 28–May 1.

Dutton, J. L., L. Fahey, and U. K. Narayanan. 1983. Toward understanding strategic issue diagnosis. *Strategic Management Journal* 4: 307–23.

Eadie, Douglas C. 1983. Putting a powerful tool to practical use: The application of strategic planning in the public sector. *Public Administration Review*, September/October: 447–52.

_____, and John B. Olsen. 1982. *The game plan: Governance with foresight*. Washington, D.C.: The Council of State Planning Agencies.

Eckert, Philip C. 1986. A public sector model for strategic planning: An overview of the Hennepin County process. Report prepared for Hennepin County government, April 6.

Foresight Task Force. 1983. *Foresight in the private sector: How government can use it*. Washington, D.C.: U.S. Government Printing Office.

Halstead, J. Philip. 1985. Issues management and issues networking: A national and regional plan. Report prepared for the Clorox Company.

Hennepin County strategic planning manual. 1983. Minneapolis, Minn.

Hennepin County strategic planning, phase 1: Executive report. 1984. Minneapolis, Minn.

Hennepin County strategic planning, phase 1: Management report. 1984. Minneapolis, Minn.

Lorange, P. 1980. *Corporate planning: An executive viewpoint*. Englewood Cliffs, N.J.: Prentice-Hall, Inc.

Lozier, G. Gregory and Kumar Chittipeddi. 1986. Issues management in strategic planning. *Research in Higher Education* 24, 1: 3–14.

Nanus, Burt. 1984. Foresight, strategy and political communications. Paper presented to the National Governors Association, Nashville, Tennessee, July 30.

Renfro, William L. 1982. Managing the issues of the 1980s. *The Futurist*, August: 61–65.

_____, and James L. Morrison. 1983. The scanning process: Getting started. In *Applying Methods and Techniques of Futures Research*, edited by J. L. Morrison, W. L. Renfro, and W. I. Boucher. San Francisco: Jossey-Bass.

Taylor, Bernard. 1984. Strategic planning—which style do you need? *Long Range Planning* 17, 3: 51–62.

Wilson, Ian. The benefits of environmental analysis. In *The Strategic Management Handbook*, edited by Kenneth J. Albert. New York: McGraw-Hill.

Zentner, Rene D. 1981. Issues and their management. Paper presented at the Critical Issues Management Program, Castine, Maine. June 14–19.

Charting the Course for Kirkwood's Future

Barbara J. Byerly

The city of Kirkwood will soon be observing its 125th anniversary. In order to keep this first planned suburban residential area west of the Mississippi River on its unerring chart of success and prosperity, its legislative body and management team came together about 18 months ago to develop a compilation of visions and strategic plans for its future.

Located in west St. Louis County, the city received its charter of incorporation from the state in 1865. A mayor and six council members, elected at large, form the city's legislative and policy-making body. A team of full-time management professionals oversee the day-to-day city service operations performed by more than 240 full-time municipal employees. Known as the "Greentree City," the city's boundaries encompass nearly nine miles of tree-lined neighborhoods and business areas. Since it owns and operates its own water plant and has electrical service available through its distribution system for about two-thirds of its residents, it has developed a reputation for being a full service community. The city has a population of about 28,000.

The need for a formal plan for the city's future was determined following a change from a commission to a charter form of city government that took place a few years ago. Mayor Herbert Jones explains, "Traditionally the council had focused on shorter range goals, such as what was to be achieved in the city and city government within the next year or two. The process of long-range, strategic planning rather than year-to-year goal setting, began in earnest two years ago."

Reprinted with permission from Missouri Municipal Review, *Vol. 54, No. 9, October/November 1989. Published by the Missouri Municipal League, Jefferson City, Missouri.*

Professional Facilitators

The city contracted with the Institute of Cultural Affairs (ICA), a private, nonprofit organization based in Chicago to conduct its strategic planning session. The exercise was conducted over a day-and-a-half period utilizing facilitators from ICA. It was generally felt by all participants that having professionals involved in this first time effort, providing limits, guidelines and leadership, was vital to the success of the endeavor. The need for a consultant has since been reduced by having several staff members trained as facilitators.

Mayor Jones reports, "We began the process by establishing a main focal point. That point makes the assumption that, basically, most citizens like the city the way it is today. The challenge lies in how we can maintain that approval as things change within the community and in the surrounding areas. If we are to continue the current quality of services the city provides and how those services are delivered through the end of the century, we simply cannot accept status quo — some things are going to have to be done differently."

Land use, how Kirkwood has been developed and how it will be developed in the next 20 years, was identified as a key issue. The planning group determined that new thinking regarding the location of industrial and commercial areas should begin immediately. The city will be monitoring the physical appearance of these industrial and commercial areas since many of them border residential space. "We must guard against any potential blighting effect on neighboring residential areas in the future. We'll also be looking at the possibility of redeveloping underutilized land or structures," Mayor Jones says.

"Kirkwood is Kirkwood because of the people who live here," Michael G. Brown, chief administrative officer, says. "It's a diverse community offering a broad spectrum of housing opportunities ranging from modest to very expensive, and we believe that the community wants to keep it that way. Few would like it to become a city made up entirely of $200,000 houses. Quality is the real issue. You can have a well-kept $40,000 house as well as a well-kept dwelling that costs much more. Our goal is to maintain all the neighborhoods and the city services delivered to them equally."

Five-Year Plan

Developing the plan was a tremendous team effort. As a direct result, members of the city council feel they have a better product and a stronger working relationship between themselves and department heads. David White, director of the city's parks and recreation department, agrees, "The process really opened up lines of communication. The session provided an excellent opportunity for all of us to explore our ideas and suggestions as they relate to every facet of city services. It became a strong team experience as department heads and council members realized we share essentially the same goals and objectives. I feel it was particularly helpful to have the individuals involved in policy-making working so closely with those of us responsible for implementing those policies on a day-to-day basis. The closeness and understanding we established during that session has carried over to our everyday activities."

The plan, with regular updating, may service Kirkwood until the end of the 20th century, but the focus is on the next five years. That updating is accomplished by following a carefully prepared action plan for each calendar year. The actions are tentatively planned, with specific assignments made for activities during each quarter. Progress is monitored at the end of these three-month periods as well as new assignments occasionally being added. Toward the end of the year, the action plan for the next calendar year is created. As part of the annual review, the entire group comes together to take another look at the overall visions, with an eye toward changes when appropriate.

Practical Visions

Following are the ten "practical visions" identified by the group as well as some of the results realized. They are not listed in any order of priority.

- *Maintain the Existing Diversity of Housing Opportunities* — Kirkwood has a heritage of offering a wide range of single-family dwellings, apartments and condominiums to serve a variety of economic needs. Our goal is to maintain this diversity of housing, assuring the city can meet the economic needs and desires of residents of all ages.
- *Increase and Broaden Citizen Involvement* — Kirkwood is justifiably proud of the number of citizen volunteers who give so unselfishly of their time and talents to make the city a better place in which to live. As a result of the strategic plan, a concerted effort has been undertaken to encourage a greater variety of residents to participate more actively in city affairs by serving on boards and commissions. In addition, the council has been conducting periodic meetings with boards and commissions to discuss the strategic plan, issues of mutual concern, working toward mutual understanding of philosophy and better communications.
- *Improve City Facilities* — A facilities task force of citizens and staff has

been formed during the past year to address this vision. The group has submitted its recommendations regarding city-owned building improvements and expansion. Architectural firms currently are being selected to provide the needed technical expertise to accomplish these recommendations. The outstanding progress in improving and maintaining the city's roads, bridges, water and electric systems and storm water drainage will continue.

- *Preserve the Quality of Residential Neighborhoods* — Few things are more important to a mature community like Kirkwood than preserving the quality of its residential neighborhoods. We will encourage upgrading homes that do not meet current standards. In order to protect land values and the character of our neighborhoods, we will guard against plans that could adversely increase density or otherwise diminish the quality of life enjoyed today.
- *Improve Underutilized Areas* — Kirkwood has long sought to attract high quality, responsible businesses and commercial developments to meet the diverse needs of its citizens. Since the strategic planning session, the city has renewed dialogue with St. Louis County and bordering residents in nearby unincorporated county areas about the mutual benefits of annexation. An industrial task force also has been organized to determine the economic viability of the city's various industrial areas and to develop strategies to enhance their viability.
- *Seek Cooperative Opportunities* — As a leader among local governments, Kirkwood is seeking possible opportunities to work with other governmental bodies, institutions and businesses for their mutual interests. As a result of the strategic plan, the city has more aggressively sought to market its services to other cities in an effort to obtain full cost-effectiveness of city services. The city has since worked out an agreement with the neighboring community of Oakland to handle its code enforcement inspections.
- *Enhance Downtown District* — Kirkwood's downtown business district has long been vital in servicing the needs of our citizens and in helping preserve the distinctive character of our community. As a result of the strategic plan, there is a renewed emphasis on rebuilding a good relationship with all merchants in general and with downtown businesses in particular. Further, the council recently committed funds to specific downtown improvements. This new climate laid the groundwork for the Civic Progress Committee's popular "Shop Kirkwood First" program, which is designed to encourage residents to purchase needed goods and services, whenever possible, from Kirkwood merchants.
- *Expand Recreational Opportunities* — Kirkwood has an outstanding parks and recreation system that serves the needs of its citizens well. We intend to maximize the potential of any underutilized park and recreation

facilities within that system. Based on emerging trends and changing needs of the community, we plan to explore such innovative concepts including an expanded Community Center or a full-service recreation complex.

- *Provide Environmental Stewardship* — Kirkwood is dedicated to preserving and protecting the environment for future generations. The city's recycling center has and will continue to be a model for other communities. An innovative leaf pickup and composting program recently was launched by the city in conjunction with the strategic plan.
- *Maintain Financial Stability* — Kirkwood currently is in a very stable financial condition. Sufficient reserves have been maintained to protect the city from unexpected adverse economic conditions. Constant attention to cost savings will maintain the future financial stability of the city.

Benefits of Planning

The timing of the plan could not have been better as the city looks to observe its 125th anniversary of receiving its charter from the State in 1865. Indeed, the focus and work being done for this upcoming milestone [are] also the result of the strategic plan.

"The entire planning process has been a totally positive experience for us and we wholeheartedly recommend it to all city governments," reports Mayor Jones. "It made it possible for us to focus on exactly what needed to be done. From that point it has been a case of implementing what was identified. For instance, everyone agreed that we should strive to improve two-way communications with residents, the business community and employers. As a result, we are planning to add a communications specialist to the city's staff."

Brown adds, "There is a good possibility that none of these things would have happened without the use of the strategic planning process. Most certainly they wouldn't have occurred within the first nine months of utilizing the program."

The Results of Strategic Planning in McKinney

Debra B. Forte

McKinney, Texas, has embarked upon a long-term approach to fiscal policy planning that, while not unique, is unusual for a community of only 20,100. The city was once a typical agricultural-based county seat, located sufficiently far from the sprawling Dallas–Fort Worth metroplex to consider itself immune and untouched by the strong currents of 20th century development. In recent years, however, McKinney finds itself directly in the path of major northward growth trends. Preparing for the transition to a more metropolitan environment and providing for stable financial conditions during the growth era called for comprehensive and long-term fiscal planning.

Since December 1984, McKinney has completed a series of advanced fiscal planning programs that have transformed the city's reactive management style into a more proactive posture and enabled the city to unequivocally exert positive control over its destiny. City staff now perform major financial functions that heretofore would have been unthinkable for a city the size of McKinney. Much of this has been made possible by computerization and an efficient use of consultant services. McKinney's proactive fiscal posture has nurtured an unprecedented degree of community awareness, and city staff and council enjoy a high level of confidence regarding fiscal planning and programs.

To implement McKinney's fiscal programs, fundamental issues were addressed by city council and a pragmatic policy planning approach, designed to foster a cohesiveness among all council members, was adopted. This exercise helped to shape a consensus on issues and to provide positive feedback to staff in the policy direction desired by the

Reprinted with permission from Government Finance Review, *Vol. 5, No. 4, August 1989. Published by the Government Finance Officers Association, Chicago, Illinois.*

council. The continually reinforced process has resulted in the annual development of formally adopted council policies.

Significant technology applications were essential to the fiscal planning process, as each component depended on computerization expansion. Some of McKinney's fiscal planning projects were the result of consultants' labors and expertise; however, with each consultant engagement, the city negotiated for not only a report of findings, but also for a software model that would enable staff to conduct the analysis in the future. This was accomplished without additions of personnel and at considerably lower cost than the continuance of contracting these particular professional services to an outside provider. The value received in return for the time and money invested in the fiscal planning described in this article is difficult to quantify, as the projects were not accomplished overnight, but were progressive, continuing efforts on the part of the professional staff.

A number of analyses and reports, as well as their underlying computer programs, contributed to the evolution of McKinney's fiscal planning. An annual cost-of-service study (CSS) has become a foundation document enabling the city to better understand and control the myriad of factors that contribute to the cost of providing a service to the public. A fiscal impact model has been developed to gauge the impact of major land developments in McKinney's extraterritorial jurisdiction, or those specific areas requesting annexation. A long-range financial plan, which spans a five-year projection period and five years of historical data, allows staff to review a series of financial plans and develop various scenarios for management's examination.

These analyses and documents provide input to the annual budgetary process and provide the necessary linkage of programs, developing continuity and conformity. The comprehensive annual financial report, sometimes referred to as the city's "report card," affirms budgetary incentives and essential fiscal positions as they relate to original forecasts.

No single project, but rather a consolidation of all programs was responsible for the success of McKinney's proactive fiscal planning posture. The GFOA's Award for Excellence in Financial Management also contributed by providing an additional incentive; it reinforced the belief that this was not an impossible task for an entity of this size to undertake. In the following section, each of the major components of McKinney's fiscal planning is briefly described.

Cost-of-Service Study

As a prerequisite to future software models and fiscal strategies, the cost-of-service study was developed. This study became the foundation document, enabling the city to better understand and control the myriad of factors that contribute to the cost of providing a service to the public. The CSS is reviewed every year immediately prior to the budgetary process in order to establish a basis for the pending year's fee structure. Based on expenses required to generate the service, the revenues are individually analyzed. Levels of economic recovery are determined by the political body upon presentation of realities by staff. These issues, as to which services would be subsidized *vs.* full cost recovery, are the fundamental components of the council's desired direction for the community.

To prepare the cost-of-service analysis, a schedule of factors driving each activity level was designed. The data are now updated on a regular basis. These criteria, unique to each department, deal with workload measures and indicators of services provided by all levels of the work force. This schedule allows managers to rank departmental functions according to the proportionate share of time devoted to each, as well as by employee responsibility and cost factors. Table 1 illustrates the activity bases used as productivity measures in the personnel office.

The CSS process is also the basis for costing the city's general and administrative services, for which the enterprise activities reimburse the general fund. The amount of general government time devoted to administering enterprise funds is analyzed through the CSS.

Fiscal Impact Analysis (FIA)

As growth encroached upon McKinney, management and council perceived the necessity of attempting to forecast the cost associated with a planned development community. To do so utilizing a 40-year schedule was an uncommon task, but the joint efforts of a variety of professionals created such a FIA model for McKinney. They were led by a study team comprising the city executive team, a development team, fiscal consultants, and planning/engineering consultants. Using the software created for the FIA, the city has been able to absorb this process in-house as well.

McKinney's first fiscal impact analysis examined a 6,250-acre development and annexation. Two additional analyses have been prepared, one for a 2,100-acre development, and one for an 1,100-acre development. All projects involved multidimensional projects of significant magnitude and were requesting annexation for city services. They involved zones for residential (single-family, multi-family, estates, etc.), commercial, office and retail, as well as parks and open space. Figure 1 illustrates the diversity of the second FIA project and reflects the flavor of the other two as well.

Table 1. Activity Level Factors Personnel Office

Activity Bases	Existing	Recommend	Adopted
1. # of vacancies	80	80	80
2. # of persons interviewed	300	300	300
3. # of persons tested	400	400	400
4. # of class sessions	20	20	20
5. # of appraisals	600	600	600
6. # of insurance claims/changes	200	200	200
7. # of employees processed	300	300	300
8. # of calls received	65,000	65,000	65,000
9. N/A	NA	NA	NA

The study approach taken at McKinney is illustrated by the following description of the steps taken to understand the fiscal impact of the Flying M Ranch Development on the city of McKinney. A microcomputer model depicting the build-out of the Flying M Ranch Development was constructed using probable densities, land mix in accordance with the zoning ordinance and a staging schedule which was believed to be aggressive but realistic. A 40-year period was considered in the build-out model.

The developers initially had a tendency to use the maximum densities allowed in the zoning ordinance even though it was their belief that the actual densities would be lower. After assurance was given that the study team was interested in presenting the most realistic picture, the densities were assumed to be lower than the maximums. The study team further reduced the densities to a level believed to be most probable. This was done with the knowledge that the resulting changes in densities could be tested to determine the impact on key financial numbers without having to produce additional sets of detailed schedules.

The overall impact of reducing the densities and stretching the build-out time frame did not alter the overall fiscal story to any great degree. The fiscal impact is slightly higher with greater densities because of the percentage shift in services and revenues from the residential category to the nonresidential. The break-even period shifts by two years, but the overall magnitude is not significant within the ranges under consideration. The cost figures presented in the report demonstrate the influential variables from which conclusions about land mix, density and build-out rates can be made.

Concerned that the new growth not be a burden to the existing community, McKinney officials had the FIA allow for development in stages and projecting the resultant revenue and expenditure bases. The parallel forecasting of cost and benefit to the community as the facilities were expected to be in place allowed council to see the tax base and sales tax base

Figure 1. Franklin Ranch Land Use Summary

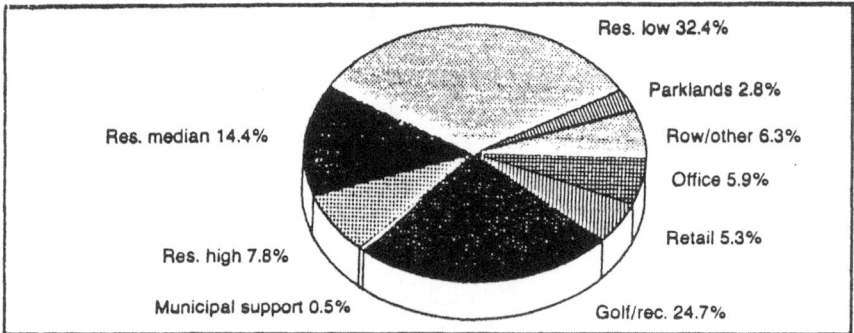

Res. low 32.4%

Parklands 2.8%

Res. median 14.4%

Row/other 6.3%

Office 5.9%

Retail 5.3%

Res. high 7.8%

Municipal support 0.5%

Golf/rec. 24.7%

that would be created. They also could preview the services required of fire, police and eventually, libraries and government substations.

Capital Improvement Program

The capital improvement program (CIP) in McKinney was developed from a professional staff base, supported by community input, and prioritized by needs. All projects are grouped by three major types: streets and drainage, water and wastewater, and public facilities. Projects are further categorized within each group and a source of funding identified for each project. Status reports describe each project by narrative, by mapping locators, and by projected cost estimates. An example of the public facilities schedule is shown in Table 2. Accompanying the preparation of the CIP is a financial review of funding capabilities. As bond financing was considered for funding the program, a sizing of the proposed bond issue was developed which demonstrated the city's fiscal ability to fund a level of projects without a tax increase. This, provided as a component of the long-range financial plan, will be discussed in the next section.

Long-Range Financial Plan

The long-range financial plan (LRFP) spans a five-year projection period and is supported by five years of historical data for comparative and projection purposes. The computer model allows staff to view the financial plan in accordance with assumptions regarding revenues, expenditures and fund balances. A significant component of this process is the set of fiscal policies that were developed and subsequently adopted by the city council as management and community goals. These goals are listed in Table 3.

Among the various computer models used in McKinney's planning process, the long-range financial planning package is the most comprehensive. It requires 21 diskettes for a back-up of the model. Its basis is line-item detail, similar to the basic line-item budgetary process. Factors driving the model include: inflation, demand for service, salary, benefit assumptions and any supplemental programs. Enhancements to the revenue base include user fees and tax provisions. Fiscal restraints were exercised in the area of expenditures, with scrutiny in every department.

With these tools the city of McKinney has sized its capital improvement projects and has been able to recognize the operational impact of capital expenditures in future years as each facility comes online. Expenditure items are calcuated into the plan with forethought rather than afterthought, and their impacts are associated with specific revenue sources to balance the budget. For example, if a fire station is funded by a bond sale in year 4, in year 5 the staffing and the utilities reflect a corresponding adjustment to the general fund costs.

Bond Financing

As an established and older community, McKinney had substantial infrastructure to be replaced in addition to keeping up with growth. However, management and citizens were concerned with the tax rate and its relationship to improvements. Thus, the challenge was to determine what level of improvements could be accomplished while balancing these two factors. McKinney's funding program encompassed these two basic concepts and the structure of bond issuances for the city's capital improvement program was established. The capital improvement program was ranked and sized according to McKinney's ability to pay while maintaining a level tax rate.

A group of local community leaders, "Citizens for Progress," supported and promoted the program through the referendum process. The election was approved by approximately two-thirds of the population, showing the community's need for not only physical infrastructure improvements, but increased public safety and expansion of the library and parks systems. The enlargement of Wilson Creek Park was among the park projects receiving this strong public approval. McKinney received significant state support through grant funding for the Wilson Creek project, which is part of a major parks master plan.

A bond program was designed to provide improvements of $21 million in $5 million increments spanning the five-year projection period. The first issue was determined necessary in the spring of 1988. An analysis to identify a window for issuance involved closely monitoring the interest

Table 2. Capital Improvement Program Public Facilities Projects

Project Description	Funding	1987–88	1988–89	1989–90	1990–91	1991–92	1992–93
Airport:							
Airport improvements/Land	Grant/Other	$3,000,000	$3,965,000	$1,300,000	$1,300,000	$1,300,000	$ 0
Facilities:							
City Hall expansion							
Down payment & remodeling	Current	25,000	0	0	0	0	50,000
Wysong municipal building and parking	Current	130,000	0	0	100,000	0	0
General site acquisition/devel.	Land sale/Current	187,000	0	75,000	100,000	75,000	100,000
Fire:							
Fire station #3 and #4	GO bonds	40,000	0	915,000	0	980,000	0
Central fire station improvements	GO bonds	40,000	0	0	0	0	0
Golf course:							
Golf course acquisition/devel.	Land sale	0	2,500,000	2,500,000	0	0	0
Library:							
West McKinney Branch	GO bonds	0	0	0	0	0	900,000

Parks and recreation:

North Park improvements	GO bonds	0	0	200,000	0	0	0
Community center parking/roads	GO bonds	0	0	300,000	0	0	0
Soccer complex I & II	GO bonds	0	0	36,000	200,000	200,000	0
Comegy's Creek bike/hiking trail	GO bonds	0	0	150,000	0	0	0
Wilson Creek Phase I & II initiation/bike trail	Grant/ GO bonds	110,000	0	0	150,000	100,000	0
Wilson Creek Phase III & IV	GO bonds	410,000	0	375,000	0	0	0
Wilson Creek land acquisition	GO bonds	0	0	0	0	40,000	0
Pool renovation II	GO bonds	0	0	110,000	0	0	0
Park land acquisition/devel.	GO bonds	0	0	300,000	0	0	0
Finch Park improvements	GO bonds	0	0	0	200,000	0	0
Parks maintenance center	GO bonds	300,000	0	0	0	0	0
Mouzon Park improvements	GO bonds	0	0	40,000	0	0	0
Tennis complex—Wilson Creek	GO bonds	0	0	0	0	0	250,000
Stonebridge Park	GO bonds	0	0	0	300,000	0	0
Equestrian center	GO bonds	0	0	0	0	100,000	40,000
Park playground/picnic improvements	GO bonds	0	0	0	75,000	95,000	95,000
McKinney median landscaping	GO bonds	0	0	60,000	0	0	0
Park irrigation	GO bonds	0	0	35,000	35,000	35,000	35,000
Public safety:							
Public safety facility	GO bonds	300,000	0	225,000	0	0	0
Total bond funds		$1,200,000	0	$2,746,000	$ 960,000	$1,550,000	1,320,000
Grand total		$4,542,000	$6,465,000	$6,621,000	$2,460,000	$2,925,000	$1,470,000

Table 3. Management and Community Goals of the City Council

The city council adopted this set of financial goals in conjunction with the presentation of the long-range financial plan which was presented prior to the budget review process.

- The city will maintain a working capital reserve equal to 5 percent of the total operating expenditures of the general fund. This balance will ultimately reach the equivalent of one month's operating needs, or 8.33 percent, by the end of the planning period (1992).

- The city will maintain an undesignated reserve for the purpose of providing for emergency and other unplanned expenditures and revenue shortfalls which might occur during a fiscal year. This reserve should be increased to reach a level equal to one month's operations by the end of 1992.

- The city will maintain a reserve designated for insurance purposes. This fund is to be used to pay for extraordinary losses or for substantial, unplanned insurance premiums.

- The city will begin charging the water and sewer utility fund an amount equal to 4 percent of gross sales. This is to compensate the general fund for the loss of franchise taxes that would be payable from a privately owned utility.

- The city will continue the current program of leasing large capital equipment needs from short-term leases, in order to "smooth" the on-going financing requirements.

- The city will strive to reduce the length of maturity of its long-term debt in order to lower net interest cost and to maintain future flexibility by paying off debt earlier. The target shall be 15 years and no longer than 20 years.

- The city will reduce the balances in the debt service fund from the current level, equal to approximately six months, to a level of two months. This is to be done in a fashion which will minimize dramatic fluctuations in the taxing structure. Also, the draw-down should be substantially completed by the fourth year (1991) of the planning period so that the subsequent year will be funded from current revenue streams.

- The city will issue bonds in increments of not more than $5 million and will provide for a bond program of $20 million over the five-year planning period.

- The city will begin a more aggressive program to reduce the level of delinquent taxes. The current collection rate will be targeted to improve by at least 1 percent per year over the planning period. This will be accomplished by utilizing available legal alternatives.

- The percentage of the tax rate allocated to the general fund will increase from its present amount of 56 percent to at least 65 percent over the planning period. Conversely, the allocation of the tax rate for debt purposes will decrease from the current level of 45 percent to no more than 35 percent by the end of the planning period.

• The tax rate will continue to be reduced with the objective of reaching a level not greater than $0.60 by the end of the planning period.

• Property tax exemptions presently allowed by the city will be continued with no allowance for additional exemptions.

• The applied tax rate will not exceed the effective tax rate by more than 8 percent in any planning year and will be no more than 3 percent of the effective tax rate by the end of the planning period.

• The city will take the necessary actions to negotiate a new franchise agreement with Southwestern Bell and will incorporate a 4 percent franchise fee into the new agreement, effective October 1, 1987.

• The city will put into motion, at the appropriate time, an action to increase the current occupancy tax rate from 6 percent to 7 percent effective 10/1/89.

• The city will implement an infrastructure replacement fund. The contributions made to this fund are possible due to revenues generated from new and accelerated growth.

---

rates. After what was considered a positive rating presentation and further feedback from the investor industry, the sale was accomplished in April.

Producing the official statement (OS) for the bond issuance in-house in an effort to contain costs was a major undertaking. Staff worked with bond counsel on the details associated with the format and content of an OS and conducted extensive research on alternatives of presentation. Timeliness and completeness were the primary consideration while preparing the OS. A GFOA Educational Services Center seminar on disclosure guidelines was of great assistance.

Financial Newsletter

As part of the bond financing program, a fiscal and planning newsletter was developed to communicate to the public and to the financial market information on what is happening in McKinney. Designed to promote the community, the newsletter has been circulated semiannually to citizens of McKinney, investors, banks and existing bondholders. Its content focuses on administration, economics, finances, debt and planning.

Summary and Conclusion

Since it first undertook proactive fiscal planning, McKinney has completed five cost-of-service studies as well as three fiscal impact models and two long-range financial plans. As the city embarks on the second year of its bond sale program, staff is currently compiling information in preparation for the next issuance scheduled for the fall of 1989.

A significant team effort is required to accomplish such ambitious goals. The finance officer must have the support of the city manager's office throughout the process. Keeping the council briefed on pertinent issues, so that they are informed and knowledgeable at all times, requires persistence. These progressive efforts, consistently applied over a series of years, will continue to accrue benefits to the community well into the future.

Scenarios for Milwaukee—
Citizen Participation
in Projecting Futures

Belden Paulson

One of the greatest challenges of futurist programs such as goals projects is to translate futures thinking into the thought processes and life-style of the ordinary citizen. The average individual in the local community continually asks: how do the sweeping projections of Alvin Toffler, Willis Harman and Herman Kahn relate to my life? What do they have to do with me and my needs?

One approach is being tried in the nation's heartland, Milwaukee, Wisconsin. Since 1980 citizens of the four-county metropolitan area have been developing Goals for Greater Milwaukee 2000. The project has involved more than 600 people working through committees and task forces to preserve the positive elements of today's community while developing new responses to tomorrow's needs. The hardest task is identifying what those needs are.

Even the more sophisticated leaders of Goals for Greater Milwaukee 2000, tend to be entrenched in the assumptions and paradigms of the present and recent past. For the businessman the balance sheet of the next quarter, or at best the next year or two, has overwhelming importance. For the educator the great struggles of the 1960s and 1970s that dealt with the crisis of educational relevance, the war on poverty, desegregation, and institutional survival in times of declining enrollments, leave little creativity to envisage emerging trends that could make today's thinking obsolete.

It is in this context that the Futures Subcommittee of Goals for Greater Milwaukee 2000 has been working with the Board of Directors and nine

Reprinted with permission from World Future Society Bulletin, *Vol. XVII, No. 3, May/June 1983. Published by the World Future Society, Bethesda, Maryland.*

task forces to develop alternative scenarios to illustrate factors that are likely to influence the future of Milwaukee. The scenarios help to illuminate one's assumptions about the future of issues that have central personal importance. They force one to make choices: what do I really want to have happen, and what price—in terms of policies and resources commitments—am I prepared to pay to facilitate my preferred future?

Our Futures Subcommittee has also developed a simple "game" which a large number of citizens can play. It takes the form of a short questionnaire where respondents take a stand on key assumptions underlying the scenarios. By stating what they think will happen and what they would like to happen, they are in effect opting for particular scenarios. These data, along with other citizen input and task force materials, bring the views of many citizens into the formulation of the central thrust of this future-oriented community planning project.

In developing the alternative scenarios, we have stressed variables that have economic implications, as well as encompassing a broad range of value questions. For example, one of the major controversies the task forces have been discussing is the way untrammeled economic growth and development relates to preservation of the environment and husbanding of natural resources.

For simplicity's sake, we have identified four main variables and have limited ourselves to two salient aspects of each. Some of the variables may reinforce one another. Others are in direct conflict. In real life they tend to combine and mesh but analytical clarity is served by focusing on each one separately (see Figure 1).

Alternative Scenarios

Utilizing sharply contrasting perspectives on the future, and discounting the Disaster scenario of nuclear war or other catastrophic possibilities (which may be quite realistic but is even less predictable than the other alternatives), we hypothesized four broad scenarios for Greater Milwaukee toward the year 2000. For analytical purposes the scenarios are described separately although the most likely reality would be combinations. Any member of the Goals Project—in fact any citizen in the community—can identify his or her tendencies toward particular scenarios by responding to a limited number of questions that focus on the four variables listed in Figure 1.

The scenarios are summarized as follows:

Scenario 1—Shrinkage

This scenario holds that the economy is experiencing a long term downturn and that people should accept this trend and prepare to cope

Figure 1.

1. Economic growth
   A. Level and nature of employment
   B. Availability and utilization of particular technologies

2. Natural resource availability and use
   A. Availability, cost, and use of energy (oil, gas, nuclear power, coal, etc.)
   B. Availability and use of non-energy natural resources (land, soil, water, air, minerals)

3. Policy and activity of major institutions (e.g., government, corporations, unions)
   A. Degree of emphasis placed on untrammeled economic growth and development versus degree of emphasis on preservation of the environment
   B. Degree of emphasis placed on utilizing resources and developing policies to deal with social and racial problems

4. Life-style attitudes and values
   A. Degree of emphasis placed on high material consumption and affluence versus degree of emphasis on voluntary simplicity and frugality, in eating, dress, transportation, use of energy, etc.
   B. Degree of emphasis on personal gain versus degree of emphasis on the larger community and relating individual benefit to the benefit of the whole

---

with the consequences. Much of the Midwest economy has been based on heavy industry, and oriented to high resource- and energy-consumption, the most obvious example being the automotive industry. To reverse the current downturn would require massive recapitalization in new technologies, as well as imaginative leadership and entrepreneurship, and broad scale work retraining. This view believes that economic opportunities for such large investment do not favor the Midwest relative to some other regions and that no national government policies are likely to draw in large subsidies from other areas of the U.S. to assist redevelopment of the Midwest economy in the way that the Midwest once subsidized the economic growth of the South and the West. Already there is a significant shift in the Midwest from manufacturing to service industries, and average incomes are decreasing because the only available service jobs pay at lower wage scales. The population in the city of Milwaukee and the county has been static or in decline for some time, and now the southeastern Wisconsin region is no longer growing. As in most large Midwestern cities, a decentralizing process is occurring with the population moving toward the smaller towns or to other regions such as the Sunbelt. With the number of jobs decreasing and those jobs that are available being less attractive because they pay less, this scenario holds that Milwaukee's population will continue to decrease. At the same time, the proportion of lower income population is likely to increase in the city as more mobile and higher skilled people leave, further decreasing the city's attractiveness. This in turn will require greater governmental assistance to meet social needs. Efforts at downtown revitalization, and re-entry of the middle class into the city may slow these trends but they are unlikely, according to this scenario, to reverse the basic process of shrinkage.

Scenario 2 — Stabilization

This scenario holds that the pace of shrinkage will be reversed and that the quality of life will remain approximately as it has been in the good years of the recent past. At the same time, it is believed that little significant growth can be anticipated in the economy, in jobs, and population. Undoubtedly there will be cyclical ups and downs but no significant trend in either direction. The skilled labor force, and the solid local businesses which bring incremental technological change to keep a degree of modernization, will preserve this area's relative ranking in the national spectrum. The reputation of Wisconsin and Greater Milwaukee for honest government, the natural environment, the cultural amenities, and the rich ethnic pluralism of this metropolitan area will continue to serve as attractions both to hold the present population and industries and to draw in some new people and jobs, so that Greater Milwaukee maintains a plateau of well-being for the foreseeable future. This scenario holds that future scarcities of resources will not take place to any significant degree, or that if they do they will not dramatically influence local life. Prevailing values and life-styles will continue.

Scenario 3 — Growth

The future in this scenario, will be characterized by growth, be it slow, moderate, or rapidly accelerating. New technologies will modify or completely replace what now exists. New job opportunities will open up in a whole range of areas from microelectronics and robots to genetics and space applications, and jobs in service industries will expand. With the need for new discoveries and new skills, the education and information industries will draw in new resources and provide opportunities as knowledge and innovation burst forward. Like the internal combustion engine in 1920, the computer may usher in a maze of industries. This view holds that science and technology will overcome the limitations of natural resource scarcities through new discoveries of raw materials, and more productive and efficient ways to utilize what is available. Government will reduce regulations and taxation so that private enterprise can take full advantage of emerging opportunities. This view believes that industrialism, rather than nearing the end of an age of cheap abundant natural resources, will enter into a new period of rapid and sustained growth because of technological breakthroughs. Incomes, consumption, and the standard of living will increase, perhaps dramatically, while improved productivity is likely to reduce the work week and offer more leisure time, which in turn will expand leisure-related industries. Undoubtedly there will be problems emanating from this period of growth, from the unknown consequences of new technologies, or from hazards to the environment because of heavy emphasis on growth and development or from lack of sensitivity to longer term trends related to expending of natural resources; but these will be the problems of an expanding rather than a contracting economy.

Scenario 4 — Change of Direction

This scenario holds that the conceptual model we use to view the future is itself outdated. As we formulate new criteria for looking realistically at the future we must alter some of our basic assumptions and values which will result in significant changes in the ways we approach the economy, technology, use of natural resources, and our life-styles. This scenario takes the view that limits hitherto unrecognized may force us to change our worldview. This will include the need to drastically increase our sensitivity to ecological and environmental factors as we perceive dangers from such trends as loss of top soil for sustainable agriculture, and increasing pollution of water and air due to the aggregation of wastes. This scenario sees the coming years as a possible "historic turning point" in our culture, a time when we begin to recognize that there is an impassable barrier to the onward and upward progression of production and consumption of the past. Values will slowly change, with people taking more interest in cooperation and working together for the large common good (of survival and fulfillment), in contrast to mainly emphasizing pursuit of self interest and immediate material gain. New technologies will enter as the old high-natural — resource-consuming industries decline in scale and importance. One of the likely burgeoning new areas of jobs according to this view, will be the "natural economy" where people do more for themselves. With less cash, more time, and less pressure from a high consumption market economy, many people will reduce their heating costs with strategies which use energy conservation and renewable energy; they will reduce costs of health/medical care with more attention to preventive health and nutrition; they will take more interest in either raising some of their own food or developing cooperative arrangements with other people for food production and distribution. This view believes that a process of

Figure 2. Impacts of Selected Scenarios for the Future of Greater Milwaukee

Scenario	Economic Growth		Natural Resource Availability		Institutional Policies		Lifestyle Values	
Key Dimensions	*Job Levels*	*New Technologies*	*Affordable availability of energy*	*Availability of non-energy resources*	*Emphasis on conservation of environment*	*Emphasis on social problems*	*High consumption*	*Emphasis on community*
1. Shrinkage	Low	Low	Low	Low	High (government plays larger role because fewer resources for costly remedies)	High (increased demands to aid needy)	Low	High (needed to maintain social cohesion in downturn)
2. Stabilization	Medium	Medium	Medium	Medium	Medium	Medium	Medium	Medium
3. Growth	High	High	High	High	Low	Low	High	Low
4. Change of Direction	High (trend toward many jobs outside of market economy)	Medium (some new technology will focus on eco-sensitive industries)	Low (increased recognition of resource finiteness and need to respect the earth)	Low	High (much more public attention to ecological/environmental systems)	High (heightened interest in social justice)	Low (lower consumption not simply due to less buying power but to changed values)	High (increased sensitivity to community: planetary and local)

increasing decentralization will place more power with the individual and the local community and neighborhood, although government will maintain key traditional functions, including responsibility for aiding society's most disadvantaged.

In Figure 2 we present a summary of these four scenarios. It should be repeated that these are polarized models although the real life versions would undoubtedly integrate shades of various scenarios and their underlying assumptions.

The *Shrinkage* and *Change of Direction* scenarios, it should be noted, are similar in most of their rankings, but are conceptualized differently. *Shrinkage* is the result of an economy in decline, but is based on a conceptualization of the major variables similar to that used in the *Stabilization* and *Growth* scenarios. *Change of Direction*, in contrast, uses a significantly different conceptual framework. Over time, should the *Shrinkage* scenario become chronic/permanent, *Shrinkage* and *Change of Direction* could merge. However, the conceptual distinction is considered important.

Conclusion

Goals for Greater Milwaukee 2000 has aimed to enlist maximum citizen involvement in thinking about the future. At least 600 people have been serving on the board of directors, the four standing committees, the nine task forces, and several ad hoc committees. A twelve page supplement to the *Milwaukee Journal*, Wisconsin's major newspaper, summarized the preliminary recommendations of the task forces. More than 10,500 citizens completed and returned a lengthy and detailed newspaper ballot which indicated their opinions on many key issues.

In all this involvement, however, there is still the tendency to think in "the present" rather than project the future. The scenario approach, which to date has been used with the Executive Committee, the task forces, and some citizen groups although not with the broad public, provides some structure in helping people to think through their expectations about the future. It relates the "big picture" of Kahn's "growth model" and Harman's "coming transformation" to the context of metropolitan Milwaukee. It helps people to pin down their assumptions and see the relationship of their beliefs and premises to the alternative futures that are likely to result.

Our experience to date indicates that many people think that *Shrinkage* or *Stabilization* is most probable, but that *Growth* and/or *Change of Direction* represent the preferred future. People in business/industrial/labor/political groupings tend to favor growth, according to our findings, while members of "alternative" organizations that relate to ecology, energy, politics, education, and "new economics," emphasize change of direction. Whatever the combination selected we have found that playing the "scenario game" invariably generates much discussion and debate even among people little disposed to think about the future.

Oak Ridge — Strategic Planning for a Strategic City

Joseph C. King and David A. Johnson

Oak Ridge, Tennessee, is not a typical American city. It was secretly created by the United States Army during World War II on a remote site 25 miles west of Knoxville. Using TVA power, Oak Ridge provided the refined uranium for the atomic bombs of the Manhattan Project. Forty years later, Oak Ridge was no longer an Army camp of 75,000, but an incorporated city of 28,000.

From the outset Oak Ridge was a planned community. But because it was planned for a purpose other than housing people and commerce, its initial character and subsequent development yielded conditions that by the mid-eighties called for a stronger commitment to immediate problem solving, as well as long-range urban planning. The community and its municipal government met this challenge with an approach that successfully combined traditional elements of master planning with components of strategic planning. This chapter documents the process and suggests that such a synthesis is both desirable and practical.

Setting the Stage

Oak Ridge today faces a variety of problems comparable to other boom towns, communities with highly educated populations, university communities, and company towns. Some problems simply relate to the fact that Oak Ridge began as an "instant" city; built and populated in a short period of time, its population, economy, and housing stock all show signs of aging at the same rate. Other problems are those usually

Reprinted with permission from John M. Bryson and Robert C. Einsweiler, Editors, Strategic Planning: Threats and Opportunities for Planners, *1988. Published by the Planners Press, American Planning Association, Chicago, Illinois.*

associated with company towns, only in Oak Ridge the "company" is the
federal government. The government employs nearly 20,000 people,
dominates the local economy, owns much of the land and, in the view of
many residents, does not pay its fair share of taxes. Indeed, it generates
no taxes at all, instead making a much lower in lieu payment. Still other
problems derive from the special nature of Oak Ridge and its original
mission — the promotion and exploitation of nuclear energy by a cadre of
highly educated scientists and technicians. Justified or not, the suspicion
of things nuclear eventually cast a pall over Oak Ridge, the "Atomic City."
The discovery in the early eighties of mercury contamination in local
streams and significant environmental problems on the U.S. Department
of Energy's 37,000-acre reservation tarnished the city's favorable image.

The creation and operation of Oak Ridge as a federal reservation
shaped the city from the beginning. At the point of its incorporation in
1959, the city found itself without a taxable industrial base and lacking a
vigorous commercial sector. The hilly, isolated site selected for the
Manhattan Engineering District served well in providing for safety and
security required for development of the atomic bomb during the Second
World War, but was not at all conducive to residential, commercial, and
private sector industrial growth. Moreover, the manner in which land and
improvements were transferred from the federal to the private sector yielded
very little developable property to support future growth. Unlike the surrounding area, the work force in Oak Ridge traditionally had been
unionized. This, coupled with the relatively high wage rates paid at the
federal facilities, created an environment not well suited to the types of industries that were likely to locate in East Tennessee communities. Consequently, new industries and new populations, so attracted to East Tennessee's share of the growing Sun Belt, were not especially drawn to the
Atomic City.

During the fifties and sixties, Oak Ridge's isolation diminished as
Knoxville's suburbs developed. The construction of a four-lane divided
parkway in the early seventies linked Oak Ridge to the interstate highway,
greatly facilitating movement in and out of the community. While residential development in Oak Ridge occurred at a respectable rate, the surrounding communities began to house an increasing share of the city's
work force. The maturing of families that had moved into Oak Ridge during the forties and fifties yielded declining household sizes and a steady
drop in school enrollment during the seventies and early eighties.

Oak Ridge had received considerable planning attention over its short
life from the Army Corps of Engineers and, in 1948, from Skidmore, Owings and Merrill (SOM), which had laid out some of the elements of a new
town combining Garden City principles with Bauhaus buildings. The plan
called for self-contained neighborhoods as well as a town center to provide

civic identity and urbanity. Much of the SOM plan had been carried out, but the town eventually sprawled down its long valley, exhibiting some of the less desirable aspects of American highway commercial development. The generally well-educated population demanded and enjoyed a high level of municipal services – schools, in particular – but the city lacked physical amenities and a high quality of public landscape and urban design. Oak Ridge ended up looking more than a little like a retired Army base with a gateway commercial agglomeration incorporated into the jurisdiction. Conventional city planning and zoning in later years had brought some order to the development process, but not enough to prevent the accumulation of serious economic and environmental concerns.

During the late seventies and early eighties, the city suffered several economic development setbacks. Plans for a $2 billion synthetic fuels plant were scuttled, as were hopes for a large uranium fuel reprocessing plant. The much contested Clinch River Breeder Reactor Project was cancelled by Congress after years of engineering and site preparation work. The in-lieu-of-tax contract between the city and the Department of Energy expired and subsequent payments made on a year-by-year basis were subject to termination without notice. The Department of Energy's pending decision to mothball the inefficient K-25 Gaseous Diffusion Plant and terminate uranium gas centrifuge research development and manufacturing activities, plus the potential loss of 2,000 jobs, caused concern to grow to deep apprehension regarding a future tied to the uncertainties of the federal budget. A strong consensus was building among Oak Ridgers that it was time to take actions that would guide the community toward a more stable economic future.

Another important event occurred in 1982 when, after nearly forty years of managing Oak Ridge energy operations for the federal government, the Union Carbide Corporation terminated its contract and a new management contract was won by the Martin Marietta Corporation. The arrival of Martin Marietta and small branch offices of several other national firms such as Boeing, Bechtel, Westinghouse, Gilbert/Commonwealth, Lockwood Greene, and Science Applications International brought to Oak Ridge companies committed to quality community growth. Martin Marietta's executives, and those of other national corporations with branches in Oak Ridge, were enthusiastic about the concept of strategic planning. Why not, they suggested, apply the principles of strategic planning to the problems of Oak Ridge?

Oak Ridge had long enjoyed a reputation of being a well-managed provider of municipal services. A strong emphasis on efficiency and increased productivity resulted in significant staffing reductions during the early eighties and by 1984 cost savings resulting from such efforts exceeded $1 million. Telephone surveys conducted by the city revealed a high level of public satisfaction relating to delivery of services. However, the surveys indicated that the public also saw its municipal government as being responsible for solving long-range problems relating to the issues of growth and development. While the city was seen as performing well in terms of program implementation, it was not perceived by community business leaders as being effective in planning for and managing change. Several expressed a need for a comprehensive plan to better articulate policies, goals, and strategies. Interested citizens formed the "Coalition for a Master Plan," composed of representatives from the regional planning commission, the municipal environmental advisory board, the chamber of commerce, the local chapter of the League of Women Voters, and two growth-oriented groups, to encourage the Oak Ridge City Council to fund and undertake such a planning process.

A Plan for a Plan

The assistant city manager was assigned responsibility to design and implement a master planning effort for the community. In March 1984, a proposal to develop a comprehensive plan was presented to the city council as part of the city manager's proposed budget. In addressing the development of a comprehensive plan, the proposal cautioned against falling prey to the failings of past efforts. Two land use plans and several special topic plans had been prepared by the city since the 1948 Skidmore, Owings and Merrill master plan. While each served a purpose and to a certain extent had guided development, none was officially adopted, none served as a foundation for day-to-day decisions, and all soon became outdated and of relatively little use. Deficiencies of past planning efforts were obvious — inadequate community involvement; weak commitment and participation on the part of the city council and staff; poor linkage between the plan, policymaking, and operational decisions; and a tendency to be too long-range in scope. Four important criteria were therefore suggested by the assistant city manager as objectives of the planning process:

- The entire community was to be involved.
- The city council was to directly participate in development of the plan and would formally approve the finished product.
- The resulting plan would be easily understood and readily available to the public.
- The plan would be *useful.*

As depicted in Figure 1, it was anticipated that the comprehensive planning process would integrate long-term considerations with more incremental

Figure 1. Integrating Strategic and
Long-Range Planning: The Oak Ridge Process

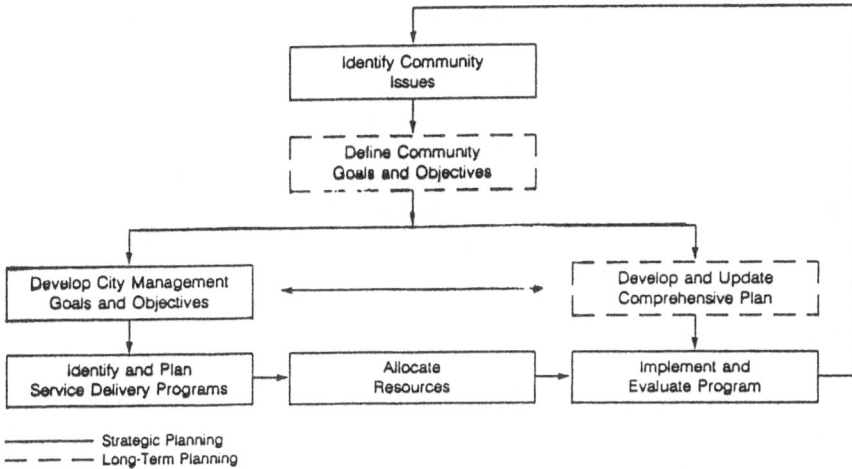

```
                              ┌─────────────────────┐
                              │  Identify Community  │
                              │       Issues         │
                              └─────────────────────┘
                                        │
                              ┌─────────────────────┐
                              │   Define Community   │
                              │  Goals and Objectives│
                              └─────────────────────┘

┌─────────────────────┐                         ┌─────────────────────┐
│ Develop City Management│◄──────────────────►  │  Develop and Update  │
│  Goals and Objectives  │                       │  Comprehensive Plan  │
└─────────────────────┘                         └─────────────────────┘

┌─────────────────┐    ┌─────────────┐    ┌─────────────────┐
│ Identify and Plan│──►│   Allocate   │──►│  Implement and  │
│ Service Delivery │    │  Resources   │    │ Evaluate Program │
│    Programs      │    └─────────────┘    └─────────────────┘
└─────────────────┘
```

──────── Strategic Planning
— — — Long-Term Planning

Source: SRI International, *Picket Fence Planning in California* (Menlo Park, Calif., 1978).

short-term management systems already in place. The finished product was to be practical in that it would focus on policies and strategies rather than on unrealistic or restrictive prescriptions. To remain current and responsive to community needs, it would be maintained and regularly updated.

The city staff initially envisioned that the desired integration of long-range planning and existing administrative and budgetary processes could be accomplished with minimal outside assistance from planning consultants. A review of the literature suggested to the staff that small cities making heavy use of outside consultants too often found themselves with documents that were of relatively little use because elected leaders and the general citizenry did not participate sufficiently in the planning process.[1] The city staff therefore recommended that the bulk of work associated with development of the plan be done in-house. A majority of the budgeted funds were to be spent on engineering studies of transportation and utility systems and any outside assistance that was needed would be sought from the faculty of nearby University of Tennessee. The business community, particularly those national firms with branches located in Oak Ridge, urged more extensive use of outside experts. The final proposal to the city council recommended a compromise that featured extensive staff involvement with support provided by an outside planning firm.

The issue of how the proposed comprehensive plan would look also was deliberated. The city staff saw the need for a detailed working document that might serve as a constant reference to those involved in setting and implementing policy. Some in the business community expressed preferences for a glossy, summary document formatted like a corporate report that could be used to market the community and recruit industry. Again, a compromise allowed both documents to be produced.

The city council approved a $125,000 budget for the comprehensive planning project in its FY 1986 budget. The appropriation subsequently was increased to $144,500 to complete a supplemental traffic study. Under the direction of the assistant city manager, the project team included the planning director and other city staff members, a graduate student serving a special internship, and outside consultants. Rather than use a single planning firm, the city chose to retain three. After evaluating proposals submitted by comprehensive planning firms, the city selected Bennett, Ringrose, Wolsfeld, Jarvis, Gardner, Inc. (BRW) of Minneapolis, Minnesota, as its primary consultants. Robert C. Einsweiler, Inc.[2] was selected as a special consultant to assist the city in arriving at an operational definition of its comprehensive plan, establishing development goals and objectives, and resolving conflicts between participants in the planning process. George E. Bowen and David H. Folz, both faculty members at the nearby University of Tennessee and doing business as Cherokee Planning and Development Associates, were hired as economic development consultants. The assistant city manager and planning intern assumed responsibility for coordinating citizen participation.

Initial work with the comprehensive plan project team revealed a fundamental conflict between advocates of long-range master planning and those of strategic planning. Traditional comprehensive planning proponents tended to be goals oriented, while those preferring strategic planning were more concerned with community issues. The traditional comprehensive planning proponents suggested a systematic inventory of conditions, setting of formal goals and stating of policies, and development of general plans and programs. Specific, detailed action plans were seen as less important at this stage than was the need to establish policy direction. Adherents of the strategic planning approach expressed a stronger bias for action, arguing that formal goal and policy setting were less important than determining what action the city would take to address major community issues. Ultimately the project team blended the two approaches. The mix of traditional and strategic planning processes balanced the perceived need for a formal policy structure with the desire to focus on specific actions necessary to resolve identified community problems and take advantage of available opportunities.[3]

The Planning Process

As indicated in Figure 2, the project was divided into four basic components. The first provided for the framing of community issues and a general inventory of the community—its demographics, physical design, land use and topographic characteristics, and its economic base. This helped the project team focus its assessment of social, economic, and land use trends within the context of problems and opportunities perceived to be the most important to the community. The second component aimed at achieving community consensus regarding major issues, objectives, and policies identified during the initial analysis. The third focused on specific plans and strategies to accomplish identified objectives. The final phase brought all the inventory, issue, policy, and strategy elements together into a formal comprehensive plan that provided a framework from which short-range actions could be taken, the results assessed, and future actions directed. Following adoption of the plan, it was anticipated that the initial product would be embellished with an additional detailed traffic network study that would yield specific roadway improvement plans for the next five to ten years.

Several informal advisory groups were established at the project to represent the interests of major employers, various components of the commercial sector, growth-oriented organizations, social agencies, and organizations concerned with quality-of-life issues. Interactions with these groups were augmented by sessions with the city council, planning commission, board of zoning appeals, environmental quality advisory board, and the general public. Depending on the project phase, general public input opportunities ranged from neighborhood meetings to community workshops and symposia. Opportunities were provided to interact with the informal advisory groups, city council, planning commission, and the general public during each of the four project phases.

As reflected in Figure 3, it was anticipated that from an identification of community issues the project team would construct policies that could serve as a framework for specific strategy components. Emphasis was placed on consensus building from the start. The project team sought to reach an agreement among the public and community decision makers regarding not only the issues that should be addressed in the plan, but also on the specific actions that would be taken to solve community problems or take advantage of opportunities. As expected, the process turned out to be a reiterative one. As the focus became more and more specific, earlier assumptions regarding consensus on issues and policies were tested and, where appropriate, issue descriptions, policy statements, and strategy descriptions were modified. The process for developing initial consensus on strategies in group sessions, as introduced by Einsweiler, follows:

Figure 2. City of Oak Ridge, Tennessee: Comprehensive Plan Project Schedule

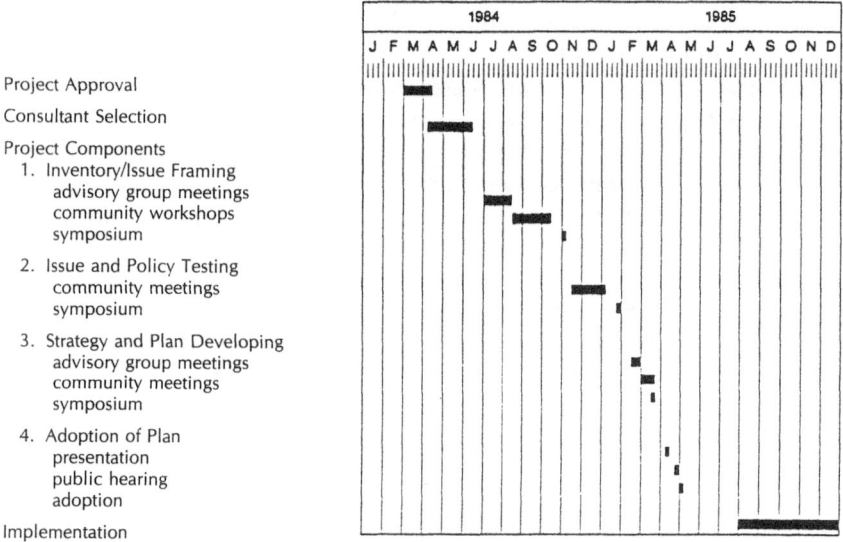

1. Survey the concerns of the group.

2. Capture those concerns insofar as possible in the exact language of those who stated them.

3. Organize stated concerns under headings that appear to reflect larger issues.

4. Test the "quality" of capturing concerns by presenting them back to those who stated them and also sharing them with other groups.

5. Test the range of acceptable solutions by asking the same people to propose ways of dealing with those issues and concerns.

6. Coalesce behind proposals that possess desirable attributes and are shorn of undesirable or unacceptable negative effects.

The issue-framing and inventory phase of the comprehensive planning process was initiated in July and completed in early November. Meetings with the consultants and the city council, planning commission, various municipal boards, the city staff, and several of the informal advisory groups were conducted, as were tours of the community, municipal facilities, and Department of Energy installations. The consultants were provided with copies of previous land use and special topics plans, budgets, and other studies. From such interaction and research, a preliminary identification of major community issues was accomplished.

Figure 3. Development of a
Comprehensive Plan: The Oak Ridge Process

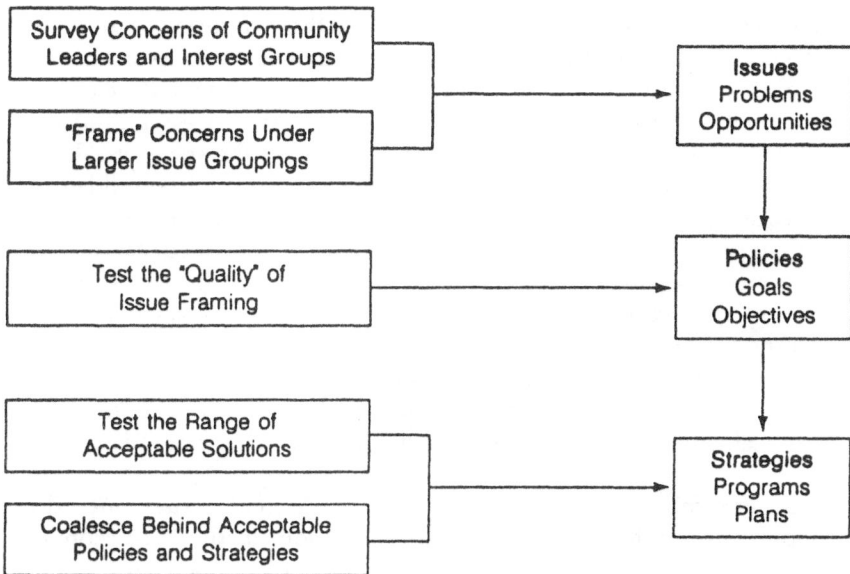

Survey Concerns of Community Leaders and Interest Groups

"Frame" Concerns Under Larger Issue Groupings

Issues
Problems
Opportunities

Test the "Quality" of Issue Framing

Policies
Goals
Objectives

Test the Range of Acceptable Solutions

Coalesce Behind Acceptable Policies and Strategies

Strategies
Programs
Plans

Seventeen workshops were conducted, the first three with the help of the planning consultants and the balance by the city's staff. Sessions were held for the city council and planning commission, advisory groups representing major employers, quality-of-life organizations, lending institutions, builders and developers, real estate agents, retailers, community college and high school students, the clergy, social welfare agencies, and the general public. An analysis of general conditions followed by a review of issues identified in the initial round of meetings and concluded by a solicitation of strategy suggestions by those present was the agenda used for all the workshops. Participants were asked to identify the major community problems and opportunities that should be addressed in the comprehensive plan and to describe the specific means for dealing with them. While participants produced few strategy and program ideas not already under consideration by the project team, suggestions did reveal the extent of municipal involvement considered appropriate in attempting to resolve problems and take advantage of identified opportunities. From this information, the project team compiled policy statements and where appropriate identified alternative positions for city council and planning commission consideration. The issue-framing, inventory, and analysis phase ended with a public symposium conducted by the planning consultants.

A review of the project team's analysis of conditions was conducted along with a presentation of suggested planning policies.

During the late seventies and early eighties, the city council and planning commission frequently found themselves caught between community interests favoring expanded development and those favoring preservation of the community's quality of life. The city staff consequently anticipated two basic concern groups would emerge: one pro economic development and the other pro environmental quality. As the process unfolded, it became apparent that differences centered not on the issue of whether development should take place, but instead on how growth should occur. Consequently, the planning process focused on how development could occur so that both concerns could be adequately addressed. With minor exceptions this pattern repeated itself with regard to other issues. The degree of conflict anticipated by the city staff regarding key community concerns did not materialize. While there were differences of opinion on how problems might be solved or opportunities seized, there was general agreement regarding the issues that should be addressed. The framing of issues yielded four focal points for the comprehensive planning effort:

1. *Employment and economic development issues* including economic uncertainty; conflicting attitudes about methods of economic development; the need for jobs, a balanced economy, and economic self-sufficiency; the adequacy of infrastructure; and the appropriate role of government in fostering economic growth.

2. *Population and housing issues* including declining population; unbalanced age distribution and household status; the type, value, and availability of housing; and deficiencies in the marketing of available housing.

3. *General development issues* including the original town plan's neighborhood concept versus a more market-based approach; urban sprawl, service extension problems, and the availability of land for development; and the location of special uses.

4. *Quality-of-life issues* including the image of Oak Ridge, the attitudes of its citizens, and the impact of both on housing and economic development policies; concepts of ambience and aesthetics; the need for activity spaces for varying age groups; the need for increased diversity; social issues; and the quality of services.

The second project phase was initiated with work sessions for the city council and planning commission to confirm proper framing of issues and to review and respond to the inventory analysis. Policy choices were then presented to the public in a series of eight neighborhood meetings. A second public symposium was held in late January 1985 to finalize policy formulation and focus on selection of specific strategies and plans. At this session, a preliminary draft of the comprehensive plan was introduced for review.

The plan adoption phase included a round of seven workshops for the city council, planning commission, and informal advisory groups followed in March by three special subject symposia — one on population and housing, one on economic development, and the third on land use and general development. A final draft on the comprehensive plan was presented to the Oak Ridge city council in early April. One month later, following a public hearing and several modifications, the plan was formally adopted.

Implementation of the Plan

The adopted plan includes chapters on population and housing, economic development, general land use and development, public facilities and utilities, parks and public open space, quality of community life, and administration. Each identifies major issues and provides an extensive inventory of conditions, policies expressing community goals and objectives, and specific programs and action plans. For example, with regard to the condition of the community's housing stock, statistics on the age, tenure, condition, and vacancy rates have been collected. Concerns relating to deterioration of housing and maintenance of neighborhood quality have been noted and policy statements regarding stabilization, rehabilitation, redevelopment, and land use control have been adopted. Programs featuring housing rehabilitation loans and grants, scattered-site rehabilitation, maintenance standards, public facility maintenance, and housing inspections have been identified and/or implemented.

The plan has been extensively integrated into the city's management process. Nearly all of the city management's adopted performance objectives are linked directly to the plan. For example, one of the city manager's goals and measures of performance include implementation of a reoccupancy inspection program. The plan provides the framework from which this strategy is launched.

The city's annual and six-year capital improvement budgets are now based on policies and programs prescribed in the comprehensive plan. Based on the outcome of the process, the adopted plan includes a priority framework from which to make capital and operations expenditure decisions. As indicated in Figure 4, the first of four priority groups focuses on provision of basic services. The second, third, and fourth groupings represent strategic investments in opportunity areas and address issues of economic development, housing development and preservation, and quality of life.

Figure 4. Relationship of Comprehensive Plan Priority Framework to Budget Resources

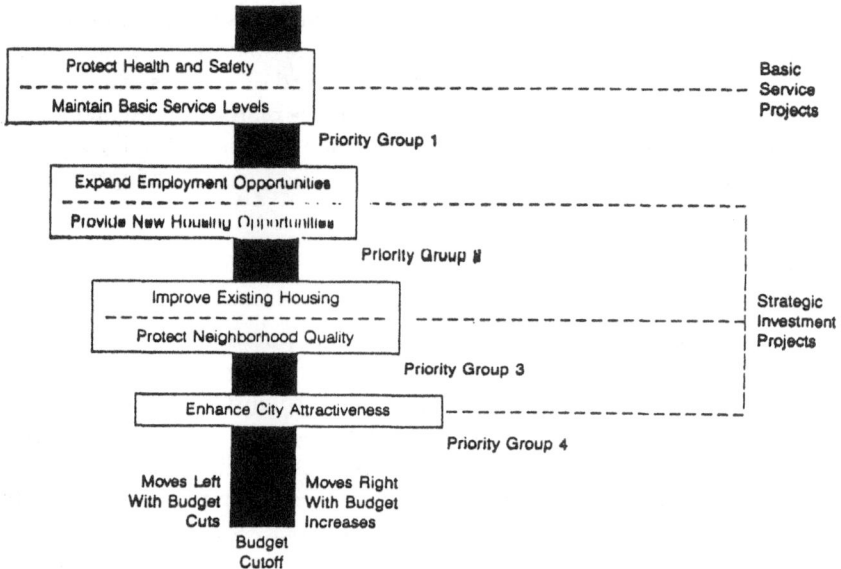

In short, the comprehensive planning project has produced a *strategic* plan based on a firm foundation of broad, long-range goals and objectives.

Strategic Planning in Oak Ridge

What can be learned from the Oak Ridge comprehensive planning process? Perhaps the primary lesson is that strategic planning and traditional comprehensive planning are not mutually exclusive; they can be blended successfully. The Oak Ridge process embodies most of the key elements that are said to characterize a strategic planning process:

- It is a focused process that concentrates on selected issues.
- It explicitly considers resource availability.
- It assesses strengths and weaknesses.
- It considers major events and changes occurring outside the organization or jurisdiction.
- It is action oriented — with a strong emphasis on practical results.[4]

For students of practical strategic planning, the Oak Ridge experience provides an interesting case study. The stimulus to undertake the planning process was provided by community leaders frustrated by slow economic and population growth and the downturn of federal funding cycles critical to the city's economic well being, but the process evolved from the traditional approaches to comprehensive planning. The final product does not reflect a growth-at-all-costs philosophy. The city council was directly involved in the process, as were the planning commission and other citizen boards, but elected and appointed groups generally responded to concerns, issues, and strategies generated by the community-based planning process rather than setting their own planning agendas.

The Oak Ridge process generated issue statements by aggregating and clustering specific citizen concerns. Prioritized policies were derived from these statements and specific actions to achieve those stated objectives have been implemented by the city. The Oak Ridge operating and capital budgets, as well as the city staff's management objectives, now are directly linked to the comprehensive plan.

The planning approach undertaken by Oak Ridge has not differed greatly from conventional comprehensive planning approaches that use a high level of citizen and interest group input. It is unique in its direct linkage with short-term strategies and programs. This should be reassuring to planners who have been told by some writers that comprehensive planning and strategic planning are polar opposites, with the former being all-encompassing, goal and plan oriented, idealistic, and ambitious, and the latter being focused, practical, and results oriented.

The Oak Ridge approach is not without risks. Early in the process, a local newspaper editorial questioned the focus on community concerns rather than positive attributes and potentials. Indeed, had the process ended with the cataloguing of problems, little of anything constructive would have been accomplished. But the process in Oak Ridge went beyond consensus on what the problems were to coalescing behind action plans aimed at resolving problems.

The ultimate success of the process will rest in part on its ability to survive changes in key personnel. Since adoption of the comprehensive plan, both the city manager and assistant city manager have moved on to work for different cities. Changes have also take place in certain private sector positions. Time will tell whether the process was overly dependent on the actions of specific individuals or is successfully institutionalized.

Another problem for Oak Ridge, as for all cities attempting to apply strategic planning, is that many of the strategic decisions affecting the future of the city will be made not by city government alone, but also by other community actors such as the Department of Energy, Martin Marietta, and absentee commercial landowners. The city has its comprehensive strategic plan, but the city is only one among a number of key players. The question is: Are the city's plan and action agenda adequate to structure and guide the actions of the other players whose interests may or may not coincide with those of the city and its residents, or is it necessary to demand that these players also provide strategic plans for their involvement and responsibilities in Oak Ridge? One citizen participant, who is fond of sculling the Clinch River, proposed that Oak Ridge change its nickname from the Atomic City to Rowing Capital of the World. It won't take very long to see if all the strategic rowers in Oak Ridge are pulling on the oars together.

Notes

1. In an extensive review of local government planning efforts in California, SRI International found this to be true in a number of locations. See Steven A. Waldhorn, Edward J. Blakely, James R. King, and Phyllis A. Guss, 1978. *Picket fence planning in California: A study of local government planning,* Menlo Park, Calif.: SRI International, September.

2. Robert Einsweiler is a professor of planning and public affairs at the University of Minnesota's Hubert Humphrey Institute of Public Affairs, Minneapolis.

3. The successful blending of these approaches can be credited to Robert Einsweiler who brought to the process an effective method of framing community issues and articulating strategies. With a clear reading of community issues and associated strategies that were acceptable to policymakers, the project team was able to back into the process of formally setting goals and policies.

4. Donna L. Sorkin, Nancy B. Ferris, and James Hudak, 1984. *Strategies for cities and counties: A strategic planning guide,* Washington, D.C.: Planning Technology Incorporated, p. 1.

The Placentia 2000 Project — Long-Range Planning in Local Government

Robert W. Kuznik and Roger L. Kemp

The Need

Long-range planning has long been a common practice in the private sector. Strategic planning enables the organization to successfully cope with change in a complex environment through the efficient use of its resources. While the future may be uncertain, existing and emerging trends can be identified, analyzed, and successfully used to develop policies and management practices which respond to change. In local governments, the one-year budget cycle has been the common frame of reference for public officials. The single most important planning instrument has been the general plan, which guides the growth of a community in the area of land use. Long-range strategic planning, however, is seldom used in other service areas of local government.

In the City of Placentia, long-range planning as a community effort began in the mid–1960s, with the creation of the Placentia Tomorrow Project. This project called for a small group of council-appointed citizens to identify goals for the city for a ten-year period. Their plan laid the groundwork for the growth of a quality, primarily residential, community with a limited commercial and industrial base. It also set the course for the development of needed parks and recreational facilities. Nearly 20 years later, the city council created a second major long-range planning project to involve the citizens in their government's plans for their city.

Long-range planning is becoming an increasingly popular subject of study. The recent teleconference on "Local Governments in the 1990s and

Reprinted with permission from Nevada Government Today, *Vol. 10, No. 3, Fall/Winter 1984. Published by the Nevada League of Cities, Carson City, Nevada.*

Beyond," cosponsored by the National League of Cities, the U.S. Conference of Mayors, and the International City Management Association, is an attempt to make local officials aware of the need for and processes necessary to prepare local governments for the future. The future soon becomes the present, and successful planning will smooth the transition and enable public officials to plan for, rather than merely react to, events that are now shaping their environment. One successful long-range planning model, the Placentia 2000 project, may assist other local leaders shape the future of their governments in a world beset by change and complexity.

The Project

In July 1983, the city council publicly approved a program titled "The Placentia 2000 Project." News releases were subsequently prepared announcing the 25 vacancies on the Placentia 2000 Project Committee. Over 30 citizens applied to serve on this important planning body. In late August, after all the appointments were made, the council held a formal "kick-off" meeting to set forth the purpose of the program, the importance of long-range planning, and their desire to get citizens involved in helping determine the city's direction for the year 2000. Each citizen was appointed to one of five subcommittees. Each subcommittee's chairman served on a Steering Committee to eliminate duplication and work-out conflicting goals. The elected officials set February 1984, as the target date for completion of the "2000" report.

Each subcommittee consisted of five citizens. These groups were organized around five facets of community life — residential, commercial and industrial, cultural and recreational, city services and finances, and communications and new technology. The charge of each subcommittee was to assess the present conditions of the city in their respective area, identify desired goals for the year 2000, develop strategies to achieve those goals, and present their findings to the city council at the end of a six-month period. The elected officials highlighted several "community issues," which are noted below.

- *Residential* — Explore the city's housing patterns and policies. Will the present direction meet the needs of families in the future?
- *Commercial and industrial* — Most citizens now work and shop outside of the city. Should the commercial and industrial base of the city be expanded to create a more viable local economy in the future?
- *Cultural and recreational* — In the past, the city has made a substantial commitment to recreational programs and neighborhood parks. Will

these meet the recreational and cultural needs of the community as it matures by the year 2000?

- *City services and finances* — A full range of services are now provided in the community. Are these services adequate? If additional services are desired, how should they be financed?
- *Communications and new technology* — The world is entering an age of newly-sophisticated communication technologies. Should the city act now to take advantage of these "tools" to better serve the public in the future?

The Goals

After many public meetings, including a city-wide town hall meeting, the final Placentia 2000 Project Report was prepared by the committee, and presented to the city council. The entire citizen participation process spanned several months, and included press releases, citizen participation forums, a questionnaire distributed to all citizens, contacts with numerous community leaders in all walks of life, and many subcommittee meetings. The several Steering Committee meetings were also well publicized and attended by members of the news media. All public comments were welcomed by the various subcommittees and all input, regardless of its source, was taken into consideration during the preparation of the final report. Some of the more important community goals identified in the final report for the year 2000 are summarized below.

- Residential goals
  - Maintain the present "residential image" of the community.
  - Encourage a full range of housing types for all segments of the community.
  - Utilize available open space to create a healthy and attractice living environment.
  - Investigate the potential for city participation in future housing programs.
  - Develop all remaining vacant land in accordance with the city's adopted housing goals.
  - Continue to maintain the same high quality standards for residential development.
- Commercial and industrial goals
  - Encourage increased commercial and industrial development to raise revenue and employment without sacrificing the city's low-density residential image.
  - Pursue light industrial development without significant adverse environmental impacts.

The Structure of the Placentia 2000 Project

- Twenty-five citizens appointed to five subcommittees:
  - Residential
  - Commercial and Industrial
  - Cultural and Recreational
  - City Services and Finances
  - Communications and New Technology

- Each subcommittee was asked to:
  - Assess the present condition of the city.
  - Identify community goals for the year 2000.
  - Develop strategies to achieve these goals.
  - Report their findings to the city council.

  - Seek out a quality hotel with regional convention facilities.
  - Develop a cultural complex for the arts with facilities for classes, exhibits, and performances.
- Cultural and recreational goals
  - Expand the community building to include a large kitchen and banquet facilities to better serve the public.
  - Pursue joint ventures with the school district for a performing arts center, the remodeling of a high school auditorium, and upgrading an athletic facility.
  - Acquire surplus school sites for the athletic fields and playgrounds needed in the future.
  - Construct an outdoor performance platform at Tri-City Park, the city's largest park.
- City services and finances goals
  - Expand the city's redeveloped area to foster development which expands the property tax base for financing new services.
  - Assist property owners with development in the Santa Fe Avenue area, the city's oldest commercial district, to create a healthier business climate.
  - Provide cultural and recreational services to an increasingly aging population.
  - Aim to make all cultural and recreational facilities self-supporting in the future.
  - Form an assessment district, or use subscription fees, for paramedic

Significant Events of the Placentia 2000 Project

1983

Council Approves Project at Public Meeting	July
News Releases Prepared to Fill Vacancies	July
Council Appoints Members at Public Meeting	August
Council Conducts "Kick-off" Meeting	September
Subcommittees Formed	September
Questionnaire Distributed to All Citizens	September
Brochure Prepared on Project	October
Bilingual Public Notices of Town Hall Meeting	October
Committee Holds Town Hall Meeting	October
Steering Committee Holds First Meeting	October
Local Radio Program Does Special on Project	November
Subcommittees Identify Goals	December
Goals Distributed to Press and Public	December

1984

Steering Committee Drafts Final Report	January
Draft Report Circulates to All Members	January
Final Report Presented to City Council	February
Final "2000" Report Approved by Council	February

services, and other services that may be added in the future in response to new technology.

- Communications and new technology goals
  - Explore the possibility of an emergency two-way cable television system to service the public in the future.
  - Set-up training programs to acquaint citizens with the use of the city's cable television equipment for community-based programming.
  - Videotape key city events for historical preservation in the city archives.
  - Form a Communications and Technology Committee in the future to make recommendations to the council in these evolving areas.
  - Consider after-hours time-sharing of the city's computer facilities.
  - Establish an annual Communications and Technology Fair to help citizens keep abreast in these areas.
  - Underground all utility lines, including transmission lines, by the year 2000.

The final Placentia 2000 Project Report was presented to the city council in February. It will serve as a guide when establishing future policies in those areas of community life discussed above. The city's elected officials will be reviewing these recommendations with the goal of preparing one California city for the year 2000. Rather than merely reacting to events as they unfold, an active posture of planning will be used to better serve the public and enable a smoother transition into the future. The broad-based citizen input used to identify community goals will provide the council with valuable ideas when considering policies and programs to cope with an ever-dynamic and changing environment.

The Outcome

One key outcome of the "2000" project was that the council quickly realized that the final report was the result of a difficult and time-consuming process, and that that process was just as important as the completed project. Since obtaining citizen participation in community goal-setting was so important, the plan will be periodically reviewed and revised to ensure that long-range goals continue to be consistent with the wishes of the citizens. The entire planning process received only minor criticism. Those few who criticized were invited to participate, keeping in mind that goal-identification cannot accommodate every single wish. The democratic system must prevail, and the goals identified must reflect overall the majority of the citizens in the community.

The "Placentia Planning Model" was relatively simple and straightforward. The process used is transferable and easily adapted to other cities, as well as other types and levels of local government. As future policies and programs are implemented, few can condemn the outcome that involved so many citizens and different segments of the community. Since the political environment in most local governments is highly charged, such a "grass-roots" approach to planning gives greater legitimacy to future actions of the legislative body. Long-range strategic planning for local governments will become commonplace as elected officials adapt their agencies to ever-present change and complexity. The recent efforts of the National League of Cities, U.S. Conference of Mayors, and International City Management Association help stress that need for government preparing for tomorrow. It is hoped that the planning model used in Placentia will assist other public officials as they undertake similar endeavors.

San Francisco —
The Unveiling of a Strategic Plan

Richard Morten

In the spring of 1975, when New York City was forced to acknowledge the mess it was really in, headlines like these shocked the nation: "New York Sinks," "Crisis in Stink City," "Going Broke the New York Way" and "Beyond Apocalypse."

Five years later, amid reports of billion-dollar deficits, borrowing beyond the breaking point, more than one million lost jobs, mass deterioration in its neighborhoods, roadways on a 200-year replacement cycle, and graffiti-splotched, decrepit subways, a *Forbes* magazine article entitled "Grim Times in Fun City" asked "Can New York make it in the Eighties?" and replied, "On its own, no."

Today, that prediction appears to be unfolding. New York City is facing a $341-million fiscal shortfall in June 1983, and with tax revenues running below expectations, a terrifying $1.3 billion deficit in '84. A *Time* magazine article recently told of bandage-like repairs on the 99-year-old Brooklyn Bridge where a snapped cable recently killed a man, of a transit system that nears collapse, and of the city EPA commissioner's fears about an impending overflow of the sewer system. And despite a housing shortage, blocks and blocks of homes are boarded up, awaiting demolition.

While San Francisco wasn't included in the *Time* story, the Mayor's recent proposal to spend $20 million of the city's estimated $150-million surplus on public works — infrastructure — repairs indicates that this city too has seen neglect. But even though some maintenance has been deferred, the city has, during extremely trying times, managed its financial resources prudently.

The dynamic of San Francisco's service economy has created many new jobs, sheltered it from the decline in wholesale and manufacturing

Reprinted with permission from San Francisco Business, *Vol. 18, No. 2, February 1983. Published by the Chamber of Commerce, San Francisco, California.*

activities, and provided a sound fiscal base. The city's housing stock has been well maintained and new units added despite the slumping market. San Francisco is well-served by a comprehensive regional and local transportation network. And the simple existence of a budget surplus is indicative of healthy circumstances.

San Francisco's comparatively rosy circumstances might lead some to ask why its business community recently pooled together $600,000 to fund an in-depth study of the major problems threatening this city's future. The answer: to make a great city greater.

San Francisco's Strategic Plan, now being prepared for implementation, has thus far been an 18-month survey involving a partnership between business and government which concluded that this city's future is neither bountiful nor bleak. While it is not faced with crises like those confronting New York, indicators show San Francisco's fiscal health has declined steadily in the past decade and its economy could falter unless preventive action is taken.

Much will depend on the resolution of certain closely related key issues — housing, city finances, job and business opportunities, and transportation. It was around these topics that the Strategic Plan's four task forces were developed. These groups launched painstaking studies of each strategic issue, evaluated upwards of 200 possible solutions and forwarded 39 strategies to the Strategic Plan Management Committee.

After consultations with city officials and evaluation of each proposal in terms of its amenability to public/private-sector partnership, its ability to take maximum advantage of the city's strengths and mitigate negative outside forces, and its consideration of resource constraints, 19 key strategies were selected for implementation in the first year. The following is a brief discussion of the four task force issues and the chosen strategies.

The San Francisco Strategic Planning Process

The strategic planning process has been conducted in four phases:

- Phase I — Issue Identification and Forecast
  Phase I was completed in May 1982, and a report was issued at that time. Historical data on demographic, economic and fiscal trends were collected and analyzed, and projections were made to the year 2000. In light of the many trends analyzed, four key issues were identified as having particular importance to the city's future:

  - Housing
  - Transportation

- City finances
- Job and business opportunities

These are clearly strategic issues where business and public interests converge and which the business community, working in concert with the public sector, can best address.

- Phase II — Strategic Issue Analysis and Forecast
Phase II was completed in September 1982, and a second report was issued. Task forces of business, city and community leaders studied the four strategic issues identified in the first phase. The purpose of this analysis was to identify and prioritize the factors which will either facilitate or impede the city's future progress in these four areas. Based on a careful analysis of the high-priority factors, the task force defined a series of assumptions which formed the basis for setting realistic goals, objectives and strategies.

- Phase III — Goals, Objectives and Strategies Formulation
This report marks the completion of Phase III. The task forces have identified the specific goals and quantifiable objectives related to the four strategic issues and have recommended over 200 strategies. Given resource and manpower constraints, the Management Committee prioritized the strategies and selected 19. Implementation of these strategies will begin in 1983, recognizing that some will be completed in the short term while others may require many years to complete. As the plan is updated in future years and as conditions change, additional strategies may be adopted.

- Phase IV — Plan Implementation
A mechanism has been developed to implement the recommended strategies and to periodically assess the validity of the underlying assumptions. Key business leaders have volunteered to monitor each of the strategies and to assist in the implementation. It will also be essential to continue the positive dialogue among business leaders, regional and city officials, and concerned members of the community which has characterized the first eighteen months of this planning effort.

Job and Business Opportunities

According to the president of the Embarcadero Center and co-chairman of the Job and Business Opportunities task force, "San Francisco's economy cannot operate as an island unto itself; it must compete in a highly interdependent world economy and to do so, we must create an environment that allows for reasonable business growth." In the words of the president of Bayshore Metals and task force co-chairman, "Not only must we be competitive, but we must create employment opportunities for San Francisco residents." These two thoughts, "reasonable business growth" and "employment opportunities," guided this task force in its analysis and strategy development.

Between 1965 and 1979, San Francisco had only a 7 percent increase in the number of new business establishments — slightly greater than that in Cleveland. Largely behind that growth were expansions by companies already located here, particularly firms in the financial, transportation and utilities sectors. This increase by major existing corporations is one of the key factors separating San Francisco from many of the nation's fiscally weak cities.

More recently, however, there is growing concern that San Francisco may have lost its competitive advantage to suburban communities in the retention of the labor-intensive, back-office functions of these headquarter companies. There is ample evidence that companies are making relocation decisions which could have a long-term impact on resident jobs and the economy.

The key industries for San Francisco's future are finance and head-quarters, business-support service, retail, visitor and convention activity, and professional services. These represented 35 percent of the city's employment in 1979, a slice expected to reach nearly 50 percent by the year 2000. They will also account for about 75 percent of all new jobs created here from now to the end of the century. These projections are, of course, dependent on San Francisco's internal strengths and weaknesses. If strengths diminish and weaknesses become more pronounced, the employment growth rate will not reach these targets and may actually decline.

One goal of the Strategic Plan is to maintain and enhance the city's strength as a financial, headquarters and services center. To work toward this goal, the following strategies were developed:

Diversification and Retention of Business

The annual addition of thousands of new jobs created by companies already in San Francisco has masked the fact that very few new companies have joined the city's economy. This has left both the business community and city government complacent, spurring no aggressive efforts to attract businesses or establish new enterprises here.

San Francisco has a number of attributes — its status as a world-class city with a strong financial and headquarters core, quality institutions of higher education, a good transportation network and sound fiscal health. These must be promoted if additional regional, national or international firms are to locate here. To accomplish this end, the Strategic Plan proposes that the San Francisco Chamber of Commerce and the Mayor's Office of Economic Development collaborate to develop a marketing plan that will identify 50 to 200 companies that might be attracted to San Francisco. Once identified, the companies would be contacted by City officials and business leaders and encouraged to relocate to San Francisco.

Of course, the task force recognized that attracting new companies to an area is considerably more difficult than working to retain existing businesses. For this reason, a business retention task force of key private and public sector individuals will be formed and meet regularly with major San Francisco employers to discuss the benefits of remaining and growing in this city. It would be an ongoing effort to promote the strengths of the city and its positive impact on business.

Office Cost Differentials

If San Francisco is to successfully convince new or existing employers to locate or remain here, one hurdle that must be overcome is its expensive office space. A comparative cost analysis indicates that San Francisco Financial District space averages about $7–15 more per square foot than most alternative Bay Area locations. Secondary office space South of Market Street, however, exceeds competitive suburban sites by just $7–8 per square foot.

The intent of this Strategic Plan strategy is to reduce that disparity by reducing the cost of developing new office space in San Francisco. To do so, a task force representing the Department of City Planning, the Mayor's Office of Economic Development, and the business/development community will be established to identify, compare and monitor total office development costs — including taxes — in competing headquarters and secondary-office cities. The group's objective will be to devise a plan to make San Francisco office space more affordable.

Secondary Office Space

America is in the process of rehousing its work force. And as San Francisco has led most central cities in the shift from a manufacturing to a service-dominated economy, it has experienced a boom in the construction of office space to house these new workers. Despite this buildup, rents from October 1978 to July 1981 increased by 150 percent. Fortunately for the long-term health of the economy, the laws of supply and demand are working. As office supply increase this year, there has been a corresponding reduction in rents and an increased vacancy rate allowing tenant mobility. But, as noted earlier, rents here remain comparatively high.

In a recent statement to the Planning Commission, the mayor said, "I am extremely concerned that we maintain our competitive position with respect to 'back office' and office-serving employment. I am not satisfied to have our hometown office buildings occupied by a relatively few executives in the 'front' while the bulk of the employees are moved to the suburbs. Back office employment provides many job opportunities for San Franciscans ... and contributes to the tax base. We cannot allow our employment base to emigrate to the suburbs."

The mayor has called on the Planning Commission to develop "affirmative policies" encouraging the creation of secondary office space at a cost which is reasonably competitive with that of neighboring counties. The Strategic Plan supports the mayor's position and suggests that a joint task force of developers, secondary office space users, and the City Planning Department be formed to determine the necessary requirements for this type of office space and, if necessary, to amend the planning and zoning laws in appropriate areas to allow for its construction.

Education and Training Advisory Committee

Business and education leaders agree the skills of workers need to be enhanced for them to compete successfully in an economy demanding an increasing number of service and computer-trained employees. They also concur that education and training programs need to be designed to more closely match the future needs of employers. The task force has chosen to form a committee composed of top-level private and public representatives to develop programs that will ensure that city residents have the skills necessary to fill future jobs in the city.

Preserve Retail Core

Compared to most central cities, the vitality of San Francisco's Union Square retail center and its many neighborhood commercial strips is unique. Some of the factors accounting for this strength are high disposable income, a strong tourist and downtown service economy, and a good regional and local transportation network.

Even though retail employment is not expected to rise above the current 18,000 jobs, the city needs to ensure that zoning and other public policies allow for reasonable growth for downtown and neighborhood retailers. The encroachment of inappropriate uses into retail areas should be minimized. And the business community and city government should consider implementing a marketing program to attract additional premier retailers.

Convention Meeting Space

There are significant economic and job opportunities in the nation-wide growth of convention and trade show activities. San Francisco's beauty and competitive stance — further enhanced by its retail and restaurant facilities, the number of existing and planned hotels, and the many cultural and recreational activities available in and around the city — put it in prime position to capitalize on this lucrative area.

The task force, however, was surprised to learn that the recently completed Moscone Convention Center lacks adequate meeting space to accommodate major conventions, and as a result, San Francisco is losing business to competing cities. Negotiations have already begun to plan and develop increased meeting rooms in or near the center. This strategy encourages continued negotiations and support from the business community to ensure that such space is constructed.

City Finances

To assist in its analysis, the City Finance Task Force constructed a five-year fiscal model assessing the impact of external and internal policy decisions on the city's General Fund. Research showed that San Francisco's financial position has deteriorated over the past 10 years, and the model indicated that the city's fiscal health will be uncertain over the next five years. The current General Fund Surplus will be completely sapped in the next two to five fiscal years, demanding careful attention to plans involving increased expenditures or decreased revenues. The city must have a consistent financial plan and practice careful fiscal management if it is to maintain essential services without raising taxes.

Fiscal Health

Through the Mayor's Fiscal Advisory Committee (MFAC), a set of fiscal indicators and standards linked to economic data should be established to monitor the city's fiscal performance and forecast its financial position. These key indicators and standards would be used to evaluate policy, impacts and trends. The five-year financial forecast would encourage planning and discourage crisis management.

A vice chairman of Wells Fargo Bank and task force chairman said, "This strategy will establish a monitoring process that will help maintain the city's financial strength and help it in dealing with an uncertain fiscal future."

Pensions

City pension costs are rising faster than the overall General Fund budget. In two key departments — police and fire — these costs now represent almost half of their yearly expenditures. This strategy will focus on controlling pension costs and evaluating alternatives to bring city pensions into line with other city expenditures.

Infrastructure

Between 1975 and 1982, in constant dollars there has been a 45 percent decrease in the public works budget. From the city's General Fund alone, Strategic Plan findings indicate an additional $40–50 million annually should be spent on capital improvements and $15–25 [million] on maintenance.

In recent years, the city has elected to defer maintenance and new capital investments — a relatively easy decision since the consequences are not apparent for many years and there is little public clamor for increased spending on roads or other capital needs. Nevertheless, failure to address the infrastructure spending gap will result in an ever-increasing backlog of deferred maintenance which will become increasingly more expensive in later years. San Francisco's backlog is currently manageable, but without adequate attention it will become a major burden.

The business community can be instrumental in this area by helping the city prepare a fixed-assests record system. The MFAC could develop a process whereby the condition of the city's public works could be monitored, and the amount of the city's General Fund to be spent on capital improvements and maintenance could be determined. Once there is an accurate accounting of the need, then a process for funding the unmet portion could be developed.

Housing

"For San Francisco residents and businesses, the expenses and scarcity of rental and owned housing is a significant problem" — *Frances Davis, Housing Task Force chairman and Potlatch Corp. vice president and general counsel.*

Though housing is an issue that has been extensively studied and discussed, there are no simple "quick fixes" to national or local problems such as financing, rent control, or construction and land costs. Only by working in concert can City Hall and the business community establish policies and actions that will increase housing production and reduce cost.

Building Permit Process and CEQA Changes

A major institutional constraint on the city's capacity to increase its housing supply is the permit approval process. The uncertainities and delays involved in obtaining a permit discourage developers from undertaking residential projects and add to the cost of the final product by as much as 25 percent. And the longer the permit approval time, the slower the flow of new units onto the market. In the recent past, analysts have reviewed the operation and organization of both the Department of City Planning and the Bureau of Building Inspection and have recommended actions to improve the process.

During the Housing Task Force's deliberations, questions arose about the implementation of those existing proposals and whether the changes increased efficiency and reduced costs. The mayor shares these concerns and supports the Strategic Plan strategy to have the MFAC assume ongoing responsibility to monitor, evaluate and recommend improvements in the building review and permit process.

Throughout the state, local officials and development communities are evaluating proposals to revise the California Environmental Quality Act (CEQA). The state-mandated environmental impact reporting requirements and process seem to have become overly burdensome, costly and hinder housing protection. Carefully crafted amendments could ensure that the environmental protection remains in force while streamlining project review and thus reduce cost and increase production. Work on these CEQA amendments has already begun.

Pro-housing Coalition

The lack of a broad-based, politically organized pro-housing constituency is recognized by city officials as a major barrier to the formulation of aggressive housing production policies. Rarely do residential developers find project support at Planning Commission hearings.

During hearings for the proposed City Residence Element, a loose-knit coalition of business, union and community-based groups developed a unified position. The Strategic Plan recommends that such a coalition be formalized, and charged with actively supporting proposals that will increase housing supply, enhance its affordability, and reduce appropriate regulatory controls.

Secondary Units

The task force did not view the construction of additional secondary units as an affordable-housing panacea. Rather, they believe that a city ordinance legalizing new secondary units in appropriate residential areas which can handle the additional density should be pursued.

Housing Zoning and Density

The city and county of San Francisco instituted a comprehensive rezoning of residential districts in 1978 which set allowable densities in established residential areas at the level of generally prevailing density. It is unlikely that impetus for another such undertaking will materialize in the near future.

However, there are opportunities for selective rezoning in the city for mixed-use rather than exclusively commercial or industrial use. The proposed Residence Element identifies Rincon Hill, the Van Ness – South Van Ness corridor, South of Market and parts of the North of Market (Tenderloin) for rezoning. In addition, certain neighborhood commercial areas that could accommodate greater density could be rezoned to enlarge residential areas and preserve a viable mix of commercial activities to serve residents. Careful planning and zoning can ensure that the quality of new or existing residential neighborhoods is enhanced.

Regardless of the rate of employment growth, there is a need for both resident and non-resident employees to get to and from work, whether by public or private transportation. Considering both automobile traffic and planned expansion of public transit, there appears to be adequate capacity to handle a larger number of commuters from the North Bay, East Bay and Peninsula, as well as within San Francisco, at least through 1990. At the present time, there are no plans to expand the road or transit capacity beyond expected 1990 levels. But unless additional capacity is planned and funded, the transportation system serving San Francisco will be severely taxed by the year 2000. According to the Transportation Task Force Chairman, a Bechtel Power Corporation vice president and director, "Transportation is an area which requires a long lead time to plan and acquire the needed facilities to accommodate additional demand. We must think and plan for the end of the century."

Muni and BART Capital Programs

The city and the business community share the goal of expanding transit capacity and facilities to satisfy projected need. Business can take an active role in supporting the implementation of BART and Muni five-year capital-improvement plans, and can assist public officials in lobbying for federal, state and local money to finance these programs.

A BART board member and the BART General Manager have commended San Francisco's business community for its aggressive support of the BART capital program at the federal level. This pattern of support would be continued under the Strategic Plan's transportation strategies.

BART Extension

A high percentage of Peninsula commuters drive to the city. New commercial development along Highway 101 in northern San Mateo County will only increase the congestion on the roads leading into the city. Even if Southern Pacific's CalTrain and SamTrans buses expand their city-bound transit service, it is questionable whether this is the best long-range solution to easing the Peninsula commute. A possible alternative is extending BART from Daly City to Peninsula cities, as was originally planned. This strategy will focus on political, economic and transit requirements to encourage such a BART extension.

Muni Advisory Committee

Based on his extensive experience in transit operation, Muni's general manager believes the private sector can contribute considerably to the improvement and expansion of Bay Area transit programs, and the business community concurs. This Strategic Plan strategy calls for the creation of a technically oriented group of business volunteers to assist Muni in improving its performance and containing costs. The business community and Muni patrons both will benefit.

The Chamber Executive Vice President, who is a Wells Fargo & Co. vice chairman, has been charged with overseeing the implementation of the Strategic Plan. He indicates a key element in the plan's success is the continuation of the dialogue between the public and private sectors. During the development of the Strategic Plan, constructive communication channels were opened that have resulted in a mutual enlightenment of the concerns and problems facing these two sectors of our city. An objective underlying all Strategic Plan strategies is the continual effort to improve business and government communications. And the Strategic Plan's theme — "Making a Great City Greater" — will continue to be the guiding principle throughout its implementation.

Santa Barbara County's Transformation Program — Meeting the Challenge of a New Reality

Lea Brooks

Santa Barbara County is designing a new vehicle to make government operations more effective, efficient, accountable and flexible. "We're restructuring county government and changing the way we do business," explained Tom Rogers, Board of Supervisors' chairman. "It is mainly a financial goal. We want to provide for ourselves the resources to respond to the community's priorities."

County officials found they could no longer adequately deal with declining financial resources and increasing demands for services. "Our government structure and methods of communication and resolving conflicts weren't set up for problem-solving, and we needed to move faster," Rogers said.

After a rocky start more than two years ago, Santa Barbara County's "transformation" program is in full swing. Two recent milestones were largely the result of thousands of hours of work by the 28-member Public/Private Sector Advisors Task Force, which has representatives from five "stakeholder" groups — the Board of Supervisors, department heads, management-level employees, employee groups and the public.

On May 22, supervisors unanimously adopted the county's first-ever goals and mission statement.

The statement, which includes program priorities that will be revised annually, "represents a commitment on the part of the board to lead and

Reprinted with permission from California County, *September/October 1990. Published by the County Supervisors Association of California, Sacramento, California.*

put our money where our mouth is," Rogers said. "It is kind of like staking your claim on the future."

On Aug. 20, supervisors unanimously accepted the Santa Barbara County Administrative Office Management Review/Strategic Plan, which proposes 20 major "prescriptions for change."

The report was prepared by the consulting firm of CMSI, which was hired in November 1989 to develop a strategic plan for the administrative office. It recommends that the county administrative officer be given a lot more responsibility and authority.

"We have a good start," Rogers said. "It's a long process and we've already made some changes and have a lot of good feelings about what we can do and what we can change."

For example, the board agenda process has already been revised to make the meetings more efficient. Rogers noted that despite a "huge agenda" at a recent meeting, everything ran smoothly and on time, including a "major controversial issue that was handled in 45 minutes."

County Administrative Officer Chuck Wagner called the report "a significant step, but still only a first step in our overall county transformation program to develop more effective and efficient county operations."

Wagner is developing a budget, timetable and recommendations for implementation. In October, supervisors will begin clearly defining the respective roles of the administrative officer, Board of Supervisors and department heads.

The county administrative office was the first to undergo an evaluation so a model process could be developed to examine each of the county's major areas of service.

Change Agent

Wagner was elevated from public works director to county administrative officer in November 1988 to oversee the transformation program. Wagner, who has worked for Santa Barbara County for nearly 30 years, considers himself a "change agent."

He finds himself in a unique position. His contract terminates June 30, 1992 — his planned retirement date.

"The board had this problem and asked me to help solve it," he said. "I had enough of an ego to believe that I had certain skills I could bring to this problem and could actually make a significant contribution to this county and retire feeling I had done something worthwhile."

Many county employees are upset at the prospect of change and don't understand why Santa Barbara is undergoing an intensive self-examination.

"It's not that anything is broken," Wagner explained. "My analogy is that we're trying to run a very good operating Model A Ford in a 1990 road race. Even though it is working well, it is still a Model A Ford.

"Proposition 13 significantly changed the fiscal situation in which we operate. Generally, I think most counties, including Santa Barbara, have done an excellent job of coping with the change. However, we have not really made the changes that are necessary to live with the fiscal reality — a fixed bottom line.

"We're changing our whole attitude in Santa Barbara about cost effectiveness, accountability and program performance. We're not accusing people of not working hard. They may not be working as effectively as they could because they may not have the proper training or tools. We're committed to giving them the necessary training and tools to become more cost effective and efficient so in the end we can do more with less. We're expecting people to work smarter, not harder.

"I'm convinced that what is happening in Santa Barbara County is going to happen in every county in this state. We need to get county government operating under today's expectations and fiscal realities to take us on into the next century."

The most unusual aspect of Santa Barbara County's evaluation is the open, participatory process, according to Wagner. There have been numerous task force meetings, workshops and public hearings.

"We made a conscious decision to do our business in a fishbowl," he said. "We invited everyone to participate. The five stakeholder group concept has proven to be an innovative and effective method of problem identification. In the end, I think the changes we're going to make will be more readily accepted and understood.

"One thing I've learned is how traumatic change really is for people, especially when you have not quite been able to explain to them exactly what changes you have in mind. We didn't have a set agenda or a set plan. The only thing agreed on by the board was that it had to be a public process."

David Nichols, retired county manager of San Mateo County and a member of CMSI's Santa Barbara project team, said, "The board was anxious that it not be done in a vacuum. There was extensive interaction with the stakeholders. It was very courageous for the board to ask for that kind of review — a willingness to examine themselves in a way that would be very public. There are risks. It was a very public review that involved the community."

Bob Klausner, a Santa Barbara businessman and public member of the task force, called the Santa Barbara board a "rare bunch of supervisors" and praised them for tackling the issue of government structure. "This is not a sexy issue," he said. "The state is laying its responsibilities on counties without resources and the federal government is laying its responsibilities off on the state. The system that has evolved is topsy — it was built by adding additions to a house. It's not a system anyone would start out with today. The issue is how do you modify the structure without tearing it down because it has to keep running to provide these services."

Implementing the changes will "require a lot of education and sustained interest. We're on the road; how we do remains to be seen."

There will be many benefits if the changes are fully implemented, Klausner said. "Supervisors will find that they can produce more for constituents. For the bureaucrats, there will be clear lines of authority, responsibility and accountability. Their working conditions will be easier — less stress, headaches and backaches. They will know what's expected of them and be able to hold the political body accountable. It's hard to work for a political body when the political winds blow different directions."

Strengthening the County Administrative Office

Now that Santa Barbara County supervisors have accepted a strategic plan to strengthen the administrative office, the next step is implementation. One of the main hurdles facing supervisors is how to pay for the report's 20 recommendations when money is extremely tight.

"Doing business in a new and better way will require an upfront investment in additional staff for this office," said Administrative Officer Chuck Wagner. "While some people are going to argue that this is not the time to be taking a look at adding to the administrative officer's staff, there couldn't be a more critical time for administrative officers throughout the state to be operating at their top efficiency. The administrative office is the key arm of the board to implement its policies."

Supervisors will consider a timetable and funding for the recommendations during budget reduction hearings in mid–September. To date, the county has spent $140,000 for the strategic plan, $78,000 for subconstracts and thousands of hours of staff time on transformation. The plan's major recommendations include:

- The county administrative officer should have the authority to recommend to the Board of Supervisors one candidate for non-elected department head vacancies. If the board rejects the candidate, the county administrative officer will make another recommendation until the board accepts one.
- Build into the structure an annual performance evaluation process between the county administrator and the board-appointed department heads based on board-adopted goals.

- The county administrator, based on performance evaluations, can set a department head's salary anywhere in the board-established salary range. This authority gives the county administrator muscle in dealing with department heads.
- Reorganize the administrative office by creating three deputy administrative officers who — with the assistant administrative officer — will support management and strategic planning in environmental management, law and order, human services and infrastructure.

   The county currently has an adminstrative officer, an assistant and seven analysts.
- Automate and improve the budget process to include financial planning and forecasting, interdepartmental impacts on new programs and program performance measurements.
- Hire a part-time lobbyist in Sacramento and coordinate departmental lobbying.

Donald D. Stilwell, executive vice president of CMSI, the firm that prepared the plan, said, "We gave the county administrator a lot more responsibility and authority, cleaner lines of authority and better coordination of activities."

David Nichols, a member of CMSI's Santa Barbara project team, said the "plan upgrades a number of important management functions and identifies who is responsible for them. The county administrator is responsible for most of them, but others will be delegated: training; affirmative action; intergovernmental relations; management development; communication; recruitment; budget; employee relations; strategic planning; agenda policies; and meeting management — how to conduct efficient meetings."

A Commitment to the Public

Health and human services, community planning and resource management, and public safety were given high priority in the first-ever goals and mission statement adopted by Santa Barbara County supervisors.

"The Santa Barbara County Board of Supervisors and the entire county workforce are committed to providing the best possible public services, within available financial, natural and human resources, to promote a life of quality for all county residents," the statement says.

"The board recognizes that, in this era of increasingly limited financial resources, county government cannot provide the maximum levels of services everyone may desire. Instead, the challenge will be to provide the best possible services within given financial constraints. This may mean that levels of service in some areas may not be ideal. It may mean that extremely difficult choices will have to be made, pitting worthy programs and projects against each other. The board sees its responsibility to assess needs, set priorities and make these critical choices on behalf of all county government."

The board's major goals are:

- Annually adopt clear and achievable goals and program priorities that address the community's most important needs.
- Achieve the goals and program priorities by optimizing managerial and organizational effectiveness.
- Adopt and manage cost-effective county budgets, within available resources, that optimize results in providing effective public services based on the goals and program priorities.
- Recruit, hire, train, motivate and retain the highest quality workforce which reflects the ethnic and gender makeup of the county population.
- Provide consistent, well-informed, helpful and timely public service and communication to maximize understanding of, participation in and satisfaction with county government.

Resistance to Change

When Rogers initially ran for county supervisor in 1986, he told prospective voters that the county needed to do a better job of managing its resources.

"I was idealistic," he recalled. "I had an expectation that county government could respond to the public's wishes. When I came on the board, I couldn't get where I wanted to go. I saw lots of great ideas, but a failure to accomplish them because of inappropriate management. I realized that you have to do more than say, 'these are my goals.'"

Rogers recalled an incident at a meeting shortly after being elected. "A member of the public told me, 'I trust you and I think you're a good guy and I know you'll do your best, but I don't have any faith in county government's ability to deliver what the public wants.' That really shook me up."

Rogers was also frustrated by a unanimous vote of the Board of Supervisors in 1987 that directed two county agencies to figure out a way to control flooding while protecting the environment. "Essentially, nothing happened for two years," he said.

Both incidents made Rogers realize that the county's management structure lacked clear lines of authority, accountability and communication. He was surprised at the resistance to improve the system.

"I thought people would be interested in results—that there would be enthusiasm for change and getting better," he said. "The challenge became showing people how change could benefit them."

Employees were downright hostile toward a productivity program developed in 1988. "It got a bad name," Rogers explained. "Employees thought it meant they weren't doing a good job. The county went through a lot of tumult in 1988 and 1989. Employee morale was low, there were budget shortfalls and a lack of public confidence. There were strikes and sickouts."

In an effort to improve employee relations, supervisors declared 1990 the year of the public employee. An employee suggestion award program pays cash awards to employees who find ways to save money and improve services. Another ongoing program presents a cash award to the county employee of the month.

Wagner's promotion in 1988 and the seating in January 1989 of two new supervisors — Dianne Owens and Gloria Ochoa — really started the transformation process rolling.

With 14 years in office, Supervisor Bill Wallace is the senior member of the board. Employees initially resented change because the county's internal structure was not broken, he said. "It's not like this county is a disaster zone. We're not going bankrupt and there have been no horrible cuts."

The supervisors in office before Rogers, Owens and Ochoa were often polarized on issues and there were a lot of split votes, Wallace said. "We did not look at the county's internal structure.

"The transformation program has coalesced the [current] board. It's been a good process for all the board members to go through," he said. "We've gotten to know each other."

Owens agreed that the current board works well together. "While it does not always agree, it agrees to work together," she said. "Members are very like-minded, which is pretty unusual."

Owens said she is still amazed that the county did not set goals until this year. She surmised that since money wasn't a problem until Proposition 13 reduced taxes and limited local government's ability to generate taxes, county officials didn't worry about setting goals.

She believes that the transformation program will pull all the elements of county government together. "We're all in the same business of providing county services. The health department should not be competing against the probation department. The end result is we're serving the same people. We have to look at the county as a whole."

Agriculture Commissioner Ron Gilman, also a member of the task force, said one of the benefits to department heads will be a "clear understanding of the responsibilities of the board, the administrative officer and the department heads. There should be a clear message of what the board expects from the departments and a clearer way to determine a department's accomplishments.

"The board recognizes and we [department heads] recognize that times aren't the same as in the past. We have to make changes to stay current."

Strategic Planning in Local Government — The West Hartford Approach

Richard Russo and David Penchoff

The economic changes which have confronted the country in the last five years have had significant impact on the municipal bond market. The recognition and response to these new conditions has varied. One response has been developed by the town of West Hartford and deals with the new realities of the market place as well as the traditional perspectives of the policy making arena. The success of the approach is a result of the strategic nature of the planning which went into its development. These successes notwithstanding, the article indicates the need for a greater emphasis on the use of a strategic planning perspective in policy formulation and some of the vehicles which can assist in the development of such a perspective.

A good deal of attention has been focused over the past year on "creative" approaches to capital financing. These approaches have evolved in response to the high long term interest rates and increased market volatility which represent a major shift in this formerly benign area of municipal finance. As a result of this shift, the development of policies for the issuance, structure and management of debt must be integrated with the long range plans for the maintenance and development of the infrastructure of a municipality.

The town of West Hartford has recently embarked on a program which is intended to provide an extensive degree of integration of capital

Reprinted with permission from Connecticut Government, *Vol. 34, No. 2, Spring 1983. Published by the Institute of Public Service, the University of Connecticut, Storrs, Connecticut.*

improvement planning and programming with capital financing and debt management. The program evolved after the full effect of high term interest rates on total capital project costs was articulated by the department of finance and understood by the Town Council.

Defining the Problem

The first indications that there would be pronounced changes in the nature of the municipal bond market came to the attention of the Department of Finance after bond sales in 1978 and 1979 had resulted in interest rates which began to exceed the five percent mark. In June of 1980 the department published an analysis in the town's annual financial report. The analysis pointed out that the effect of interest rates which are sustained at the six percent level is to increase the portion of annual budgetary debt service which is dedicated to the repayment of interest. The analysis further indicated that within a few years at such interest rates and with regular bond sales of twenty year maturities, interest will exceed principal in annual debt service. The net effect of the trends which were pointed out in the analysis is that more dollars would be required in annual debt service but less debt would be retired.

Seeking Solutions

In order to mitigate these trends it was recommended that a cash reserve be established and utilized to allow for shortened maturity schedules (reduced to ten years rather than the traditional twenty) and hence reduce total interest costs. The cash reserve would serve as a form of "endowment" to provide cash infusions from interest earnings as an offset to the increased annual principal payments which would be required with ten year issues.

The analysis was well received although the link between theory and practice was still to be developed. That link was to be provided in 1981. It was at that time that long term interest rates had begun their ascendency to beyond the ten percent level. As a result, total financing costs for major capital projects with twenty year bond issues would be double the cost of actual construction.

Impetus for Action

With the awareness that the new market conditions could have a serious effect on the town's ability to sustain a responsible capital improvement program, the town council responded to administrative recommendations to step back and take a strategic approach to the entire question of capital programming and financing.

To address the question of capital improvement programming, new emphasis was placed on the development of a capital program document which could be used as a vehicle for installing discipline and setting priorities for the town's future capital maintenance and development. (Figure 1 represents a conceptual framework for that process.) At the same time research was being conducted as to effective ways to finance that program. As indicated previously, these approaches were initiated at a time of high long term interest rates, coupled with an unprecedented degree of volatility. This made the financing question much more difficult while placing greater emphasis on the use of priorities in the structuring of the capital program.

State of the Art

At the time, and to the present there are very few financing alternatives available which would provide any long term advantages to the town in its debt management program. Many of the approaches being put forth in journals and at various conferences have dealt with alternative marketing methods which could be utilized by lesser rated jurisdictions to enhance the marketability of bonds but would not necessarily result in lower borrowing costs. Fortunately, West Hartford has maintained triple-A ratings from both major rating agencies and has therefore had to contend with the more fundamental questions of the level and volatility of the market itself.

A New Opportunity

One development did arise after discussions with the town's then newly selected financial advisor, the First National Bank of Boston. It was indicated that tax exempt commercial paper could be utilized in place of traditional Bond Anticipation notes (BAN's) to provide cash for projects which had bond authorizations but were not yet issued. The advantages of this instrument over traditional BAN's are twofold; first, the interest rate for commercial paper was up to one hundred basis points, or one percentage point, less than six-month BAN's and secondly, commercial paper could be structured with the cooperation of the Connecticut State Association and with much greater flexibility than BAN's which must have fixed maturities (usually six or twelve months).

Figure 1. West Hartford Approach to a Strategic Programming System: Capital Programming and Budgeting Component

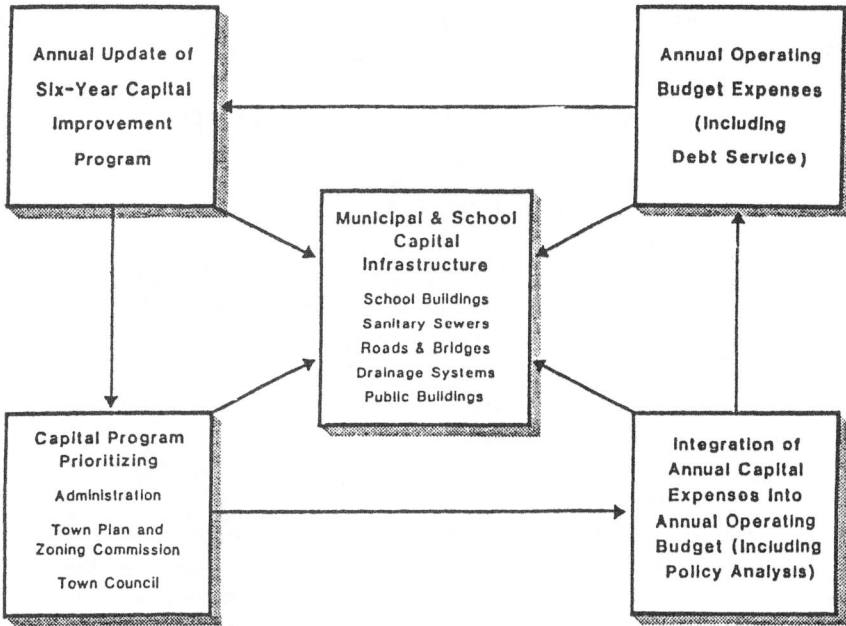

The use of commercial paper would provide the town with three distinct advantages relative to total capital financing costs. The first was the cash flow and reinvestment opportunities, the reinvestment advantage or "spread" of the interest cost of the commercial paper compared to what the town could earn through the reinvestment of the unexpended portion of the borrowings ranged from three to five percentage points. With a commercial paper program in excess of two million dollars and projected to be at times over four million, this provided a potential of over two hundred thousand dollars in additional interest earnings for the town.

The second advantage was the flexibility for bond issuance. Because the maturities for commercial paper can be less than thirty days and can be altered with each successive sale, the town would be in an advantageous position to enter the bond market should a "window of opportunity" present itself. This element of the program was essential in dealing with the volatility factor which was a new phenomenon in the municipal bond market.

A third advantage of this approach was that it did not preclude the town from reverting to traditional methods of financing through the use of BAN's or utilizing the town's cash position for current projects and issuing bonds every spring.

With the advantages of the commercial paper program made apparent to policy officials, the Department of Finance then developed a strategic framework for the development of an administrative operation which could implement the commercial paper program and, more importantly, begin to integrate the development of the capital improvement program with an organized and long range approach to capital financing.

Commitment of Resources

The result of these efforts was the establishment of the Program Planning Office in January 1982 with funding and staffing of the office effective July 1, 1982. The office is contained within the Department of Finance under the Director of Finance. The responsibilities of the office are the implementation of the newly developed debt management program and the coordination of that program with the capital programming processes of the town. In addition, the annual operating budget and selected policy analyses are administered by the office.

This comprehensive planning and management capacity provides the basis of the town's strategic programming system. As Figure 2 indicates, these formerly distinct elements are, for the first time, focused in one office for coordination and development of further enhancements to the system.

Current Status

The Program Planning Office has been in place for approximately eleven months. While eleven months may be a limited timeframe for a retrospective review, a number of comments can be made.

1. The commercial paper program and its flexibility were shown to be of significant value in early November 1982 when a sudden drop in long term interest rates afforded the "window of opportunity" for market entry. With the flexibility of commercial paper and the staff capacity in program planning, a bond sale was completed within a five week period inclusive of preparation of a prospectus. This compares with the three to five months previously required for bond sale preparation.
2. The bond issue was structured with a ten year maturity and received a very favorable interest rate of 7.6%. This provided a major

Figure 2. West Hartford Approach to a Strategic Programming System: Program Planning Office Component

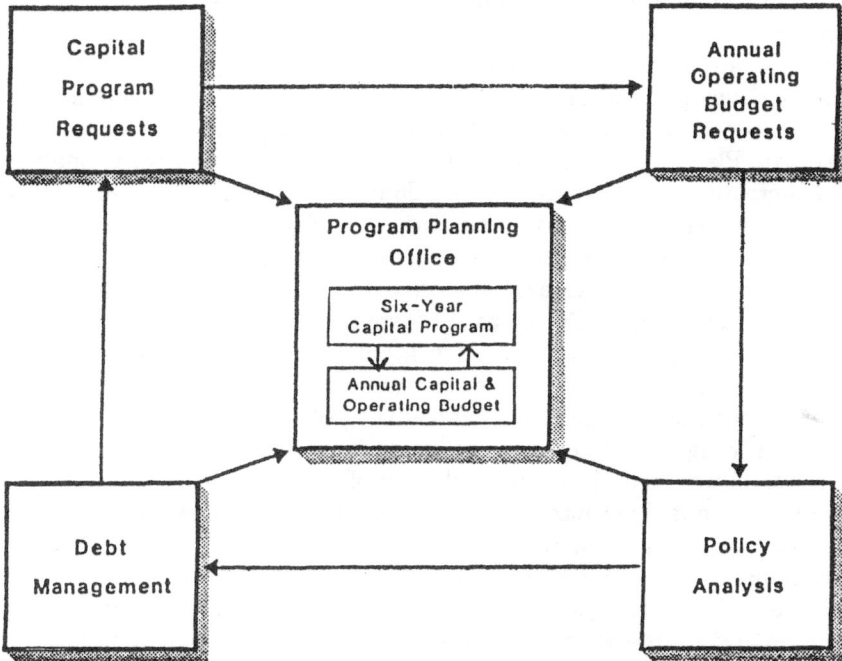

achievement in attaining the policy goal of lessening total interest costs.

3. The reinvestment advantages of the commercial paper program and related debt management operations are already projected to result in over $500,000 in interest earnings to the town. These interest earnings will ultimately serve to reduce financing costs in the future.

4. The expanded research capability of the Program Planning Office has provided the Town Manager and Town Council with a greater degree of financial and statistical information to assist in developing a strategic perspective in dealing with the town's capital program.

Prospects for the Future

From a financial management perspective, the above-cited achievements are notable. The strategic approach to capital financing was clearly shown to be viable from a procedural and direct cost/benefit standpoint. However, these successes represent initial success in only the debt management component of the overall strategic planning process and, while significant, will be limited without further advancements in the remaining areas of capital programming and long range analysis of both capital and operating budget policy issues. It is only through that process that a strategic approach toward achieving pre-defined community objectives can be developed and pursued. Such a process can only be implemented by the commitment of the policy bodies themselves. A resource such as the Program Planning Office can provide a good deal of assistance in analyzing alternatives and coordinating the administrative procedural mechanisms but procedure is only a tool and without a clearly defined direction to which the procedures can be applied, the advantages are lost.

To provide the necessary perspective for articulating policy direction, the Program Planning Office has put forth the concept of a multi-year approach to budget planning and development. Such an approach would utilize the concept of a biennial budget as a means of reducing the "budget crunch" perspective which either forces key policy decisions to be made in an already highly charged atmosphere or, if the issues are of a longer term nature, allows decision making to be put off to future years when the options will probably be narrowed to the least favorable alternatives. Under the multi-year approach, the Council could adopt a two-year budget at the beginning of its term which would represent a maintenance of existing policies. They would then establish the policy areas in greatest need of attention and address them in a more reflective and objective manner. The final determinations of policy direction could then be reflected and incorporated in a revision of the second budget year as well as the adoption of a comprehensive five-year strategic plan.

Initial discussions with policy officials have indicated an awareness that such a process could be of great assistance to them. At the very least, there is a growing recognition that the traditional budget process does not provide a rational basis for long range policy development. Such recognition on the part of policy officials may provide the impetus for further enhancements to the strategic planning process in West Hartford.

PART THREE

The Future

The Future of Strategic Management

William Earle Klay

What follows is a set of conjectures about the future of proactive strategic management. As such, it shares with strategic management the quality of uncertainty. Uncertainty about the future cannot be eliminated, but it can, at times, be managed through the development and implementation of strategy. In doing so, strategists can learn much about their organizations and about the environment within which they live. Similarly, the development of well-ordered conjectures about the future of strategic management may help to better understand strategic management itself.

The issue at hand is not whether strategy formulation has a future, for certainty it does. The making of strategy is as old as organized human endeavor. There can be little doubt that leaders will always involve themselves in the formulation of strategy. Nor is the issue here whether academicians will continue their relatively recent forays into the making of organizational strategy. If academia truly hopes to understand the behavior of organizations, and especially the behavior of senior leaders within organizations, then it will continue to study strategy. To do otherwise would be an open invitation to academic irrelevancy.

What is in doubt is the future of anticipatory strategy formulation and, particularly, the emerging body of prescriptive theory intended to guide the development and implementation of proactive strategy. In their landmark study, Cyert and March (1963) concluded that organizations typically try to reduce complexity and its accompanying uncertainty by reacting to feedback rather than developing anticipatory capabilities. Clearly, many organizations continue their reactive styles in spite of the environmental turbulence that so concerns the proponents of proactive strategy formulation.

Reprinted with permission from Jack Rabin, Gerald J. Miller, and W. Bartley Hildreth, Editors, Handbook of Strategic Management, *1989. Published by Marcel Dekker, Inc., New York, New York.*

The future of prescriptive strategic management, the body of theory that prescribes methods for proactive strategy formulation and implementation, may well depend on three factors—perceived need to anticipate, practicability of prescriptions, and perceived utility of implementing such prescriptions. It is assumed here that the future environments of organizations will be sufficiently turbulent that there will be a need to anticipate. Competitive pressures and fundamental structural changes in our economy and society will prompt many organizational leaders to seek ways to cope with changing conditions. Therefore, the future of strategic management will depend mostly on the degree to which potential users will perceive the set of prescriptions derived from the theory to be useful and doable.

There can be little utility from a body of theory if its prescriptions are not practicable, and there seems little likelihood that prescriptions will be put into continuing practice if there is not sufficient utility for key decision makers. In forecasting the future of strategic management, then, the task is twofold—to examine whether its prescriptions are practicable, and whether there are sufficient reasons for decision makers to seek to undertake them.

Prescriptive Strategic Management

The dimensions of prescriptive management have been most fully described by H. Igor Ansoff (Ansoff 1965, 1984; Ansoff et al. 1976). The chronology of his writings show how a desire to understand the nature of corporate strategy evolved into a concern as to how organizations could better plan to cope with a changing future. Thus, from an awareness of the importance of organizational strategy, coupled with a growing concern that organizations were failing to properly prepare themselves to deal with an uncertain and changing environment, emerged his prescriptions for strategic planning. Subsequently, Ansoff and others realized that the prescriptions for strategic planning were encountering substantial resistance. This realization gave rise to the set of prescriptions known as strategic management.

Ansoff has posited four distinctive types of management systems, each of which is a response to the level of turbulence and predictability of an organization's external environment (1984, p. 14). When the external environment is stable and essentially unchanging, "management by control" predominates. The primary concern is with the development and implementation of financial, personnel, and other process controls. When change occurs but is essentially continuous, an extension of past experience, "management by extrapolation" prevails in which emphasis is placed on long-range planning of an extrapolative nature utilizing such methods as econometrics and time-series forecasting.

Discontinuities in the environment, according to Ansoff, prompt the emergence of either "management by anticipation" or "management by flexible/rapid response." If the nature of discontinuities can be understood sufficiently well in advance, then attention can be focused on improving anticipatory capacities and on strategic plans to place the organization in a desirable position vis-à-vis its environment. If, however, signals related to the nature of unfolding environmental change are especially weak, and there appears to be a likelihood of unpredictable surprises, then management's attention is likely to focus on the identification of such signals and on the development of an organization that is capable of rapid learning and response.

There is much definitional confusion regarding strategic planning and strategic management. The long-range plans developed through extrapolative techniques have sometimes been labeled as "strategic plans," and critics of strategic planning have faulted such processes, predicting the demise of strategic planning precisely because it failed to consider the possibilities of discontinuity. Such strategic planning, says Gray, tends to excessive reliance on "rationality" and, ironically, contributes to a "dangerous, short-term financial orientation" among top managers (1986, p. 89).

To others, strategic planning is worthy of the definition only if major emphasis is placed on the anticipation of discontinuities. However, even when strategic planning does emphasize preparing the organization for a future that may be significantly different than the present, the problem of resistance to such plans and the planning processes from which they emerge still exists. Gray surveyed senior managers in firms that had tried some form of strategic planning, and found widespread discontent. A majority of these executives indicated that their discontent was due "mainly to difficulties encountered in the implementation of plans" (p. 89).

Prescriptive strategic management includes the full range of strategic planning activities, but it is not limited to these. Because prescriptive strategic management is expressly intended to improve the abilities of organizations to deal with discontinuities in their external environments, it does not limit itself to the more narrowly conceived strategic planning of an extrapolative nature. The strategic planning dimension of prescriptive strategic management is of the type defined by Sufrin and Odiorne, who speak of it as a "process of adjustment by anticipation" in which special attention is focused upon risk, uncertainty, and unintended side effects (1985, pp. 5–6).

Strategic management is also a response to failure, the failure of strategic planning to (1) provide methods to overcome the resistance to strategic plans and to the planning process from whence they come and (2) provide methods to build a systematic learning and adaptive capacity throughout an organization. Sufrin and Odiorne, for example, speak of the necessity to somehow deal with the "change resistors" (1985, p. 10). Gray (1986) is of the opinion that strategic planning is a temporary process, from which an organization will either exit with a sense of failure, or progress further to strategic management. Either the obstacles to strategic planning will prevail, he says, or management will develop a capacity to manage resistance and promote change which will move an organization into the realm of strategic management.

After reflecting on the results of previous strategic planning efforts, Ansoff concluded that "it became increasingly evident that top management support is a necessary, but not a sufficient condition for assuring effectiveness of strategic planning within a firm" (1984, p. 197). It is necessary, he says, to extend the processes of anticipation introspectively, so that possible causes of resistance *within* an organization might be anticipated, and subsequently minimized or otherwise controlled. It is evident, however, that the qualities of "management by flexible/rapid response" extend well beyond simply devising means to manage resistance to "management by anticipation." Prescriptive strategic management includes both dealing with resistance to change *and* building a systemic capacity to learn and respond effectively.

Strategic management, then, is a combination of analytical methods and managerial behaviors. T. K. Das (1986, p. 15) says that theory with respect to strategy must consider two different dimensions of strategy making. One is the "rational-analytic conception," which encompasses the array of methodologies that are intended to assess the status of an organization and its environment so that the former might be better positioned within the latter. The other dimension is the "subjective side," which deals with the sociological and psychological propensities of organizational members, and especially with the processes of perception.

In order to assess the future prospects of strategic management, it will be necessary to explore both the rational-analytical and subjective dimensions of strategy making. Only then will it be possible to examine whether the prescriptions of strategic management are practicable and sufficiently attractive to prompt decision makers to seek to undertake them. The utility of a set of prescriptions is, after all, a matter of how they are perceived by potential users.

A Model of Strategic Management

Figure 1 presents a graphic depiction of the analytical and behavioral dimensions that are involved in prescriptive strategic management. These

Figure 1. Strategic Management Activities
DIRECTION

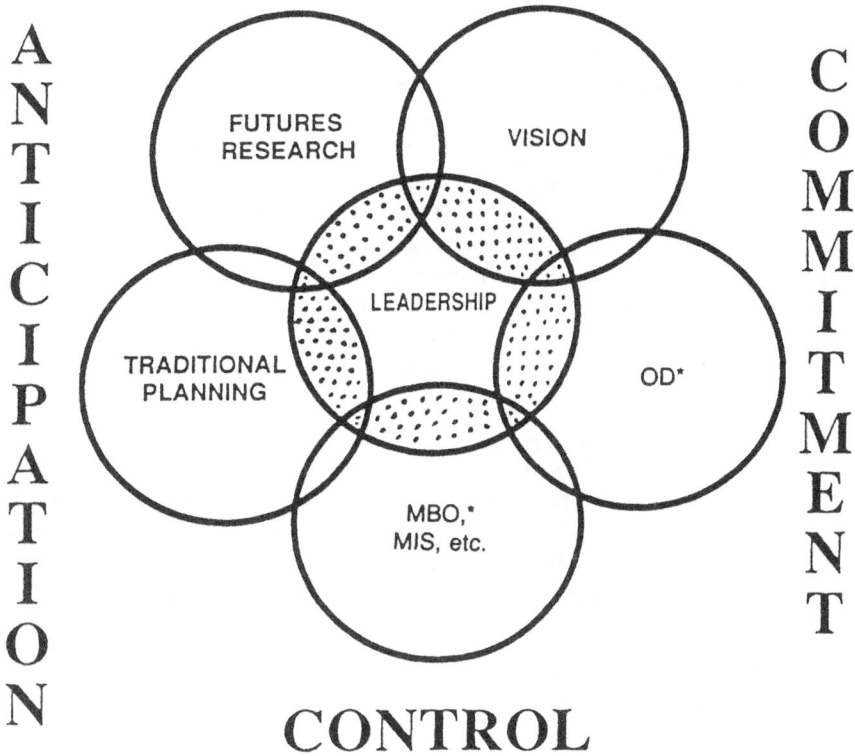

A
N
T
I
C
I
P
A
T
I
O
N

C
O
M
M
I
T
M
E
N
T

CONTROL

STRATEGIC MANAGEMENT

dimensions involve the interplay of six circles of activity within an organization. The six activity circles, in turn, are related to the accomplishment of four broad organizational purposes, each of which is essential to the achievement of the full potential of an organization.

Anticipation: Traditional Planning

Proponents of strategic planning often use biological or military metaphors associated with the notion of "survival" to underscore the importance of anticipation as a basis of successful adaptation. To fail to anticipate sufficiently well is to risk the loss of markets, loss of political support, and ultimately, if failure is of the worst kind, loss of the organization itself or of control thereof. Strategic planning therefore is inherently oriented toward anticipation.

In its earliest stages, strategic planning relied primarily on the extrapolative analytical techniques of traditional planning. Regression-based econometric forecasts, time-series analyses of such things as market share, and demographic projections of potential clients or customers are among the methodologies of traditional planning that are of particular relevance. Strategic planning, however, does not necessarily encompass the full range of an organization's traditional planning activities. It only includes those planning activities that are closely related to the deliberations of top leaders about the basic nature and fundamental directions of the organization. Capital facilities planning that is guided by strategic decisions, for example, has more to do with the operational implementation of strategy than it does with the making of the strategy itself.

Thus, strategic planning requires a nexus between planning and leadership activities. If planning fails to penetrate the activities of leadership, it can scarcely become strategic. Strategic planning can be said to exist only when leaders use planning to guide their fundamental decisions about strategy. Conversely, the use of planning processes to make strategic decisions is by no means the full extent of leadership behaviors. Strategic planning exists at a point of overlap between the spheres of planning and leadership, where planning helps leaders to anticipate, and leaders guide the planning process to better serve their most fundamental decision needs.

Anticipation: Futures Research

The failure of traditional planning techniques to contribute substantially to the anticipation, much less understanding, of many fundamental changes has led scholars and practitioners to explore the possibilities of adding the newer methodologies of futures research to strategic planning. Futures research is a relatively recent interdisciplinary field that applies a variety of techniques, often qualitative and group-oriented, to explore the nature of change with a particular orientation toward anticipating future threats or opportunities. Methods such as Delphi panels, environmental scanning, and scenario development have become a part of strategic planning (i.e., Becker 1982; Neufeld 1985).

Together, traditional planning and futures research comprise the set of methodologies that are used to accomplish the anticipation dimension of strategic planning. Futures research activities within organizations must be guided by the information needs of top managers if they are to serve the strategic planning needs of the organization. In turn, prescriptive strategic management theory requires that futures research be accepted and used by organizational leaders in the making of fundamental strategy.

The personal attention of top leaders to all details of futures research in organizations is unnecessary, but some degree of mutual penetration between the activities of futures researchers and leaders is essential if informed decisions are to emerge from the process. Further, because there are potential areas of conflict between futures research and traditional planning, and in large organizations the two forms of anticipatory activities may be divided between different specialists, leaders may be required to devote time to assure a necessary measure of mutual interaction and synergy between them.

Direction: Vision and Meaning

Few, if any, organizations engage in anticipatory processes merely for the intrinsic pleasure of doing so. Strategic planning is inherently oriented toward the establishment of direction. Strategic decisions are, by definition, those that establish and reaffirm the fundamental purposes and directions for an organization to follow. In other words, directional guidance for the making of myriad operational decisions is accomplished through strategic decisions.

> Strategic planning concerns itself with establishing the major directions for the organization, e.g. what is its purpose/mission, major clients to serve, major programs to pursue, its major geographical area, its major delivery approaches [McConkey 1986, p. 51].

When strategy is developed from traditional, extrapolative planning, the future is seen as an extension of models of reality that are already well accepted in an organization. Consensus as to the purpose of the organization, and resultant power relations within the organization, may be relatively unaffected. When environmental dislocations occur, however, giving rise to the futures research activities, past models of reality are subject to challenge. If it becomes apparent that some elements of an organization are more vital than others in achieving new strategies, resistance to the newly defined directions can be expected from those whose relative prestige and power may suffer.

Thus, a challenge of great magnitude to leaders using strategic management is to articulate organizational direction in a way that will be sufficiently appealing to the members of the organization. The directional dimension of strategic management, therefore, involves much more than crafting mission and goal statements, for these may have little or no appeal. Bennis and Nanus conclude that an essential element of leadership is the articulation of direction, "vision" in their terminology, which has an inherent motivational appeal to members in an organization, and which helps to coordinate their many operational decisions:

> To choose a direction, a leader must first have developed a mental image of a possible and desirable future state of the organization. This image, which we call a *vision*, may be as vague as a dream or as precise as a goal or mission statement. The critical point is that a vision articulates a view of a realistic, credible, attractive future for the organization, a condition that is better in some important ways than what now exists [Bennis and Nanus 1985, p. 89].

The collaboration of Bennis and Nanus symbolizes the establishment of linkages between anticipation and the management of change in strategic management theory. Nanus is a well known author in the field of futures research, while Bennis is one of the foremost proponents of organization development methodologies to accomplish planned organizational change. They do not argue that futures research is explicitly present in the formulation of successful vision for all organizations. Indeed, they are unable to explain fully how some leaders have formulated guiding perspectives that have become sources of motivation and that have given a sense of meaning to members of their organizations.

What Bennis and Nanus do argue, however, is that futures research can be conducted in ways that involve numerous members of an organization participatively in examining their future environment. Nanus's quick environmental scanning technique is offered as a set of techniques to permit leaders, managers, and planners to interact while scanning trends and issues, and then to continue such interaction in choosing among options to strategically position the organization.

The fusion of participatory mechanisms and futures research, it is argued, will enhance a sense of ownership about the resulting strategic direction and purposes of the organization. Such a sense of ownership, in turn, will prompt organizational members to commit their energies in a creative manner toward achieving a common purpose. The achievement of the common purpose gives a higher sense of meaning to the members' lives, while a shared sense of direction serves to better coordinate their individual decisions.

Organization Development

Narayanan and Fahey (1982) stress that a comprehensive theory of strategic decision making cannot ignore the internal political influences, the micropolitics of an organization. These political factors, they suggest, will influence whether and how views are expressed and, therefore, how strategy is formulated and whether it will be accepted. The theory of strategic management adds to strategic planning a prescriptive dimension that is intended to avert the prospect that micropolitics will thwart either the formulation or the implementation of effective strategy. This prescriptive dimension is drawn essentially from the theory of organization development.

In their book that describes the progression from strategic planning to strategic management, Ansoff, Declerck, and Hayes describe prescriptive strategic management to be a synthesis between two approaches to organizational change — "rational planning processes" and "adaptive psychosocio-political processes" (1976, p. 78). They criticize much of the literature of planned organizational change for having focused almost exclusively on either one or the other of the two approaches. To do so, they say, is "to swing a pendulum between two inefficient extremes" (p. 78). It is the addition of planned organization change strategies that most distinguishes strategic management from strategic planning (see also Eadie and Steinbacher 1985).

Control: MBO, MIS, etc.

What is also needed, however, are mechanisms to translate strategies into specific operational objectives and to obtain feedback about the process of the organization in achieving these. Control systems include such activities as accounting, inventory control, and routine personnel management (including performance evaluation), which are well known and need no further explanation except to stress that it is frequently these control activities that occupy much of the time of top executives. The control-related activities, however, that are most important to implementing strategies are those addressed by the theory of management by objectives (MBO).

The literature of strategic planning has always evidenced a concern about translating strategic objectives into operational ones and establishing appropriate mechanisms for monitoring and rewarding progress toward these objectives. It is unlikely that a strategic management system can be implemented without some variation of MBO. (In addition, few organizations are likely to implement strategic management systems without taking advantage of computer-based management information systems [MIS] to monitor the progress of the organization toward its objectives. When computers are used to gather information about the external environment as well, and help managers to perform both extrapolative planning and futures research activities, the systems become decision support systems.)

Properly understood, MBO is not based simply in a theory of control, although MBO systems are sometimes implemented as if they were. The foremost proponent of MBO, Peter Drucker (1954), stressed from its inception that MBO was intended to be a set of interactive procedures to achieve growth and motivation, as well as greater control. Properly understood, MBO prescribes steps through which individual organizational members might be helped to enhance both themselves and their contributions to the organizations, for which they are held accountable. To be properly implemented, MBO requires that other control activities such as cost accounting and personnel reward systems be made to serve the MBO processes.

Control mechanisms that contradict the direction of strategy or that enervate the implementation of strategy become obstacles that must be dealt with in the theory of prescriptive strategic management. Hence, it becomes necessary to also subject the control mechanisms themselves to close scrutiny and to devise planned organizational change strategies to ensure that they are working in harmony with the goal of achieving the commitment of organization members' creative energies.

Leadership: Prospects for Failure and Synergism

The activity circles model serves to underscore the pivotal role that leadership activities must occupy in the formulation and implementation of prescriptive strategic management theory. Although subordinates can and should interact directly across the various circles of activity on the perimeter, only the top leaders themselves are in a position to achieve much of the necessary linkage and integration. The model does not require that all of the daily activities of top leaders, or all of leadership theory, be exclusively concerned with matters of strategy. It is not by accident, however, that the circle of activities that represents leaders' behaviors is the circle that is most fully overlapped by the other circles of activity.

Strategic management does not necessarily include all of the activities that take place within each of the activity circles (with the possible exception of the circle of activities associated with identifying and instilling a sense of vision and meaning). For successful strategic management to occur, however, some of the activities within each circle must be coordinated in an integrated fashion if progress in each of the four dimensions of strategic management is to be accomplished. The achievement of such integration is an essential aspect of leadership.

The theory of strategic management need not encompass the totality of the disciplinary theory associated with the activities in any of the activity circles, but prescriptive strategic management theory must be soundly related to each of these bodies of theory and associated research.

Conversely, if the theorists who study behavior within an activity circle wish to relate their theory to change within the organization as a whole, strategic management theory is a promising, perhaps compelling, vehicle for doing so.

To develop a set of informed conjectures about the future of prescriptive strategic management, it is necessary to review some of the findings about the success of previous prescriptive efforts within the realms of each of the activity circles. In a sense, prescriptive strategic management, incorporating elements of each of these bodies of theory, becomes potentially susceptible to the causes of failure in any circle. On the other hand, the failure of prescriptions for the performance of activities within a circle can be due, at least in part, to the absence of requisite change in other activity circles. Prescriptive strategic management is an explicit attempt to build synergy between the activity circles, thereby creating a greater potential for change that can be achieved by confining attention to one or a few of the circles.

The potential for failure of prescriptive strategic management can be expressed in a manner analogous to an equation:

Probability of failure of strategic management = Sum of probable causes of failure in each activity circle — offsetting synergy

The sum of causes of failure will be affected by the presence of major failure in any one circle, or by the presence of lesser failures throughout several of the circles of activity. Integrative strategic management should, presumably, lessen the likelihood of both forms of failure. If a breakdown is occurring in one circle, the integration achieved through strategic management should provide warning signals elsewhere, especially in those circles of activity that overlap the activities where major failure is occurring. If lesser failures are occurring in several circles, the leadership is likely to become aware of these when it attempts to achieve the integration necessary for synergism to occur.

The achievement of offsetting synergy is a function of leadership. The goal of prescriptive strategic management theory, therefore, should be to enable leaders to achieve such synergy insofar as is possible. The activity circles model illustrates that leadership is the foundation upon which strategic management is built. Its prescriptions can succeed only if leaders themselves act to build the necessary synergy. That they will do so, or even be inclined to try, is by no means certain. The model also reveals that strategic management places a momentous burden on leaders.

As mentioned previously, there can be little utility from a body of theory if its prescriptions are not practicable. Leaders are unlikely to believe that there is utility to prescriptive strategic management theory if they believe it places a burden on them that exceeds their physical or cognitive capacities. It is for this reason that prescriptive strategic management theory must encompass the concept of bounded rationality. Hrebiniak and Joyce, for example, conclude that recognition of bounded rationality is an essential ingredient of a theory of strategy implementation:

> The major consequence of limited rationality is to require that large strategic problems be "factored" into smaller, more manageable proportions for implementation [1984, p. 5].

This factoring process is the application of what Eadie and Steinbacher (1985, p. 427) call the concept of "selectivity." They describe a strategic management effort in a public agency in which much energy was expended on mandated, routine operational planning, which produced reams of uncoordinated plans. "The challenge was," as they put it, "to rise above the routine operational agenda through the selection of issues involving high stakes, and to identify pressure points or levers through which significant change might be effected" (p. 427).

The importance of selectivity is evidenced by the observation of the chief executive officer (CEO) of General Electric that the usefulness of his organization's strategic plans had decreased as their size and complexity had grown (Hayes 1985). Selectivity is a fundamental issue that must be addressed by both prescriptive strategic management and leadership theory. How much knowledge about each activity circle must a leader have, and how much personal involvement in each circle is necessary? Under what conditions do the answers to these questions vary? For now, perhaps the best advice for leaders is that if leaders perceive themselves to be overburdened, they probably are and should take this perception as an indicator to be more selective.

In the remaining pages of this chapter, our attention is turned to a review of literature as it relates to the theory and practice of the activities that take place within the activities circles. The intent is to identify the causes of failure of prescriptive efforts that have been attempted to improve performance in each set of activities. As mentioned, failure within one or more spheres can jeopardize the success of a strategic management effort. In the review that follows, continuing attention is given to potential sources of leadership overload.

Anticipation: Traditional Planning and Futures Research

Charles Lindblom suggests that focusing on strategy enables decision makers to avoid the purely reactive behaviors of "disjointed incrementalism" while also avoiding the impossibilities of synoptic analysis. One of the foremost proponents of the necessity to consider the boundedness of human cognition in decision and leadership theory, Lindblom (1979) does not accept the argument that these limits necessarily mean that decision making must be reactive in nature. Instead, he recommends focusing on specific sets of stratagems:

> For complex social problems, even formal analytic techniques — systems analysis, operations research, management by objectives, PERT, for example — need to be developed around strategies rather than as attempts at synopsis [1979, p. 518].

In addition, Lindblom calls specifically for the "supplementation of incremental analysis" by better informing leaders through futures research. Such research should be "broad ranging, often highly speculative and sometimes utopian," and its purpose would be to enable leaders to better think about "directions" for their organizations (1979, p. 522). Although complete anticipation as to what the future might hold is clearly beyond human cognition, Lindblom argues that we can do sufficiently well to help establish direction, as long as the efforts to do so are focused on manageable sets of strategies.

Unfortunately, the prescriptive literature related to both traditional planning and futures research has too often exhorted practitioners to be synoptic. One of the most important examples of this tendency occurred with the introduction of the planning-programming-budgeting systems (PPBS) approach during the 1960s and early 1970s. PPBS emerged from the disciplines of economics, operations research, and systems theory and proposed to replace the traditional, incremental, political form of budgeting in government. It was first introduced in the Department of Defense under Secretary Robert McNamara.

Ansoff has called PPBS "an advanced version of strategic planning" (1984, p. 188). It is also generally considered by scholars of public administration to have been a failure, for it is no longer practiced. President Johnson ordered all federal agencies to practice PPBS, but by the time the Nixon administration formally abandoned it, PPBS had deteriorated to a set of paper-shuffling procedures that had marginal relevance and little impact. Ansoff attributes much of the initial success of PPBS in the Department of Defense to the talent and energy of McNamara himself, but "As soon as Mr. McNamara departed, the pent-up inertia and resistance began to transform planning into the previous political budgeting system" (1984, p. 188).

In one of the most important studies of PPBS, Doh (1971) found that those federal agencies that exhibited the greatest effort to adopt PPBS were those in which senior leaders saw advantages to themselves or to their agencies in doing so. Most government officials, however, apparently concluded that PPBS threatened their authority, threatened to overwhelm them with undigestable volumes of analysis, or both. PPBS enhanced conflict, but did not include processes to handle or lessen conflict.

During its implementation, R. E. Millward warned, "Perhaps the most essential ingredient in the implementation of PPBS is acceptance at the level of each line and staff unit, on the part of the legislators, and throughout government, of the *value* and *need* for the tremendous amount of detail and effort being imposed from above" (1968, p. 94, italics Millward's). However, no effort was made to introduce PPBS in a participative manner that might have developed some sense of ownership in the agencies toward it. Instead, it was viewed by many, on whom its success depended, as an alien set of overwhelmingly complex procedures that promised little of benefit. Its program formats had little to do with the determination of operating budgets, thwarted efforts to establish accountability, and were divorced from incentives.

In short, PPBS failed because it was perceived by leaders to be neither useful nor doable. As a set of prescriptions for strategic planning, it failed on two of the critical dimensions — practitioners failed to perceive that it was practicable or that it had utility for them. They were probably right. Foremost among the flaws of PPBS was the fact that many senior officials felt their authority to be threatened. A key element of both strategic planning and strategic management is the repeatedly expressed intent to serve the needs of top officials. A set of prescriptions for the formulation of strategy that threatens, rather than serves, top officials is severely flawed.

Strategic planning has not typically been perceived as a threat to the authority of top officials in corporations, although its existence has often threatened the status of subordinates on whom successful implementation of strategic plans depends. The greater problem in obtaining top-level support in the business world is that many executives do not expect strategic planning to yield sufficient utility. The answers as to why this is so, and the efficacy of resulting prescriptions, is one of the great challenges facing us today in an increasingly competitive world.

One reason may be that the label "strategic plan" has been applied to many planning efforts that have, in fact, been rather perfunctory. Lauenstein (1986) argues that what is commonly called strategic planning in many American companies is actually an uninformed, bottom-up practice in which line managers act without exposure to information about the future. Being neither exposed to good long-range forecasts nor involved in meaningful deliberations about the future of the company, and without top leadership providing a sense of strategic vision, many act to protect themselves. Further, if the line managers' evaluations are tied to the plan, it is likely that plans will reflect objectives that are easy to accomplish (Pounds 1969).

On a positive note, the findings of Linneman and Klein's (1985) survey of 500 of the world's largest companies reveals trends that suggest growing use of the strategic approach to management. They concluded that there are trends toward more distant planning horizons, that top management is becoming more involved in assessing the environments of their organizations, and that there is greater emphasis on adaptive strategies in the face of uncertainty. Of particular interest is their conclusion that there may be a trend toward futures research techniques, finding that corporations are making increasing use of multiple scenarios to explore the feasibility of such things as major investments and new product opportunities.

Morrison and Renfro (1984) suggest that the futures research method that is most compatible with strategic management is environmental scanning. Such scanning techniques typically involve the scanning of large numbers of varied literature sources, sometimes using the services of volunteers from the organization who would otherwise not have the opportunity to show their talents beyond the confines of their immediate jobs. As these sources are scanned and digested, effort is centered on detecting emerging trends that present potential threats or opportunities. If such potential trends seem to warrant further study, forecasts and scenarios may subsequently be developed.

Environmental scanning is a variation of what Etzioni (1967) calls the "mixed scanning" approach to decision making. He speaks of "contextuating rationalism" by engaging in multiple levels of scanning that take the boundedness of rationality into consideration, but that help to "overcome the conservative slant of incrementalism by exploring longer-run alternatives" (1967, p. 390). Environmental scanning attempts to combine the scanning capacities of a sufficiently large number of organizational members, while also summarizing their results so that the resulting reports will not consume excessive amounts of time for senior officials. Only those trends or discovered events that are judged to be of particular salience are targeted for detailed study.

The most consistent finding regarding the failures of strategic planning is the absence or disappearance of support from the top leadership of an organization (i.e., Hofer 1976; Lenz and Engledow 1986; Schultz 1984; Steiner and Schollhammer 1975). There seems to be little evidence that anticipatory efforts themselves are likely to lead to worse performance, but there is frequent doubt in organizations as to whether anticipatory efforts will improve the organization's prospects. Where management believes that the environment of an organization is relatively stable — perceptions that can prevail among regulated industries, dominant members of oligopolistic markets, some public agencies, or those in markets where little product differentiation can occur — there is apparently little support for anticipatory efforts (Schultz 1984).

On the other hand, when Shrader (1984) reviewed 31 studies that have looked at the relationship between formal planning and organizational performance, he found that 20 reported a positive relationship while 11 reported no significant relationship. No negative relationship was reported. Nevertheless, when Lenz and Engledow (1986) used a panel of experts to choose 10 large American and Canadian corporations to interview as leading practitioners of environmental analysis, three were discovered to have abandoned their efforts subsequent to the interviews. In one case, the anticipatory processes stopped after the exit of a supportive CEO, which followed the firm's acquisition by another. The other two corporations revealed a cultural incompatibility with anticipatory processes, manifested in an unwillingness of line managers and executives to accept environmental analysts who were hired from outside the firms.

The clear implication here is that the implementation of strategic planning ought not to focus solely on questions of methodology and technical sufficiency. Building cultural compatibility may be even more important if strategic planning is to have a lasting presence and impact. If outsiders are hired to perform some of the anticipatory tasks, cultural compatibility can become especially tenuous and integrative measures are called for, probably involving line managers as major participants. Under such conditions, the anticipatory specialist should encourage and enable line managers to learn more about their organization's future environment, and to assist them in establishing direction.

Strategic management requires sufficient participation to assure the achievement of cultural compatibility with the processes of anticipation. If anticipatory specialists are clearly designated as facilitators of line decisions, rather than as decision makers themselves, the threat perceived by line managers may be lessened. Further, such participation may be necessary to assure that the anticipatory efforts are perceived as being based on sound information rather than on vague, perhaps even unspecified, assumptions. Achieving cultural compatibility is a major task confronting top executives in strategic management systems, one that requires personal commitment and exemplary behaviors. Even if strategic plans are developed in ways that build a basis for their widespread support, however, they may falter if their implementation is contradicted by the established mechanisms of control.

The Question of Compatible Controls

Operational controls often contradict strategic direction. The control systems are not always at fault, for strategy itself may be poorly communicated by an organization's leaders. Even if strategy is well communicated, however, control systems may become powerful obstacles.

A recent survey of executives who were experienced with strategic planning revealed that inadequate linkages between strategic planning and control systems are a primary source of difficulty. These executives reported that such difficulties are common in the development and execution of budgets, information systems, and reward systems (Gray 1986).

Information systems can easily undermine strategic efforts. A frequent finding from studies of management information systems, especially in the early era of computer-based MIS, was the revelation that these often overwhelm officials with too much undigested information. Gray concluded that information systems are often developed by financial managers and by technical specialists to serve their operational needs, rather than the need to sustain commitment to strategic directions. Thus, "[t]he information system drove the strategy rather than the other way around" (Gray 1986, p. 96).

Where organizations have already invested heavily in developing computer-based management information systems, the implementation of strategic management should be accompanied by the development of decision support systems (DSS). A DSS is also computer-based, but it is especially designed to serve the information needs of those at the top of an organization. As such, DSSs attempt to provide senior officials with an appropriate balance of information that reflects their need to maintain internal controls *and* keep abreast of changes in the external environment.

At their best, DSSs reflect the seminal work of scholars such as Gorry and Scott-Morton (1971) and Mintzberg (1972), and attempt to apply computer technology to extend leaders' abilities to handle unstructured decision-making situations while avoiding the excessive burdens of overwhelming quantities of relatively unimportant information. The introduction of formal DSSs, however, will by no means solve the problems of operationalizing strategic management. The new decision systems analysts may not be accepted, especially if they lack expertise in the organization's primary bodies of knowledge. DSSs may be poorly developed and, if so, may fail to deal with the overburdens of internal control data or to improve the leaders' understanding of external change. If a DSS fails to do the former, it is unlikely to accomplish the latter. The usefulness of DSSs is likely to grow with advancing technology, but they cannot accomplish the essential challenge of control: the assurance of coordinated behavior throughout an organization.

Strategic direction must somehow be translated into short- and medium-range operational objectives, and these, in turn, must somehow become the guiding objectives for the individual members of an organization.

A frequently prescribed method for doing so is management by objectives (MBO). First proposed by Drucker (1954), MBO was seen as a means for promoting the simultaneous accomplishment of both organizational and individual objectives. In many instances, however, little concern has been shown for individual needs and objectives. MBO has often become solely a mechanism for conveying objectives established at higher levels, and for holding subordinates accountable to these. The essentiality of at least the top-down form of MBO prompted Sherwood and Page (1976) to conclude that some form of MBO will always be a tactic of management.

As is true of other elements of prescriptive strategic management, MBO can also cause overload if measures are not taken to selectively focus it. MBO can easily degenerate into a process of excessive formality typified by extensive paperwork and consumption of time (Carrol and Tossi 1971). If applied solely to individuals, MBO can intensify peer competition and undermine team efforts on which the accomplishment of many strategies depend. Observing that such competition caused some firms to abandon MBO, Likert and Fisher (1977) proposed "management by group objectives," which stresses participative team-building processes.

Whether team-oriented or not, it is unlikely that organizational members will seek to achieve strategic objectives if the evaluation systems on which their rewards are based encourage them to do otherwise. There is no greater obstacle to the operationalization of strategic plans than widespread temporal conflicts between the longer-term strategic needs of an organization and the short-range orientations of its incentives systems.

It is essential, therefore, that performance evaluation and incentives systems reward contributions to strategic direction rather than be solely focused on such short-term objectives as a single year's profits (Banks and Wheelwright 1979; Hrebiniak and Joyce 1984). Stonich (1984) recommends that key managers should be given designated "strategic funds" for long-term investment purposes, and that compensation be linked through deferred income, which is contingent on the performance of a company over a multiyear period. To accomplish lasting change in an organization's incentive structure, however, requires changing the culture of the organization itself.

Organization Development and Strategic Management

The behaviors that are truly rewarded in an organization are manifestations of that organization's culture. Eadie and Steinbacher maintain that strategic management — as a result of its explicit concern with the prospect of unimplementable strategies — is inherently concerned with changing organizational cultures (1985, p. 424). What should be created, say Tabatoni and Jarniou (1976), is a "strategic culture" in which change is accepted as a normal state, conflict is managed to minimize the costs and impediments to change, learning is facilitated, and values reflect a desire to achieve long-term performance rather than immediate income. These qualities are fully congruent with the aspirations of practitioners of organization development.

> Organization development is an effort (1) *planned*, (2) *organization-wide*, and (3) *managed* from the *top*, to (4) increase *organization effectiveness* and *health* through (5) *planned interventions* in the organization's "processes," using *behavioral-science* knowledge [Beckhard 1969, p. 9, italics Beckhard's].

Since it involves planning the planning process itself, strategic management is a form of what Emshoff (1978) calls "metaplanning." Emshoff demonstrates that the theoretical foundations of metaplanning are in the literature of organization development. Strategic management, therefore, is also rooted in the literature of OD. Furthermore, strategic management promises to fill what has been a serious void in organization development.

Organization development is concerned with developing the capacity to change, and the willingness to do so, but OD does not include mechanisms for developing the foresight on which the determination of appropriate directions for change should be based. Lacking a capacity to think about the organization's future environment and therefore about what the mission of an organization should be in a world of uncertainty, OD efforts have often become preoccupied with such things as improving group relations in a rather directionless fashion.

Ackoff (1981) recommends that planners be viewed as facilitators of a learning process, one in which interactive planning for the organization's future becomes an essential element of organization development.

> It is through participation in interactive planning that members of an organization can develop. In addition, participation enables them to acquire an understanding of the organization and makes it possible for them to serve organization ends more effectively. This, in turn, facilitates organizational development [Ackoff 1981, pp. 65–66].

There is reason to believe that widespread participation in the anticipatory efforts of an organization might improve the quality of anticipation itself. Ascher (1978) has demonstrated that a prime cause of inaccurate forecasts is "assumption drag," the clinging to outmoded assumptions on which forecasts are based. If conducted in an organizational culture that is open to deliberations, interactive anticipation might lead to helpful challenges to the prevailing models of reality that could otherwise cause an organization to fail to anticipate either threats or opportunities.

When anticipation fails, the organization development aspects of strategic management are of paramount importance. Under conditions of uncertainty, argues Hayes (1985), the traditional model of strategic planning — which begins with identifying program strategies such as appropriate product mixes — is insufficient. When it becomes impossible to develop a detailed "road map" for the future, then the first priority is to fashion strategies for institution building, in order to develop the capacity to learn and respond flexibly.

Ramaprasad (1982) says that uncertainty is greatest when an organization is confronted with potentially revolutionary change. To assure organizational health and survival under such conditions, however infrequent they may be, strategic management must be devoted to assuring what Argyris and Schon (1977) have labeled "double-loop learning." Single-loop learning is learning that is done through extrapolative anticipatory efforts. It is appropriate when the currently prevailing set of assumptions will prevail into the future.

Double-loop learning, on the other hand, requires attentiveness to information that raises doubt as to the validity of an organization's basic patterns of behavior. It is associated with the futures research techniques that rise to importance when it can no longer be taken for granted that the future will be a simple extension of the past. The adoption of futures research methods, however, will not lead to learning if there is an abiding unwillingness on the part of the organization to question some of its most basic assumptions. It is only within the circle of activities that encompasses organization development that such a willingness to do so can be fashioned. A strategic management effort that does not include organization development strategies, therefore, is incomplete. It is also more prone to failure resulting from resistance to change.

Organization development, though, is not a certain process. OD can fail. Strategic management, therefore, is also susceptible to the potential causes of failure for organization development. In a retrospective content analysis of 67 case studies of planned organizational change, Dunn and Swierczek (1977) found that many hypotheses purported to be associated with successful planned change were not supported. Those that were substantiated stressed collaborative modes of intervention and high levels of participation.

Franklin's (1976) review of OD projects in 25 organizations concluded that only 11 had been successful. He found that organizations that were already known for innovation and that were inclined to experiment with new ideas were more receptive to further organization development. The use of change agents was inconclusive, but a commitment to survey feed-back was not. In 10 of the 11 successful cases, but only in two of the unsuc-cessful efforts, was such a commitment present. Success was also related to the level of support from top management — where such support existed, successful change was more likely.

Many change efforts are limited to brief team-building exercises that lead to transient changes. Boss's (1983) review of the literature emphasizes that regression to previous behaviors is due to such factors as lack of follow-up, missing or incompatible incentives, absence of accountability for sustained change, and unrealistic expectations at the outset. Above all, concluded Boss, planned organizational change requires sustained support from the top, including the CEO of the organization. "Without the sup-port," says Boss, "any long-range change effort is doomed to failure" (p. 69).

Direction and Synergistic Leadership

The preceding review of literature pertaining to activities within each of the activities circles of the model is consistent in that the role of senior leaders in the performance of each is seen to be crucial. Unfortunately, too little attention has been paid to the linkage between leadership skills, strategic planning, and organizational performance. "Those who have ex-amined this linkage," say Shrader, Taylor and Dalton (1984, p. 163), "are consistent in their conclusions: managerial skills are critical to the perfor-mance of the firm."

The activities of the organization's leaders overlap all other activities circles. Leadership in a system of strategic management, therefore, must be integrative. In fact, strategic management calls for an extensive, perhaps unprecedented amount of integrative activity by leaders. This may be both its greatest strength and its greatest weakness.

In a prescient article of two decades ago, Lawrence and Lorsch (1967) described the qualities and dilemmas of integration in a manner that is fully compatible with the literature of strategic management. Large organiza-tions, they said, necessarily involve the activities of numerous specialized personnel. Moreover, these specialists are largely preoccupied with prob-lems within a specific frame of time. With the exception of R&D research-ers whose concern for the long-range future may not be accompanied by appreciation for current conditions, most specialists are preoccupied with the shorter-term problems of implementation. The effective organ-izational integrators are leaders who can learn to balance the differing time perspectives of the specialists, without succumbing to short-term pressures.

What strategic management attempts to do, therefore, is reconcile the need for specialization with the need for integrated effort within the context of change and uncertainty. When an organization's efforts become greater than the simple sum of the outputs of its individual specializations, synergy is present. Synergistic leadership is a requisite at the outset of a strategic management effort, and the future of strategic management will largely depend on whether such synergy gains momentum or withers.

Synergy requires energy. If the integrative demands of strategic management place increasingly onerous burdens on the energies of senior leaders, they are likely to seek relief by lowering their aspirations and abandoning the effort. It is from this perspective that the importance of the set of activities associated with establishing a sense of direction and meaning for the organization can best be understood.

Chester Barnard (1938/1954) noted that a shared sense of common organizational purpose could serve both as a motivational force and as an instrument of coordination. He maintained that an essential aspect of leadership is to inspire cooperation by "creating faith, faith in the probability of success, . . . faith in the superiority of common purpose as a personal aim of those who partake it" (p. 259). If strategic management can help the leaders of organizations to develop a shared sense of organizational purpose, it might become less necessary for them to inject themselves personally into the making of operational decisions by the organization's specialists.

Strategic planning that is devoid of efforts to define and instill a sense of common purpose in an organization does not fulfill the requirements of prescriptive strategic management. That such a condition is possible is evidenced by firms that use anticipatory methods for portfolio management purposes, but that shy away from addressing questions related to a company's basic character and purpose. Portfolio management alone is not a source of motivation. Hamermesh cautions organizations against such an approach, arguing that what is needed is to instill "such goals as respect for the individual, customer service, and excellence" (1986, p. 116).

If strategic management helps leaders to create a sense of shared organizational purpose, it might also lessen if an organization adopts the full range of prescriptions for strategic management in each of the activity circles. Conflict is to be expected when an organization seeks to change itself to better deal with a changing environment. If, however, there emerges a growing sense of shared purpose among the conflicting specialists, then the potential for constructive resolution should grow also. If evaluation and reward systems are attuned to strategic direction, incentives can emerge to stimulate cooperative effort. Strategic management is not intended to eliminate conflict but to better manage it by focusing it on the real issues.

Conclusion: Leadership
Versus Institutional Myopia

Leadership and prescriptive strategic management are inseparable. The theory of prescriptive strategic management is essentially a theory of leadership that posits that the quality of leadership is determined by how well leaders can guide activities in the five circles to assure sound performance on each of the four dimensions—anticipation, direction, control, and commitment of creative energy. Its prescriptions are explicitly intended to serve the leadership needs of top executives. Strategic management, in turn, cannot be accomplished without the sustained support of top leaders. Conjectures about the future of prescriptive strategic management, therefore, are conjectures about the future quality of leadership itself.

Multiple causes for potential failure occur in each of the activity circles. Achieving the offsetting synergy is no easy task. When understood as a comprehensive theory for leadership, however, it is easier to see that prescriptive strategic management also includes an impressive array of strategies to deal with these potential causes of failure.

In fact, prescriptive strategic management is based on the underlying reality that failure is a distinct possibility. In attempting to deal with a changing, often threatening, external environment, strategic management theory now emphasizes both anticipation and flexible response capacity. Although continuing to be based on the assumption that anticipation is vital, the theory now recognizes that anticipatory efforts can fail, and therefore also stresses mechanisms to assure rapid learning and response when an organization is confronted with surprise.

Furthermore, it is now recognized that conflict and resistance to change are both natural and potentially debilitating to strategic planning. It is this realization, more than any other, that has prompted the "marriage" between strategic planning and organization development activities within the context of prescriptive strategic management. The concept of strategy has been extended inwardly to include the anticipation of resistance and fashioning of strategies to avert or mitigate opposition to change. In the future, tests of the workability of strategic management must include such activities as the fashioning of compatible incentives, building of team efforts, and instilling a continuing sense of direction and meaning. To do less, or to pass judgment about the workability of prescriptive strategic management where all activity circles are not brought fully into play, is invalid.

Unlike numerous other efforts to "rationalize" management, the boundedness of human cognition and energy is not overlooked. By definition, that which is strategic is not that which is something else. The concept of selectivity, therefore, is essential to avoid overburdens. By keeping their own limits in mind, leaders can determine for themselves which activities are truly strategic in nature. These are those activities of the senior leaders that are essential to the integrated performance of the activity circles.

Strategic management is not a set of prescriptions for quick and easy solutions. It is not a "quick fix." Ansoff, for example, estimates that five to seven years might be necessary to "implant" the strategic approach into a business firm (1984, p. 199). Consequently, enormous institutional biases in our society, biases that constitute barriers against long-range solutions, jeopardize the future of strategic management.

Biases against prescriptions that call for sustained effort over many years, and that do not promise immediate rewards, are especially prevalent in government. Public administrators face several peculiar differences from business administrators, including narrow ranges of discretion, the inability to abandon a program, and the close scrutiny of the press. No barrier to public-sector strategic management, however, is greater than the brief tenure of many elected officials and their appointees. Even though there is a fledgling interest by some elected officials in using anticipatory methods to form better public policy, it is questionable that enough support will be forthcoming from our elected leaders to sustain any government-wide efforts at strategic management. There is reason to hope, however, that some administrators in individual agencies might see the benefits of applying strategic management at their levels.

Institutional myopia may be growing in America's corporations as well. Studies that have compared the relative success of Japanese and American corporations have repeatedly emphasized the Japanese tendency to forego short-term profits in favor of such long-term objectives as building market share, often accompanied by carefully nurtured reputations for quality. Peter Drucker (1986) fears that the shifting ownership structure of American corporations will stress short-term profit at the expense of long-term competitiveness.

He reports that nearly one-third of the equity of publicly traded corporations, and more than half the equity of the largest ones, is now owned by pension funds. The managers of these funds are often judged on a quarter-by-quarter basis, not on the basis of long-term growth as measured over many years. The introduction of alien cultures through corporate takeovers can also destroy the fruits of a strategic management effort. Where corporate management is entrusted solely to financial specialists, the most emphasized activity circles are likely to be in the area of control and traditional, extrapolative planning. The other circles can be brought fully into play only by persons with a long-term commitment to the organization and who deeply appreciate its central processes of production and marketing.

In the final analysis, the future of prescriptive strategic management depends mostly on the willingness of top management to think about the future. This willingness is in doubt due to institutionalized myopia in both business and government. Unfortunately, strategic management does not address the causes of much of our inherent short-sightedness. It is to be hoped, however, that those public agencies and corporations that do strategic management well will succeed sufficiently to gain a noticeable competitive advantage over the others. Emulation might follow, thereby lessening the myopic bias of our institutions.

Let me close with a personal note. I have lived in Japan and, as I write this, have just returned from a visit to the site of an American plant owned by a large, highly successful Japanese corporation. This corporation seems to be actively engaged in all of the activity circles, and its leadership is especially integrative with emphasis on reinforcing a sense of meaning and direction. Some Japanese organizations are not especially well managed, but that country seems to have an unusual number of companies with similar synergy and commitment to the longer-range future. Hard as it may be to swallow, a prescription for some careful emulation is in order. We have the basis for doing so in our own strategic management theory.

References

Ackoff, R. 1981. *Creating the corporate future: Plan or be planned for.* New York: Wiley.
Ansoff, H. I. 1965. *Corporate strategy.* New York: McGraw-Hill.
_____. 1984. *Implanting strategic management.* Englewood Cliffs, N.J.: Prentice-Hall.
_____, R. P. Declerck, and R. L. Hayes, eds. 1976. *From strategic planning to strategic management.* New York: Wiley.
Argyris, C., and D. Schon. 1977. *Organization learning: A theory of action perspective.* Reading, Mass.: Addison-Wesley.
Ascher, W. 1978. *Forecasting: An appraisal for policy-makers and planners.* Baltimore: Johns Hopkins University Press.
Banks, R. L., and S. C. Wheelwright. 1979. Operations vs. strategy: Trading tomorrow for today. *Harvard Business Review* 57: 112–20.
Barnard, C. I. 1938/1954. *The functions of the executive.* Cambridge, Mass.: Harvard University Press.
Becker, H. S. 1982. Constructing and using scenarios: An aid to strategic planning and decision-making. *World Future Society Bulletin* 16: 13–24.
Beckhard, R. 1969. *Organization development: strategies and models.* Reading, Mass.: Addison-Wesley.
Bennis, W. and B. Nanus. 1985. *Leaders: The strategies for taking charge.* New York: Harper & Row.
Boss, R. W. 1983. Team building and the problem of regression: The personal management interview as an intervention. *Journal of Applied Behavioral Science* 19: 67–83.
Carrol, S. J., and H. L. Tossi. 1971. Relationship of characteristics of the review process to the success of the MBO approach. *Journal of Business* 44: 299–305.
Cyert, R. M., and J. G. March. 1963. *A behavioral theory of the firm.* Englewood Cliffs, N.J.: Prentice-Hall.
Das, T. K. 1986. *The subjective side of strategy making: Future orientations and perceptions of executives.* New York: Praeger.

Doh, J. C. 1971. *The planning-programming-budgeting system in three federal agencies.* New York: Praeger.

Drucker, P. 1954. *Practice of management.* New York: Harper & Row.

_____. 1986. A crisis of capitalism. *Wall Street Journal,* September 30: 32.

Dunn, W. N., and F. W. Swierczek. 1977. Planning organizational change: Toward grounded theory. *Journal of Applied Behavioral Science* 13: 135–57.

Eadie, D. C., and R. Steinbacher. 1985. Strategic agenda management: A marriage of organization development and strategic planning. *Public Administration Review* 45, 424–30.

Emshoff, J. R. 1978. Planning the process of improving the planning process: A case study in meta-planning. *Management Science,* 24. Reprinted in L. Reinharth, H. J. Shapiro, and E. A. Kellman. 1981. *The practice of planning.* New York: Van Nostrand Reinhold.

Etzioni, A. 1967. Mixed scanning: A third approach to decision-making.*Public Administration Review,* 27: 385–92.

Franklin, J. L. 1976. Characteristics of successful and unsuccessful organization development. *Journal of Applied Behavioral Science* 12: 471–92.

Gorry, G. A., and M. S. Scott-Morton. 1971. A framework for MIS. *Sloan Management Review* 13: 55–70.

Gray, D. H. 1986. Uses and misuses of strategic planning. *Harvard Business Review* 64: 89–97.

Hamermesh, R. G. 1986. Making planning strategic. *Harvard Business Review* 64: 115–20.

Hayes, R. H. 1985. Strategic planning: Forward in reverse. *Harvard Business Review* 63: 111–19.

Hofer, C. W. 1976. Research on strategic planning: A survey of past studies and suggestions for future efforts. *Journal of Economics and Business* 28: 261–86.

Hrebiniak, L. G., and W. F. Joyce. 1984. *Implementing Strategy.* New York: Macmillan.

Lauenstein, M. C. 1986. The failure of strategic planning. *Journal of Business Strategy* 6: 75–80.

Lawrence, P. R., and J. W. Lorsch. 1967. New management job: The integrator. *Harvard Business Review* 45: 142–51.

Lenz, R. T., and J. L. Engledow. 1986. Environmental analysis units and strategic decision-making: A field study of selected "leading edge" corporations. *Strategic Management Journal* 7: 69–89.

Likert, R., and S. M. Fisher. 1977. MBGO: Putting some team spirit into MBO. *Personnel* 54: 40–47.

Lindblom, C. 1979. Still muddling, not yet through. *Public Administration Review* 39: 517–26.

Linneman, R. E., and H. E. Klein. 1985. Using scenarios in strategic decision making. *Business Horizons* 28: 64–74.

McConkey, D. 1986. If it's not broke — fix it anyway. *Business Quarterly* 51: 50–52.

Millward, R. E. 1968. PPBS: Problems of implementation. *Journal of the American Institute of Planners* 34: 88–94.

Mintzberg, H. 1972. The myth of MIS. *California Management Review* 15: 92–97.

Morrison, J. L., and W. L. Renfro. 1984. Futures research and the strategic planning process: Implications for long-range planning in higher education. Paper presented to annual meeting of the American Educational Research Association, New Orleans, April 23–27; ASHE-ERIC Higher Education Research Report 0737-1292, No. 9.

Narayanan, V. K., and L. Fahey. 1982. The micro-politics of strategy formulation. *Academy of Management Review* 7: 25–34.

Neufeld, W. P. 1985. Environmental scanning: Its use in forecasting emerging trends and issues in organizations. *Futures Research Quarterly* 1: 39–52.

Pounds, W. F. 1969. The process of problem finding. *Industrial Management Review* 11: 1–19.

Ramaprasad, A. 1982. Revolutionary change and strategic management. *Behavioral Science* 27: 387–92.

Schultz, R. L. 1984. The implementation of forecasting models. *Journal of Forecasting* 3: 43–55.

Sherwood, F. P., and W. J. Page, Jr. 1976. MBO and public management. *Public Administration Review* 36: 5–12.

Shrader, C. B., L. Taylor, and D. R. Dalton. 1984. Strategic planning and organizational performance: A critical appraisal. *Journal of Management* 10: 2, 149–71.

Steiner, G. A., and H. Schollhammer. 1975. Pitfalls in multinational long range planning. *Long Range Planning* 8: 2–12.

Stonich, P. J. 1984. The performance measurement and reward system: Critical to strategic management. *Organizational Dynamics* 12: 45–57.

Sufrin, S. C., and G. S. Odiorne. 1985. The new strategic planning boom: Hope for the future or a bureaucratic exercise? *Managerial Planning* 33: 4–13.

Tabatoni, P., and P. Jarniou. 1976. The dynamics of norms in strategic management. *From strategic planning to strategic management* (H. I. Ansoff, R. P. Declerck, and R. L. Haynes, eds.). New York: Wiley, pp. 29–36.

Forces Shaping Local Government in the 1990s

James Crupi

The Modern City-State

First of all, we are becoming a world of city-states. In the future we will talk about Dallas-Fort Worth and St. Louis and Minneapolis and New York and Atlanta and Los Angeles and Singapore and Hong Kong and Berlin and Baghdad and Warsaw, rather than about nations as we did in the past. Two factors explain this shift. The world is moving to a totally interdependent global economy, as well as to a service/information-based economy. It is indeed ironic that the two major forces that led to the rise of city-states in ancient times are the same forces that will bring them back today.

Cities and the counties and other areas around them determine the wealth of nations, not the other way around. By the year 2000, 50 percent of the world's population will live in and around cities; the United States already has 75 percent of its residents in urban areas. The economic base of this country now includes 4 percent of our people working in agriculture, 23 percent in manufacturing, and 73 percent in services. But by the year 2000, these percentages will have changed to 2 percent in agriculture, 5 percent in manufacturing, and 93 percent in services. Since November 1989, 60 percent of all new jobs coming into the economy have been service-based jobs, and they are not positions as hamburger flippers. These individuals have an annual average income of $20,000.

The changes in process will become political as well as economic. Ten years ago, it would not have been important for mayors to go on foreign trade missions. Today it is not only important that they do so but essential.

Reprinted with permission from Public Management, *Vol. 72, No. 11, December 1990. Published by the International City Management Association, Washington, D.C.*

Cities will develop their own foreign policy approaches. Fifty-one U.S. cities took positions against trade with South Africa long before the federal government did so.

Boundaries will become increasingly irrelevant. As they now stand, boundaries often have more to do with sentiment than they do with logic. People in eastern Arkansas and northern Mississippi, for example, care a lot less about what goes on in Jackson and Little Rock than they do about happiness in Memphis, Tennessee, which is their reigning city-state. A kind of de facto sovereignty prevails in the areas around prominent cities.

Federal aid will continue to decline. We have to leave the federal government out of the equation in determining what we will do and what we will not do. Right now, 43 percent of our budget goes to entitlements, 25 percent to defense, and 15 percent to interest on the national debt. Last year's total of $150 billion in interest payments was enough to run the Department of Agriculture, Interior, Commerce, Justice, Labor, and Transportation combined. These figures do not even consider the savings and loan crisis.

Local governments will raise money in the international marketplace. Some communities are already floating bonds in yen and deutschmarks to raise capital to build up their infrastructures. This trend will increase in the years ahead.

This country will see an incredible rise in volunteerism as sweat equity replaces capital to get things done. Local officials will have to become very good at managing volunteer resources, which will be significant. The baby boomer generation will have 76 million people going through midlife crisis at the same time, asking themselves how they can give back to society at that point in their lives. The volunteer talent that will be available to communities will play a large role in determining their accomplishments as the year 2000 approaches.

Competition in the New Order

Communities today recognize that to be competitive, they have to pursue talent. In a postindustrial society, jobs follow people, not the other way around. Organizations are going to where the people are. People are not coming to the organizations. People are the new products. Twenty-five percent of workers in this country now work out of their homes. This represents a dramatic shift in that the individual now becomes an economic unit, an organizational unit. Local managers must mobilize and maximize this talent and make it work for their governments.

To be competitive, communities have to focus on six major areas. The first is *transportation*, particularly road, rail, and air systems, with international linkages when possible.

Comprehensive telecommunication services represent the highways of the future. Management decisions will become infinitely complex in a society where every individual will conceivably have his or her own telephone number. Decisions will no longer simply mandate capital expenditures. Managers will need to decide based on maximum leverage, on getting the most to the most people. A sophisticated society will demand sophisticated approaches.

Local government officials will need to *staff to win.* In the 1990s, citizens are going to demand that government get smaller and more efficient and more professional than it typically has been. Increasingly scarce resources will need to be delivered more effectively and more efficiently than in the past.

International economic diversification will become essential for survival in the 21st century. Whether local companies conduct business internationally or foreign firms have a local presence, communities will need to diversify in economic development. Failure to do so can leave areas dangerously subject to the highs and lows of any one sector or geographic area.

Quality of life is now an economic issue, having to do with health care, with crime, with art and culture, with the environment. Quality of life may well be one of the most important factors confronting local managers in the 1990s.

Finally, the most important aspect for competitive advantage is *education.* In a postindustrial society, schools and training programs and seminars represent the farms of the future. They produce the new crops. We need to change our perception of education, however. We need to believe that education is about more than the pursuit of knowledge. Education is about the pursuit of significance, about making a difference, about adding value, about giving something back, about maximizing talents. Knowledge is just something you get along the way to make everything else happen. By the year 2000, 65 percent of workers will need 13 years of education just to get a job.

The rules of the game have changed dramatically. Education is going to change as well. Teachers will not teach in the future; computers and interactive television will serve this function. Teachers will become Aristotles, motivators, guides on the side, facilitators. The very nature of the teacher's role will change. Lack of education in a postindustrial society renders one irrelevant as well as unimportant to society. The rules have dramatically changed. Without education, you do not work in this future. While our children represent 25 percent of our population, they represent 100 percent of our future.

Leadership Styles Across Generations

This country is experiencing a dramatic cross-generational leadership transition. The first modern American generation of leaders — people now in their sixties and seventies — built the country, the companies, the communities as they now stand. They are product-oriented, children of the industrial age, and tend to be authoritarian, traditional, and conservative.

The second generation — people typically in their fifties — is perceived by those coming before and after them as a transition generation. These are the individuals who were too young for war and too old for Vietnam, who grew up under McCarthyism, when stepping out of line was dangerous. As the offspring of Depression-traumatized parents, they tend to look at the conservative side of economics. This generation may well be America's finest managerial generation, having taken management and made it a science.

Then comes the third generation — people typically in their thirties and forties, who are fueling the most rapid rise of entrepreneurialism in this country's history. These individuals are conservative but not traditional. Life is too complex, information too specialized, and society too diverse for dedication to tradition. This generation is people- and information-oriented.

In the 1990s the third generation will bring ethics to a fever pitch in this country. People are going to demand integrity. They are going to demand honesty. They won't tolerate even the perception of impropriety. The dignity and the value of the individual will be uppermost in people's minds. And the power of the individual will be greater than it ever has been. With self-confidence and individual fortitude, amazing accomplishments will be possible.

The fourth generation — people in their twenties — appears in the shadow of the largest, most highly educated, most sophisticated generation this country has ever produced. We know these young people will be more liberal. We suspect they will define success not by what happens in the head, but by what happens in the heart. The first generation endorses hard work, plain and simple.

The third generation says, "If I can outthink you, I can outwork you." The work ethic is now intellectual rather than physical.

The fourth generation's work ethic will be emotional, concerned with spiritual harmony, with the value of human relationships, more interested in fixing things than in changing things. This is a generation that came into being when divorce was rampant, when day care and television defined the day. This is a generation searching for what it believes it was denied. Its members value quality of life and balance in their schedules. They are willing to work hard, but they are not easy to manage, because they want their jobs to be extensions of themselves. They are not as interested in self-control as they are in self-expression. They want full lives; they do not want full employment. They do not want to live to work; they want to work to live. They also believe in limits and not in unparalleled growth.

Change and the Second American Revolution

We're not talking about rapid change. We're talking about radical change. In radical change, the rules of the game change. You're either going to make them or you're going to live by them. Change always seems to follow the same cycle. As leaders, we need to understand that change, or we will get trapped by it. We need to beware of getting overwhelmed with rapid change, because change is likely to be the only constant in our future.

The first stage of change is uninformed optimism — blind enthusiasm. This is followed by informed pessimism — hesitancy based on the stark reality of the change. This second stage can be the most dangerous aspect of change in an organization or in a relationship. Eastern Europe can be said to be experiencing informed pessimism. Freedom of speech is available, but many consumer goods are not. The unemployment rate in East Germany has gone up 50 percent in the past six months. Radical change is always startling. Informed optimism is the final stage of change, when realism sets in, followed by hope and commitment. Change has then taken hold.

This country appears to be going through a second American revolution. The signs are many: the rise of entrepreneurialism, the rebirth of religion, the movement of business to the West (i.e., the Far East), the impact of a global world on the United States, the importance of education for values and competitiveness, the rise of the neighborhood movement (a throwback to the old town hall concept), and the new immigrants (Asians and Hispanics, who will redefine this nation in many ways).

Today we all fall under the specter of a globally integrated economy. We cannot escape it. We have gone from having 50 percent of world market share after World War II to now having 15–16 percent. We are in a world where Mitsubishi is bigger than IBM, Bank of America, General Motors, and Western Electric combined. We are in a world where the second largest trading center for the issuance of U.S. Treasury bills is Tokyo, Japan; where 13 of the top 20 banks in the world are Japanese; where you are witnessing round-the-clock 24-hour financial trading. When did we ever care about what happened on the Japanese stock exchange?

We're not talking about a bigger view of the world; we're talking about a fundamentally different view of the world. Most of our corporate and political leaders have had no serious international training. But we cannot afford this massive lack of exposure. Any business that isn't international 10 years from now will not be in business.

So many people spend 30 years with an employer serving the status quo. They never shape a new vision, and then it is too late. The very nature of the world has changed, and it demands a new kind of leadership.

The American political party is dying. People don't want to talk about ideology today. They just want to know what works. I believe we're going to have a social revolution in this country in the 1990s as we had in the 1960s. But it will be around human rights rather than civil rights. People are going to view health care, a good education, and affordable housing as fundamental human rights. That is a very different kind of orientation from what we have experienced.

Women's participation in the American economy is ever-growing. In the past seven years, 83 percent of eight million new jobs have been filled by women. Between now and the year 2000, 6 out of every 10 people hired will be women. By the year 2000, almost 50 percent of our work force will be female.

The work force in general is changing. By the year 2000, the average age in this country will be 39. In India it will be 19. Right now, 17 percent of persons coming into the U.S. workforce are either immigrants or minority members. By the year 2000, this figure will be 42 percent. Forty-one percent of all immigrants are Hispanic; 43 percent are Asians. We are talking about a different America.

What is happening today is not unlike what happened in 1910 with the European influx. This country is rebirthing itself as an immigrant nation, poised for the future. These new entrepreneurs don't believe it is an American right to own a car or a home. They believe in earning such privileges the old-fashioned way and are willing to risk their lives to cross the Texas border or go thousands of miles in dingy boats for a piece of that dream. The nation is changing, and it is going to be a very different place from the United States of our youth. But this is America, and these dedicated citizens are Americans.

In this changing world, local government managers need to surround themselves with good people. And waiting for them to come asking for a job is not sufficient. Managers must seek, find, and hire the best. Then they must keep the best.

We who serve the public should never, ever be afraid of telling people the cost and the price of being the best. We should be critical only of our own inability to lead them in achieving it.

This world has three kinds of people: those who make it happen, those who watch it happen, and those who do not know what hit them. The time for watching is over.

Cities for the Future

Royce Hanson

Everything has to happen somewhere. Most things in the modern world happen in cities. But cities are changing. In the face of massive technological transformation in the workplace and a major shift in employment from manufacturing to service industry, a new urban system is emerging.

This new system of metropolitan economies is polarizing. At one extreme are a relatively small number of large, diverse "command" and "control" centers. At the other extreme are the rest of the cities, increasingly subordinate to decisions made in the command and control centers.

Command and control centers are characterized by the high concentration of corporate headquarters, research universities and corporate research facilities, government offices, and producer services such as medical centers, arts centers and philanthropies.

These "transactional" cities, to use the phrase of geographer Jean Gottman, have become fundamentally different than they were in an earlier era. Most of them have experienced a massive replacement of manufacturing and other blue collar jobs in services and white collar occupations. They generally have strong economies, even in times of national recession. If we were to map their economic relationships with other places, we would find that the most important centers may have as much or more contact with a worldwide network of cities as with communities in their immediate regions.

The world class cities in this group — New York, Chicago, San Francisco, Los Angeles — are continuing to build their dominance in such command and control functions as international finance and corporate decisionmaking. They are spinning off other functions for which they were once famous, like routine clerical activities and distributive services, to other places.

Reprinted with permission from American City & County, *Vol. 99, No. 11, November 1984. Published by Communication Channels, Inc., Atlanta, Georgia.*

A few other major cities are edging into the world class as headquarters for growing industries and financial empires. Houston, Dallas and Miami are the likely candidates for strong competition with the others. A few dominant regional centers, like Atlanta and the Twin Cities of Minneapolis and St. Paul, also show signs of strong contention for world class status.

Subordinate cities are generally smaller and more specialized. Even large cities, such as Buffalo, that have some headquarters operations, have tended to be locations for branch plants. Others have economies strongly oriented to serving consumers and limited regional economies. In these cities, change has also been rapid, but often it has been more painful. Technological change in the industries that made Youngstown or Duluth expand have produced large numbers of structurally unemployed workers and very slow growth in alternative employment services.

Global Terms

The important point in this, for those concerned with the future of cities, is that this country is entering an economy in which cities are linked more closely than ever before. And that this new economy, only barely beginning to be understood, uses cities differently than the old industrial economy. It truly means that to act intelligently at the local level, public officials have to think in global terms, to see and understand how this new urban system works at a national and international scale.

The cities that seem to understand this, whether intuitively or as a result of careful analysis of their economies, are moving into more central roles. Akron, for example, no longer is a manufacturing center. While it remains the world capital of the rubber industry, it no longer produces tires. Instead, its economy has shifted to headquarters, research, education and related service functions. Other manufacturing centers like Detroit and Pittsburgh are shifting the functions they perform, within the industrial sectors they have long dominated.

What many of these cities are beginning to realize is that the city for the future, in an economically advanced nation, is the service-centered city. It must perform services on two levels. First, it must develop the labor force and the activities that complement the command and control functions — the talents and skills instrumental to the planning, design, control, marketing and evaluation of operations and products. Second, and as an essential corollary of the first, the city must serve the servants.

The chief executive officer of a major multinational corporation recently described how his firm "used" cities: Specifically, he used them to recruit the kind of talent he needed to run his corporation. Thus, he wants a city with a strong educational system, a good if not great research university and other research establishments, a good system of health care, and a fine set of public services, especially recreation and arts facilities and programs.

This response suggests a highly sophisticated understanding of the relationship between the quality of the urban environment and the health of the urban economy. It also puts a new light on the requirements of strategies for urban economic development, because the city for the future is not just in competition with other cities in its region that share a common resource base or regional infrastructure system. It is instead in competition with Tokyo, London, Paris and other cities throughout the world that aspire to house the same economic activities.

Intentional Cities

A second requirement for making intelligent choices about urban development strategies is to understand how a city currently fits into the larger system. That a city is now a subordinate center largely performing production functions is not necessarily a cause for despair. Nor is it written that Frostbelt cities must decline and Sunbelt cities must grow. The very footlooseness of the services sectors, and the needs of other industries to decentralize at certain stages of their development leaves a wide range of opportunities open.

In fact, it may be that there is more opportunity in the new economy than ever before for what economist-planner Richard Knight calls "intentional cities." Knight distinguishes these from the accidental cities of the past that arose due to their fortunate locations on waterways or at critical locations in resource zones. In other words, strategic thinking and planning can make a big difference in what happens to a city.

Such planning requires understanding that it may be possible to establish a strong mutually supportive relationship with a command and control center. It suggests that attention to the local education system should be a top priority in developing a labor force that is not only trained to assume today's jobs, but is trained well enough in basic skills to be resilient enough to shift occupations as technology and markets continue to shift. And it suggests that local tax rates should be far less important obsessions than the quality of services, the capacity of the city to communicate with distant places and the accessibility to business travelers.

It is somewhat ironic that this country is entering this new urban age without a national urban policy to help cities chart their futures. The current administration argues that urban policy, if it is to exist at all, should be the province of the states and cities themselves. Many would consider the essence of President Reagan's urban policy is to expect national economic growth to benefit all cities — "a rising tide lifts all boats." This is complemented by advocacy of a new federalism in which the states take over many of the urban activities previously carried out by the federal government. Finally, the administration endorses some federal urban programs, such as community development block grants, the Urban Development Action Grant program and enterprise zones.

It may be conceded that the urban pork barrel that passed for urban policy in previous administrations had outlived its usefulness and its indulgence in an ever more constrained federal budget. But the nature of the economic transformation through which cities are passing is not a uniformly rising tide. The economic functions that are leading the recovery and are prospects for building the economy of the future are not evenly distributed among the nation's cities.

Creating a climate in which those places and people left behind are capable of thinking and acting rationally about the future is indeed important national business. National policy today focuses almost exclusively on how much the economy does. It is only beginning to think hard about what it should do. And not at all about where it should be done.

It is this last element that should be the concern of national urban policy, because the capacity of American cities to house and serve this new economy will ultimately be a major factor in not only what gets done in the United States, but in how much of it we do in competition with other nations.

This suggests that a policy for America's future cities needs to proceed simultaneously at national and regional levels. At the national level, it would make sense to begin to consolidate the several programs that now exist for grants and loans designed to leverage private capital investment in cities. Taking new federalism rhetoric at face value, a consolidated urban loan fund, made available "wholesale" through state and regional urban development banks, could not only help leverage private investment in the future of cities, it could provide powerful incentive for harder thinking by states and cities on where best to make investments. And it could help accelerate the growth of the national economy by supporting industries and occupations that show strong competitive promise.

National policy could also help with the locally debilitating problems of structural change and unemployment. With few exceptions, it is hard for the mayor to talk corporate responsibility to multinational corporations facing major market shifts and technological change. Yet these changes, and the resistance to them by workers and cities, are important facts of the political economy.

A New Society

The development of a new social contract among labor, management and communities to facilitate transitions in local economies would help make the broader transition at the national level. The task is surely not one for the federal government alone, but it just as certainly cannot be managed without the participation and leadership of the national government.

Leaving the problems of structural unemployment and plant closings, refittings and moving to the invisible hand of the market places, the worker and the city are in a position of not knowing where the next blow will fall. This task is not one that can be resolved by some simple legislative expedient. It will take the best effort of all levels of government, the unions and business leadership.

In the meantime, there are some very practical things that can be done. A computerized national job bank would help workers relocate, and help those entering the labor force find work. Federal grants in aid could be redesigned, as they have been in other federal nations, to help equalize the fiscal capacity of the states and to give the states incentive for equalizing local government fiscal capacities.

This is an important step in relieving cities of the attraction of "beggar thy neighbor" policies of smokestack and chip chasing, which results in moving the action around the country, but not increasing the amount of economic activity. It also makes it possible for states and cities to think rationally about their needs, and to make it possible for all parts of the country to at least meet minimum levels of public service and education. Also, from the point of view of those who care about federalism, fiscal equalization makes it possible for cities to do the things that are expected of them, rather than pass the buck to the federal ladder.

Finally, it is past time for the United States to nationalize its welfare system, so that poor people can migrate to where the new jobs are with less risk than they now face. Such actions would remove a major burden on cities with especially large unemployment and dependency problems.

Under existing policy, they often find themselves caught in a spiral decline, as structural change increases their social costs at the same time as the tax base is disappearing. Thus, they are unable to use resources for investment on education and services so essential to competing with other cities for their share of the services economy.

Urban Policies

At the state, regional and local levels, there is also a need for deliberate urban policies. As a beginning, most urban areas need to establish economic intelligence systems that help them understand the changes taking place and how their economy fits into the national and international picture. This intelligence is a necessary prerequisite to sound strategic planning and decision-making.

Using this information, cities must target their resources more carefully. Targeting has become the name of the game in urban development, but most investments continue to be made on an ad hoc basis. Sometimes they work well, or if things are really bad, anything helps. But over the long run, cities need to direct investments into those sectors of their economies that are likely to have staying power in a competitive international economy.

Crucial Choices

One area where resources need to be invested heavily is education. Otherwise, most cities will not be able to develop labor forces that can aspire to and achieve high levels of employment and productive work. The disadvantaged populations of our cities are an invaluable resource that is being wasted as a result of undercapitalization. It is a desperately needed resource for the future economy. If it is not developed, there is a substantial danger that we will be faced with maintenance of an urban underclass that is capable of holding back the entire economy due to its inability to hold any but the dead-end jobs at the bottom of the service economy.

In this sense, cities, and the nation must choose whether to hold back from leadership of a full-scale knowledge economy in order to provide work for the underclass, or develop a labor force that can keep this nation in the cutting edge of development.

Finally, cities need to rethink what it means to be a service and knowledge-based society, and what it takes to make an urban area work efficiently and humanely in the new economy.

The good news is that cities have choices. There are important forces at work that are making cities change, but they are neither immutable nor inscrutable. Not all cities will become command and control centers, but most can find a good niche in the system of cities. A city cannot change its location, but it can change what it does and how it does it.

The Management Challenges

Susan Walter and Pat Choate

Shared Challenges

Today, the management challenges facing the Chief Executive Officers (CEOs) of corporations and the Chief Elected Officials (CEOs) of government are remarkably similar. For example, both face:

- overwhelming pressures to favor the short term over the long term, irrespective of eventual consequences;
- problems of managing large, often unresponsive bureaucracies;
- internal and external forces that resist change, regardless of how much that change is required;
- pressures of special interest groups—often the same special interest groups;
- difficulties in finding and retaining creative, productive people;
- the problems of creating or finding new ideas and new approaches;
- the difficulties of sharing decisions with individuals and institutions outside of the organization; and
- the problems of securing and allocating limited funds for virtually unlimited demands.

The similarity of the management challenges shared by public and private organizations extends beyond the apparently generic problems of managing large bureaucracies. Many of the same external forces affect the environments in which both public and private organizations operate. For example, in its 1980 report, *Looking Ahead*, the Committee for Economic Development (CED) identified some of the key issues that business will face in the 1980s (Schiff 1980).

Reprinted with permission from Thinking Strategically: A Primer for Public Leaders, *1984. Published by the Council of State Planning Agencies, Washington, D.C.*

Among the issues identified were changes in demography and the labor force; the changing character of work; growing international dependence; a new public questioning of economic decisions; inflation; taxes; government regulation; the changing social role of business; increased competition for capital; the decline of many traditional industries and the resulting loss of jobs; and the problems of maintaining fiscally sound retirement programs. Each of these business issues is a government issue as well.

Similarly, in its 1983 report, *Future Opportunities and Problems That Face the Nation*, the Commitee on Energy and Commerce of the U.S. House of Representatives identified 10 basic, long-term issues now confronting the nation (Congress 1983). Among the issues identified were changes in the labor force, international trade, information technology, governmental institutions, education, natural resources and food scarcity, public facilities, armaments, research and development, and health care. Each of these government issues is also a business issue.

Some examples illustrate the similarity of issues that confront CEOs and institutions in both the public and private sectors:

- *The Work Force* — The growth in the size of the American work force is slowing dramatically. As a result, today's workers will constitute over 80 percent of the work force in the year 2000. The nation's success in renewing its economy will therefore depend heavily on how well the *current* work force can be retained and upgraded. Workers for both government and business will come from this same pool of workers (Choate 1982).

  The future status and role of labor unions remain unclear, as unions seek to offset membership losses in older industries by expanding into services, high technology and other largely nonunionized industries.

  Women will constitute almost two of every three new entrants into the work force until the mid-1990s. Yet no major institution in America, public or private, has effectively integrated women into its work force.

  Disruptions in the work place are likely as the workers of the post–World War II baby-boom generation compete for mid-career promotions.

- *Trade and Investment* — The United States economy is intricately entwined with the global economy. Increasingly, the U.S. performance in the global economy is influenced by access to markets, competitive financing and the "industrial targeting" strategies of other nations. Even though trade will become increasingly important in the years ahead, world and U.S. trade policies and mechanisms are inadequate: the General Agreement on Trade and Tariffs does not include trade in services, which contributes $120 billion to the American economy each

year; the safeguard codes which provide remedies for tariff violations
are threadbare and ineffective; the U.S. lacks basic information about
the trade and investment practices of other nations; and our trading
partners are applying a wide range of unfair non-tariff trade and investment barriers against American products and services.

- *Public Infrastructures* — The deterioration of the nation's basic public
facilities is extensive. Adequate and well-functioning roads, bridges,
water and wastewater treatment systems, ports, school buildings,
libraries, parks and community buildings, among dozens of other types
of public works, are essential to the U.S. economy and the quality of
life of every citizen. Yet the national, state and local governments have
few policies or programs to address this fundamental challenge: priorities do not exist; adequate funding mechanisms have not been created;
research is limited, almost nonexistent; public decision-making is fragmented between and among the federal and state governments; and
there are no clear divisions of responsibilities between the public and
private sectors.
- *Information Technologies* — Today, information technologies affect
most aspects of human activity, including health, defense, politics and
education. The pervasiveness of these technologies has created a range
of critical issues that need to be addressed. Abroad, other governments
are erecting barriers to the movement of information across borders, im-
peding U.S. investment overseas. Domestically, the ability to access and
use information is magnifying the gap between segments of society. The
extensive information now available on businesses and individuals has
created an urgent need to safeguard privacy. Yet neither the government
nor most corporations have adequate policies to deal with these important information issues.
- *Government Institutions* — Government institutions have become
cumbersome. Specifically, it has become increasingly difficult to build
a consensus on basic issues; the debate on centralization versus decentralization of government proceeds more on the basis of rhetoric than
from a clear understanding of alternatives and consequences; electoral
processes leave citizens feeling powerless, stimulating referendum
movements that are sweeping state governments; and the relationship
between government, business and labor remains confrontational, even
while the need for cooperation becomes ever more critical.
- *Education* — The nation's education system is in decline. A growing
number of reports have documented the inadequacies of public education, from kindergarten through high school. At the college level, the
skills of new graduates do not match the needs of society. Nor do public
training programs meet the nation's retraining needs. Indeed, because
strategic vision is absent at every level of education and training,

deficiencies exist in pay, faculty, facilities, curriculum, and linkages with America's needs.

• *Natural Resources and Food* — The United States and its allies remain dependent on oil imports and are vulnerable to supply disruptions. Globally, over 800 million people consume less than the accepted minimum daily caloric requirement. In addition, America's growing dependence on strategic materials found only in nations such as Zaire, Zimbabwe, South Africa and the Soviet Union pose a serious threat to our economy and national security.

Domestically, the availability of potable water is a major national problem that is certain to worsen. During the next two decades, for example, the depletion of underground water resources in the High Plains states of Texas, Oklahoma, Nebraska, Kansas, New Mexico and Colorado will force most farmers to return to the low-yield dry-land farming that existed in the 1930s. Consequently, more than 25 percent of all irrigated farm production in the United States will cease. Since these farms currently produce over 40 percent of the nation's beef, changes in U.S. diets and food supply are inevitable.

• *Armaments* — The stockpile of world armaments is at record levels and arms are increasingly being diffused among less developed nations, with obvious destabilizing effects. In addition to ongoing arms negotiations, the next decade is likely to witness the emergence of related issues such as the safety of chemical and biological weapons during production, transport and storage; America's participation in efforts to curtail international terrorism; and the need for additional policymaking mechanisms on national security.

• *Research and Development* — Research and development (R&D), coupled with technological innovation, have long been mainstays of America's competitive edge. But current trends indicate a decline in U.S. innovation relative to our past performance and to that of our foreign competitors. In spite of the importance of government funding of basic R&D and government's central role in regulating and protecting improved technological innovations, the nation lacks a comprehensive policy for R&D and industrial innovation and technology. Consequently, business perceptions of government actions remain clouded.

• *Health Costs* — Even though health expenditures now exceed 10 percent of the Gross National Product, they are certain to escalate in the years ahead. As the population ages, these mounting health costs will place enormous demands on government, on employers who provide health benefit protection, and on individuals. Efforts to control health costs will force the nation to make critical choices about access to health care as well as the quality of services provided.

At the same time, the aging and increasing life expectancy of the population will create growing demands for particular kinds of health services such as acute and long-term health care. Changing migration patterns will determine where these demands will be the most intense.

This is only a partial listing of foreseeable, long-term changes that will affect both government and business. In a world of global interdependencies and fast-paced change, it is imperative for organizations to anticipate the future, plan for it, and take considered action.

This is precisely why better managed corporations, and recently some governments as well, are applying the concepts of strategic vision, so that they can better understand and operate in their complex environments. The techniques, processes and tools of strategic vision enable these organizations to identify and analyze emerging trends and specific events that shape their working environment, define the basic objectives of their organizations, create strategic plans and link these plans to their day-to-day actions.

The Lack of Strategic Vision

The refinement and replication of the concepts of strategic vision that have evolved in the private sector hold enormous promise for improving the quality of management in government. And the quality of government management does require improvement.

The deficiencies in the quality of government management can be divided into two basic categories. The first are administrative, such as incompetencies in day-to-day operations, unresponsive service by many public employees, uninspired and thoughtless management by many government managers, poor purchasing procedures and slow decision making.

The second are strategic deficiencies: the scant consideration given to identifying and assessing the consequences of longer-term trends and events, the absence of clear goals, poor or nonexistent strategic planning processes, limited linkages between plans and actions, and the absence of evaluation and feedback mechanisms.

As a consequence of both administrative and strategic deficiencies, American government today is managed as though government were somehow unimportant. The passage of legislation, announcement of policies, passage of appropriations, creation of programs, and issuance of rules and regulations are too often equated with actual accomplishment. But the chasm between intention and results is wide.

This is because management and results, per se, have been largely overlooked in both electoral politics and the actual conduct of the public's business. Consequently, virtually all of the 82,000 units of government in the United States operate without basic processes and tools for anticipating the future, preparing for its uncertainties or even operating coherently in the present.

If government really were unimportant, its mismanagement — administrative and strategic — would be of little consequence. But just the opposite is true. The federal, state, and local governments influence virtually all economic and social decisions in the country through a diverse array of tax, expenditure and regulatory actions. Government now employs almost one of every six American workers and commands more than a third of the nation's annual Gross National Product. Government's decisions, actions and inactions affect the nation's economic performance, as well as its efforts to meet social objectives and maintain a secure national defense.

The mere reallocation of powers within the federalist system, per se, will not improve government management; nor will massive government reorganizations. Improvement can come only from careful and pragmatic approaches that are deeply grounded in an understanding of the extent of the current ad hoc mismanagement, its causes, its consequences, and the actions required to facilitate change.

While the extent, consequences and costs of administrative deficiencies in the management of government have been documented repeatedly, the strategic deficiencies in government management are less clear. This is because strategic deficiencies are longer term in nature and are often masked and mislabeled as administrative weaknesses. The limited information that is available, however, outlines a disturbing situation in the strategic management of some fundamental areas of public-sector domestic responsibilities: managing the public work force, government expenditures, regulation and taxation. Some examples will illustrate the need for more systematic foresight, goal-setting and strategic planning processes, as well as improved linkages between planning and operations and more effective evaluation procedures.

The Public Work Force

Virtually all decisions in U.S. society are affected, often substantially, by government workers. Thus, competent government management is essential to the effective functioning of society.

Yet the federal and state governments are permitting the career civil service to decline. At the same time, many competent, potential political appointees are unwilling to work in government because of low pay, high burnout rates and the high costs of moving and living in cities such as Washington, D.C. (NAPA 1983). Most disturbing, neither the federal nor the state and local governments have long-term policies to reverse the deterioration of the career service, attract a diversity of political appointees, or make public service attractive to well-qualified workers.

If the private sector chose its managers as government did, the CEO, the company president, all vice-presidents, all director-level managers and most plant managers would be fired and replaced at least every four to eight years. Most of their replacements would have little or no job-related experience or even professional training for these jobs. Under such circumstances, it might be difficult to manage a business successfully. Yet this is precisely how senior positions in the federal, state and local governments are staffed.

The turnover rate among the senior advisors to governors averages almost 33 percent annually (CSPA 1976). At the federal level, during the past 14 years, there have been eight Secretaries of Commerce, seven Secretaries of State, and six Directors of the Office of Management and Budget. High turnover is found in every federal agency. Under these conditions, it is difficult to maintain continuity of programs.

In the past, high turnover among political officials at the federal level was offset by the relative permanence of senior career executives. But today, the unusually high level of resignations and retirements of these career officials threatens the effective functioning of government. Indeed, half of all senior executives—3,500 of the 7,000 highest level civil servants—have left the federal government since 1979 (USGAO 1983).

This crisis in government management is a direct, although unintended, consequence of the Civil Service Reform Act of 1978 which created the Senior Executive Service (SES). This system eliminated previous civil service protections, permitted flexibility in reassignments, and promised increased pay for outstanding work. But the system is a failure, at least in terms of its announced purposes. Specifically, the number of senior executives eligible for bonuses has been cut in half; reassignment authorities have been used to encourage the resignations of career officials; and career training has been reduced. Similar weaknesses are found in state governments as hundreds of state employees are fired with each change of administration.

The consequences of present practices are perhaps best stated by the Committee for Economic Development in [its] report, *Improving Management of the Public Work Force:*

> Some (public employees) are leaving for higher pay, prestige, or satisfaction in private employment; those whose jobs have few counterparts in the private sector feel caught and resentful; and many are resolved to fight through political action for what they perceive to be inadequate pay and working conditions. There are, in short, disturbing signs of sagging morale [CED 1977].

As the CED points out, one of the most important considerations in managing government is the effective use of people. After all, government by its very nature is labor intensive; thus, improvements in the productivity of government services are heavily dependent on the improved management and performance of government workers.

Regulation

Government regulates banks and financial institutions, labor-management relations, public utilities, competition in the marketplace, communications, transportation, public safety, health, environment, entry into many professions, and a wide array of other activities that affect most citizens and all businesses.

In recent years, governmental regulation has become a major route for meeting social and economic objectives. Unable to generate sufficient grant-in-aid appropriations to finance social and economic programs in the 1970s, the federal and state governments expanded their regulatory powers and, in the process, shifted program costs to citizens, businesses and lower levels of government. Thus, while there were only 30 federal regulatory agencies in 1970, there were over 100 by 1980. A similar regulatory explosion occurred at the state level.

These regulations have imposed massive costs on business and even on government itself. In 1980, for example, businesses spent over $34 billion on air, water and solid waste pollution abatement, while government spent over $11.5 billion. Some of these requirements, such as provision of full access for the handicapped, would have literally bankrupted many local governments if implemented. Similarly, states have mandated that local governments take actions that have forced them to devise new ways of raising the necessary funds (USBC 1983).

Despite the obvious importance of some regulations and the unnecessary imposition of others, no reliable estimates of total regulatory costs and benefits exist. There is no overall focus for regulatory policies at the federal level; nor is there any coordination of regulatory policies among the federal, state and local agencies and those affected.

Government Expenditures

A lack of strategic vision, evident in massive waste, duplication and omission, also characterizes the more than $1 trillion of annual expenditures made by federal, state and local governments.

Consider, for example, the nation's outlays for public works. America's basic public facilities are wearing out faster than they are being repaired and replaced. Over $60 billion of public works expenditures are made annually in the absence of an inventory of public facilities, standards, uniform estimates of future investment requisites, or clear allocations of responsibilities. Although the deterioration of the nation's public facilities has been documented, only a few actions, such as the 5-cent gas tax, have been taken. Yet it is clear that continued deterioration of these basic facilities will suppress the vitality of the economy, reduce the quality of life of all citizens, and raise the costs of actions when they are eventually taken (Choate and Walter 1981).

An absence of strategic vision has also characterized the nation's employment and training policies, programs and institutions. Rapid technological advances and increased competition from abroad have created enormous demands for new and improved worker skills. At the same time, a growing segment of the work force is unprepared to meet these challenges. For example, a fifth of all American adults are functionally illiterate, unable to read a job notice, fill out a job application or make change correctly. Among adults who are unemployed, the rate of functional illiteracy is 36 percent.

Over $10 billion of federal, state and local funds is expended on public training programs each year. The training problem, therefore, is not a lack of money but rather the absence of a shared strategic vision of what should be done.

As a result, basic data on current and future training needs remain limited and of little use; training facilities are antiquated; faculty skills are becoming obsolete; and federal displaced worker retraining programs are fragmented in an ineffective maze of 22 distinct efforts. Furthermore, more than 20 states still have not established linkages between their training programs and employers—a technique pioneered by the southern states in their highly successful "customized" training programs which link specific worker training to the specific needs of specific employers (Choate 1982).

Taxation

The nation's tax system is confusing and ineffective. As much as $300 billion of the GNP may now be in the untaxed underground economy; the tax laws and regulations are so confusing that experts disagree on a growing number of points; most businesses and most citizens require expert assistance to complete their tax filings; and the level and nature of most economic investments are heavily influenced by their tax consequences.

Reductions of federal taxes in the "supply-side" economic experiment have had the effect of creating the largest deficit in the nation's history. As a result, the federal government has shifted many critical responsibilities to state and local governments. For unprepared state and local governments, these additional responsibilities have created difficult fiscal and administrative burdens that may take years to overcome.

But perhaps most important, the confusion of the nation's tax system, the growing perception of its unfairness, and the increasing visibility of unpunished tax cheaters are eroding the tax system's most precious asset: the good faith and voluntary compliance of American taxpayers.

The Consequences of Limited Vision

These examples are neither unique nor isolated. They simply illustrate the disorder that is created in the absence of foresight, goals, strategic plans, operations that are linked to plans, and regular evaluations. The absence of these basic public administration functions hamper government policies, institutions and programs in six basic ways:

1. *Fragmented and disordered management practices permit no overall view of public needs and no overall specification of the roles of the respective levels of government or the private sector in meeting those needs.* Without an ordered context for overall actions, a single decision cannot be considered relative to other decisions.

2. *In the absence of clearly documented needs and well-articulated priorities, pork-barrel politics often dominate public actions and public expenditures.* Pork-barrel spending becomes a medium of political exchange, in which votes and actions are exchanged for support of other programs or projects — regardless of public needs or benefits.

3. *In this atmosphere, the short-term payoff is invariably favored over long-term goals.* When public expenditures are treated as a source of patronage, it becomes difficult to create and maintain coalitions that can sustain long-term efforts, no matter how vital such efforts may be. As a result, most political leaders support those programs that can be financed and completed in a single year. Unfortunately, most of the nation's important challenges — such as rebuilding vital infrastructure, retraining the work force for jobs in a post-industrial society, assuring a safe environment, restoring long-term noninflationary economic growth, and rebuilding our defense capacities — will take a decade or more to finance and complete. Short-term approaches to such basic national needs will inevitably produce social and economic trauma.

4. *Without coherent strategies that set investment needs and ways to meet them, specific public investment plans for defense, social programs, research and development, and public facilities cannot be systematically formulated.* Nor can government leaders and

the public determine critical linkages between various public functions, such as the role of employment and training in strengthening national defense capacities or the importance of public facilities to long-term economic growth.

5. *Disordered management practices at one level of government are easily transferred to other levels.* Thus, pork-barrel politics, a short-term perspective and start-and-stop financing at the federal level make it nearly impossible for state and local governments to plan and administer their responsibilities in a coherent manner.

6. *Disordered management practices in government limit, even prohibit, effective joint public-private sector actions.* Because of the costs, delays and bureaucracy involved, private firms often avoid doing business with government. The reluctance of private employers to participate in publicly sponsored training programs is only one of numerous examples of this fundamental breakdown between the principal institutions in American society.

The introduction of the techniques of strategic vision and management described in this book can be important first steps in bringing coherence to the management of government. Success in this effort, however, will require a thorough understanding of the forces that define the political environment in which government operates.

References

Choate, P. 1982. *Retooling the American work force: Toward a national training strategy.* Washington, D.C.: The Northeast-Midwest Institute.

_____, and S. M. Walter. 1981. *America in ruins.* Washington, D.C.: Council of State Planning Agencies.

Committee for Economic Development. 1977. *Improving the management of the public work force.* New York.

Congress of the United States, Committee on Energy and Commerce. 1983. *Future opportunities and problems that face the nation.* U.S. House of Representatives, 98th Congress.

Council of State Planning Agencies. 1976. *State planning.* Washington, D.C.

National Academy of Public Administration. 1983. *America's unelected government: Recruiting the president's team.* Boston: Ballinger.

Schiff, F. W. 1980. *Looking ahead: Identifying key economic issues for business and society in the 1980s.* New York: Committee for Economic Development.

United States Bureau of the Census. 1983. *Statistical abstract of the United States: 1984* (104th ed.). Washington, D.C.

United States General Accounting Office. 1983. *Testimony of the comptroller general on the impact of the Senior Executive Service.* Washington, D.C.

Glossary

Alternative Futures Possible forthcoming developments arrayed into sets of scenarios, or plausible futures. Alternative futures are often derived from the base scenario.

Anticipations Survey A forecasting method that involves a survey of the general public to (a) determine its intentions to buy certain products or services or (b) derive an index that measures general feelings about the present and future and estimates how this feeling will affect buying habits.

Appointed Officials Those public officials appointed by the elected officials, the city manager, or the chief administrative officer, depending upon the type of government entity involved. These officials typically include an organization's top management staff (i.e., chief executive and department managers).

Base Plan The plan of action which is consistent with the most likely scenario and the organization's mission, goals, and objectives. This is sometimes referred to as the work plan.

Base Scenario The set of trends or events which defines the initial, most likely future. The base scenario is structured so that it can be compared with a range of alternative scenarios or futures.

Box-Jenkins Forecast A forecasting technique in which the time series is fitted with a mathematical model that is optimal in the sense that it assigns smaller errors to history than other models. This type of model should be identified and parameters must be established. This is the most accurate statistical routine available but one of the most costly and time-consuming to perform.

Brainstorming An interactive group technique, specifically useful for planning, where the facilitator challenges the group into a rapid-fire generation of ideas. The evaluation process is kept separate so as not to inhibit the generation of ideas.

Citizen Participation Strategies have greater legitimacy, and are easier to implement politically, when the citizens served by a governmental entity feel that their interests and issues have been properly addressed during the planning process.

Competitive Analysis Model A private sector strategic planning approach that involves an analysis of key forces that shape an industry (e.g., relative power of consumers, products, threat of new market entrants, etc.). Competitive behavior dominates the framework of this strategic planning model.

Content The contents of a strategic planning process will vary from one organization to another. The issues selected, and how they will be addressed, generally form the content of a planning process and its resulting plan document.

Content Planning Model A private sector strategic planning approach that involves the categorization of a corporation's different businesses and the development of strategies for each business unit (or for a group of similar businesses). The goal is to balance an organization's business portfolio to meet corporate strategic planning objectives.

Contingency Plan The backup plan for an organization's work plan. Includes the plan of action that would be taken should the most probable scenario (strategic direction) not materialize as envisioned.

Cost/Benefit Analysis The relationship between economic benefits and costs associated with the operation of the department or program under study. The cost/benefit analysis may include both direct and indirect benefits and costs. Such analyses typically result in a pay-back period on initial investment.

Cost Center The smallest practical breakdown of expenditure and income into a grouping which will facilitate performance review, service evaluation, and the setting of priorities for a particular activity or service area. Typically includes a portion of a single program within a department.

Cross Impact Analysis An analytical technique for identifying the various impacts of events or well-defined policy actions on other events. It explores whether the occurrence of one event or implementation of one policy is likely to inhibit, enhance, or have no effect on the occurrence of another event.

Delphi Method A forecasting technique that includes surveying a panel of experts, all of which have access to the same information. The goal of this technique is to achieve a consensus as to a likely future or course of action. This technique eliminates the bandwagon effect of majority opinion.

Differentiating Factors The key aspects which distinguish among alternative scenarios.

Diffusion Index A forecasting method that examines the percentage of a group of economic indicators that are going up or down. This percentage then becomes the index to predict the future for these economic indicators.

Driving Forces The principal forces which lead to different evolutionary paths in the scenarios.

Econometric Model A forecasting technique that involves a system of interdependent regression equations that describe some sector of economic sales or profit activity. The parameters of the regression equations are usually estimated simultaneously. This technique better expresses the causalities involved than an ordinary regression equation.

Economic Input/Output Model Econometric models and input/output models are sometimes combined for forecasting purposes. This model is used to provide long-term trends for the econometric model. It is also used to stabilize the econometric model.

Effectiveness Performing the right tasks correctly, consistent with a program's mission, goals, and objectives, or work plan. Relates to correctness and accuracy, not the efficiency of the program or tasks performed. Effectiveness alone is not an accurate measure of total productivity.

Efficiency Operating a program or performing work tasks economically. Relates to dollars spent or saved, not to the effectiveness of the program or task performed. Efficiency alone is not an accurate measure of total productivity.

Elected Officials Those public officials that hold elective office for a specified time period. In cities, this typically includes the mayor and council members. Within county governments, it usually includes members of the board of supervisors. The titles may vary from state to state, or within a state, depending upon local laws, practices, and customs.

Environmental Scanning The process of identifying major environmental factors, events, or trends that impact, directly or indirectly, the organization and its internal operating systems. It is one of the initial steps in undertaking a strategic planning process.

Evaluation The systematic review of the mission, goals, objectives, and work plan for the organization and its various components. Evaluation occurs most frequently at the operational level by reviewing organizational objectives. The evaluation process typically results in the preparation of recommendations for needed adjustments.

Exponential Smoothing A mathematical forecasting technique similar to the moving average, except that more recent data points are given additional weight in the forecasting process.

External Environment All relevant elements or forces (e.g., social, economic, political, and technological) external to, and having an impact upon, the organization and its various components. Includes those forces that are not under the direct control of management.

Extrapolation To infer unknown information from known information. Extrapolation frequently involves a time-series analysis whereby past activities are projected into the future based on historical information. Extrapolation is sometimes dangerous because it assumes that future events are based on historical facts and circumstances.

Forecasting Techniques Those methods (e.g., qualitative, quantitative, and causal) used to project trends and predict future events or courses of action. Forecasting is an essential component of the strategic planning process. It may be used to analyze the external environment or to project organizational capabilities.

Forecasts Estimates of change or continuity in the elements developed for scenarios. A descriptive forecast is an estimate of what might happen. A normative forecast is an estimate of what is desired to happen.

Foresight Activities Planning activities that look towards and analyze the future, such as strategic planning. A general term used to group all "futures-related" planning efforts undertaken by organizations—whether public or private.

Framework for Innovation Model A private sector strategic planning approach with emphasis on innovation as a strategy. Assumes that change is unavoidable, and continuous innovation to deal with change is necessary if the organization is to survive and prosper. The ultimate strategies adopted are based on a "vision of success" to ensure future competitiveness and profitability.

Futures Research The process of collecting information from the past and present and attempting to project future conditions or desired futures. Futures research, therefore, deals with possibilities and choices within constraints.

Goals Those achievements towards which management wants the organization, and its various components or departments, to strive as it seeks to fulfill its mission. Several goals are usually identified to achieve a particular mission statement.

Harvard Policy Model A private sector strategic planning approach that involves an analysis of management's values and the social obligations of the firm. This model attempts to develop the proper "fit" between an organization and its external environment.

Historical Analogy A forecasting technique that involves a comparative analysis of the introduction and growth of similar new products and bases the forecast upon the similarity of patterns.

Input/Output Model An analytical method concerned with the interindustry or interdepartmental flow of goods or services in the economy or an organization and its markets. It shows that flows of inputs must occur to obtain certain output levels.

Internal Environment All relevant elements or forces (e.g., personnel, financial, communications, authority relationships, and management operating systems) internal to, and having an impact upon, the operation of the organization and its various components. Includes those forces that are under the direct control of management.

Issue A trend, set of elements, or event which a group decides is important for policy-making purposes.

Issues Management An attempt to manage those issues that are important to an organization. These issues typically surface after the completion of an environmental scanning process, or other practice, leading to the identification of important issues. The issues identified should fall within the scope and purpose of the organization.

Leading Indicator An analytical forecasting technique that uses a time series of an economic activity whose movement in a given direction precedes the movement of some other time series in the same direction.

Life-Cycle Analysis Involves an analysis and forecasting of new product or service growth rates based on S-curves. The phases of product or service acceptance by various groups are central to this analytical technique.

Line The personnel in those departments charged with the responsibility for those functions necessary for the day-to-day performance of the organization. Includes those departments that directly produce goods and/or services to satisfy an organization's marketplace.

Logical Incrementalism Model A private sector strategic planning approach that emphasizes the importance of small changes as part of developing and implementing an organization's strategies. Assumes that all change in an organizational setting is incremental and piecemeal in nature.

Long-Range Planning Includes a planning process that commences with analyzing the internal organization and projecting current trends into the future for selected organizational components. This planning process may not include an assessment of an organization's external environment. It may be product- or service-oriented. This term should not be confused with strategic planning.

Management Consists basically of two types — strategic and operational. Strategic management is performed at the top of an organization's hierarchy; everything else is operational management. Operational management is organized along functional lines of responsibility. Strategic management sets direction for the organization, and operational management ensures that this direction is implemented.

Management Information System An integrated information system designed to provide strategic, tactical, and operational information to management. Usually involves periodic written or computer-generated reports which are timely, concise, and meaningful.

Management Operating System The formal system of linkages between different components of the organization by which the various departments communicate with each other and by which management directs the operation and receives information on its performance.

Market Research A forecasting technique that includes the application of systematic, formal, and conscious procedures for analyzing evolving markets and for testing hypotheses about existing markets.

Mission   A statement of the role, or purpose, by which an organization plans to serve society. Mission statements may be set for different organizational components or departments. A department usually has only one mission statement.

Moving Average   A mathematical forecasting technique that involves finding the arithmetic or weighted average of a moving average or time series. A number of data points are selected to eliminate seasonal or other irregularities that may exist.

Nominal Group Technique   The process whereby members of a group are asked to identify key ideas or issues in written form. These ideas or issues are then discussed and debated before a vote is finally taken on their importance. The final result is a list of ideas or issues in order of their perceived importance.

Nonprofit Organization   Sometimes referred to as the "third sector"—the other two being the public and private sectors. Nonprofit organizations generally serve a public purpose and do not generate revenues beyond their operating expenses.

Objectives   Those tasks which are deemed necessary for an organization, or its components and departments, to achieve its goals. Several detailed objectives are typically set forth for each goal statement. Objectives include the operational implementation of goals.

Operational Issues   Those issues that relate to the internal operations of an organization, such as finance, budgeting, personnel, and technology, to name a few. Operational issues may or may not relate to an organization's external environment, and may not be of strategic importance to an organization.

Operational Management   Those tasks performed by line managers dealing with the operations of the organization. Operational managers may provide input into the formulation of strategic plans, but such plans are formulated by the planning group. Operational managers are key actors in implementing components of strategic plans.

Opportunity Cost   The cost of not taking a particular course of action. For example, if there are two issues and one is deemed to be strategic and the other is not, then the opportunity cost is the cost of not pursuing the course of action required for the non-strategic issue. If the purchase of computers is a strategic issue, and the cost to purchase typewriters is not, then the cost of not acquiring the typewriters is an opportunity cost.

Panel Consensus   A forecasting techique based upon the assumption that several experts can arrive at a better forecast than one person. These forecasts are sometimes influenced by social factors and may not reflect a true consensus of the group surveyed.

Plan for Planning   Involves setting forth the elements and steps in a strategic planning process to be undertaken by an organization. Such a plan is typically prepared by top management and approved by the policy-making body, such as elected officials in the public sector. This plan, once approved, sets forth the blueprint for the ensuing planning process.

Planner   One who has the responsibility and authority necessary to set action out in advance, or propose a course of action, for an organization. This role is usually advisory to top management, who approves plans prior to their being implemented.

Planning   An analytical process which encompasses an assessment of the environment, a determination of organizational capabilities, and the development of desired directions for the organization and its various components and departments. The process results in the approval of an action plan by top management.

Planning Group The collection of individuals given the charge of preparing a strategic plan. May include elected and appointed officials, members of the public, the internal management staff, or some combination thereof.

Policy A chosen course of action designed to significantly affect the organization's behavior in prescribed situations.

Proactive Planning Attempting to identify and manage issues at the operational, or management, level before they become political issues, which are subject to resolution through the political process. Strategic planning is one example of a proactive planning process.

Process The direction and frequency of work and information flows linking the differentiated roles within and between departments of a complex organization. Organizational processes are set forth after structure has been determined. The process of developing a strategic plan is generic and can be applied to a number of different organizations, while the content of the planning process may vary greatly from organization to organization.

Process Strategies Model A private sector strategic planning approach that involves bargaining and negotiating among two or more groups over the identification and resolution of strategic issues. Assumes that organizations are "shared power" settings in which groups must bargain, negotiate, and cooperate with each other in order to achieve their ends. The resolution of issues and strategies are achieved in a negotiated environment.

Product Strategy The direction set, relative to the goods or products produced by the organization to achieve a desired state in the future (e.g., level of products, mix of products, product market share, product pricing, etc.).

Productivity A measure of performance that includes the requirements of both efficiency and effectiveness. Includes performing the program or work tasks correctly (effectively) and economically (efficiently).

Q-Sort Helps an individual or group sort-out and set priorities among a large number of variables. Items are ranked according to what is most important and what is least important. This process continues until all variables have been ranked according to their importance.

Reactive Planning Coping or dealing with existing major issues that have not been resolved through a proactive planning process. Reactive planning typically involves using the political process to establish policies to manage issues, which are then delegated to the operational, or management, levels of an organization for implementation.

Regression Model A forecasting technique that functionally relates sales to other economic, competitive, or internal variables and estimates an equation using the least-squares technique. Relationships are primarily analyzed statistically.

Resource Strategy A plan for the distribution or allocation of an organization's resources, which details the utilization of technology, equipment, personnel, and funds. Resource strategies are necessary for the allocation of scarce, or limited, resources.

Resources The combination of technology, equipment, personnel, and funds that turns labor into goods and services in the marketplace. Adequate resources are necessary to make an organization's strategy successful.

Scenario A representation based upon an interconnected sequence of trends or events that describe an internally consistent alternative future, or course of action, for an organization to pursue and achieve.

Service Strategy   The direction set, relative to the services provided by the organization, to achieve a desired state in the future (e.g., level of services, mix of services, service market share, service pricing, etc.).

Staff   The personnel in those departments designed to serve the operating components, or line departments, of an organization (e.g., personnel, finance, general services, purchasing, etc.).

Stakeholder   Those individuals, groups, and outside parties that either affect or who are affected by the organization. Examples include constituents, special-interest groups, suppliers, unions, employees, policy-makers, and advisory bodies, to name a few. In any strategic planning process these entities must either be involved or consulted so that their views are given consideration during the planning process.

Stakeholder Management   The process of managing the interests of the various stakeholders of an organization. Involves the identification of key stakeholders and the criteria they use to judge the organization's performance. Strategies are typically developed to deal with each major stakeholder of an organization.

Strategic Issues   Those issues included in a strategic plan which are deemed important to the organization and its future performance. These issues may be either internal or external to the organization itself. Typically external issues are more difficult to manage then internal issues, due to the limited degree of control exercised by public organizations over their outside environment.

Strategic Management   Involves setting direction for the organization and is typically performed by elected and appointed officials, or some combination of these individuals, once a strategic plan is approved for implementation. While the strategic plan is approved by elected officials, top management is responsible for its administrative implementation.

Strategic Planning System   A private sector strategic planning approach that involves a system for formulating and implementing important decisions across different levels and functions of an organization. This model includes the allocation and control of resources within a strategic framework and through a rational decision-making process.

Strategic Vision   The explicit, shared understanding of the nature and purpose of the organization. It specifies what the organization is and should be rather than what it does operationally. The strategic vision is contained within an organization's strategy statement.

Strategy   A general direction set for the organization and its various components to achieve a desired state in the future. Strategy results from the detailed planning process that assesses the external and internal environment of an organization and results in a work plan that includes mission statements to direct the goals and objectives to the organization.

Strategy/Structure/Process   Three related components of an organization. An organization's process should fit its structure and, in turn, the structure should be set forth in such a way as to enable the organization to achieve its strategic direction. Strategy is determined first, structure follows strategy, and process is designed to facilitate structure.

Structure   The segmentation of work into components, typically organized around those goods and services produced, the formal lines of authority and communication between these components, and the information that flows between these communication and authority relationships.

Time Horizon   The time horizon included in a plan, or planning document, varies depending upon the type of plan being developed. Strategic plans typically have a five or ten year, sometimes longer, time horizon. Operational plans, on the other hand, frequently project a three to five year timespan into the future.

Trend Impact Analysis   An analytical technique designed to evaluate the potential effect of a set of chosen events upon a designated trend.

Trend Projection   A forecasting technique that fits a trend line to a mathematical equation and then projects it into the future by means of this equation (e.g., slope-characteristic method, logarithms, and polynomials).

Trends/Events   Those developments or factors which are external to the organization, and usually not controllable, which have a direct or indirect impact on the operation of the organization or its various components.

Visionary Forecast   A forecasting technique that involves a prophecy about the future that uses personal insights, judgment, and, when possible, facts about different scenarios of the future. It is characterized by subjective guesswork and imagination. This is not a scientific forecasting technique.

Wild Card Scenario   A scenario with a very low probability of occurrence, but high impact. A contingency plan may be developed to reduce the potential impact of this type of scenario.

Work Plan   The final planning document for the organization, or its components or departments, that contains the mission statement, goals, and objectives necessary to implement the strategic plan. Sometimes referred to as the base plan.

X-11 Forecast   A forecasting technique developed by Julius Shiskin of the U.S. Bureau of the Census. This technique decomposes a time series into seasonals, trend cycles, and irregular elements. It is primarily used for detailed time series analysis but has been extended to forecasting by incorporating other analytical methods.

About the Contributors

Affiliations are as of the time the articles were written.

Lea Brooks, Editor, *California County*, County Supervisors Association of California, Sacramento, California.

John M. Bryson, Associate Professor of Planning and Public Affairs, Hubert H. Humphrey Institute of Public Affairs, and Associate Director, Strategic Management Research Center, University of Minnesota, Minneapolis, Minnesota.

Barbara J. Byerly, Public Relations Specialist, City of Kirkwood, Missouri.

Pat Choate, Senior Policy Analyst for Economics, TRW, Inc., Washington, D.C.

Martin R. Cramton, Jr., Director, Charlotte-Mecklenburg Planning Commission, Charlotte, North Carolina.

James Crupi, President, Strategic Leadership Solutions, Inc., Dallas, Texas.

Timothy J. Delmont, Director, Master of Arts in Management Program, St. Mary's College, Minneapolis, Minnesota.

Jesse H. Duff, City Manager, Duarte, California.

Douglas C. Eadie, President, Strategic Development Consulting, Inc., Shaker Heights, Ohio.

Philip C. Eckhert, Director, Office of Planning and Development, Hennepin County, Minneapolis, Minnesota.

Skip Everitt, Associate Director, Division of Continuing Education, Furman University, Greenville, South Carolina.

Debra B. Forte, Director of Finance, City of McKinney, Texas.

John J. Gargan, Professor, Department of Political Science, Kent State University, Kent, Ohio.

Kathleen Haines, Data Administrator, Information Services Department, Hennepin County, Minneapolis, Minnesota.

Royce Hanson, Associate Dean, Hubert H. Humphrey Institute of Public Affairs, University of Minnesota, Minneapolis, Minnesota.

Harvey M. Jacobs, Assistant Professor, Department of Urban and Regional Planning, University of Wisconsin, Madison, Wisconsin.

David A. Johnson, Professor of Planning, University of Tennesee, Memphis, Tennessee.

Jerome L. Kaufman, Professor and Chair, Department of Urban and Regional Planning, University of Wisconsin, Madison, Wisconsin.

Roger L. Kemp, City Manager, Clifton, New Jersey, and consultant on strategic planning to local governments; formerly City Administrator, Placentia, California.

Joseph C. King, City Manager, Lexington, Virginia; and former Assistant City Manager, Oak Ridge, Tennessee.

William Earle Klay, Professor, Department of Public Administration, Florida State University, Tallahassee, Florida.

Robert W. Kuznik, Mayor, City of Placentia, California.

Carol Stealey Morris, Senior Planner, Charlotte-Mecklenburg Planning Commission, Charlotte, North Carolina.

Richard Morten, Associate Director, Planning Department, Chamber of Commerce, San Francisco, California.

John K. Parker, Distinguished Visiting Professor, Graduate Center for Public Administration, California State University, Long Beach, California.

Belden Paulson, Chairman, Center for Urban Community Development, University of Wisconsin, Milwaukee, Wisconsin.

Dave Penchoff, Program Planning Manager, Department of Finance, Town of West Hartford, Connecticut.

Ann M. Pflaum, Associate Dean of External Affairs, Continuing and Extension Education, University of Minnesota, Minneapolis, Minnesota.

Richard V. Robinson, City Manager, City of Cleveland Heights, Ohio.

William D. Roering, Assistant Professor of Strategic Management, College of Business Administration, University of Florida, Gainesville, Florida.

Richard Russo, Director of Finance, Town of West Hartford, Connecticut.

Susan Walter, Manager for State Government Relations, General Electric Company, Washington, D.C.

Sandy Weir, Senior Planner, Planning Department, City of Hampton, Virginia.

Index

www.ingramcontent.com/pod-product-compliance
Lightning Source LLC
Chambersburg PA
CBHW031357270326
41929CB00010BA/1222